MONTY PYTHON'S
TUNISIAN HOLIDAY

MONTY PYTHON'S

TUNISIAN
HOLIDAY

MY LIFE WITH BRIAN

Kim "Howard" Johnson

THOMAS DUNNE BOOKS/ST. MARTIN'S PRESS ✦ NEW YORK

THOMAS DUNNE BOOKS.
An imprint of St. Martin's Press.

www.thomasdunnebooks.com
www.stmartins.com

Book design by Richard Oriolo

LIBRARY OF CONGRESS CATALOGING-IN-PUBLICATION DATA

Johnson, Kim, 1955-
    Monty Python's Tunisian holiday : my life with Brian /
Kim "Howard" Johnson. —1st ed.
        p.   cm.
    Includes index.
    ISBN-13: 978-0-312-53379-3
    ISBN-10: 0-312-53379-9
    1. Life of Brian.   2. Monty Python (Comedy troupe)
3. Johnson, Kim, 1955—Diaries.   I. Title.
PN1997.L575J64   2008
791.43'72—dc22
                                          2008024759

First Edition: November 2008

10   9   8   7   6   5   4   3   2   1

For Graham Chapman, John Cleese, Terry Gilliam,

Eric Idle, Terry Jones, and Michael Palin,

who created it all and brought me along for the ride,

and for George Harrison,

who made it happen

CONTENTS

FOREWORD
BY MICHAEL PALIN

IF ANYONE CAN REMEMBER MORE ABOUT making *Life of Brian* than me, it's Kim "Howard" Johnson. He came, he saw, he got into costume. While the rest of us were fighting to up-stage each other, Howard had a notebook hidden in his toga. And he was that rare thing—a Python fan who could spell.

■ He didn't miss a trick. Not for him the long lunches after a stoning or the card schools after crucifixion. Kim "Howard"

Johnson saw it all happen, and his diary fills those gaps that none of the rest of us can remember. Or maybe daren't remember.

An essential tool for Python nuts.

AN APOLOGY FOR NOT READING THIS BOOK BEFORE WRITING THE FOREWORD

John Cleese

OF ALL THE BOOKS THAT I am planning to read in my dotage, there is none I am more looking forward to than *Monty Python's Tunisian Holiday.* This is truly one of the finest volumes I have seen in years. Beautiful binding, all the pages held securely in place in the proper order—a real feast for the eyes and a magnificent product of the bookbinder's art. Let your eyes lovingly gaze over each and every letter of the alphabet, assembled in neatly ordered rows in the traditional manner. Yes, this one surely looks like a winner. And did I mention the fabulous photographs, both in black-and-white and color? The entire package is bathed in the aroma of the finest India ink. Flip through the pages and listen to the paper rustle; run your fingers leisurely over each and every page; taste the glossy goodness of the dust jacket. Yes, this volume is truly a feast for all the senses.

Of all the books I'd love to read as soon as I get a spare moment, *Monty Python's Tunisian Holiday* is undoubtedly in the top thousand.

But then, why wouldn't it be? Not only does Howard Johnson know more about Python than anyone outside of the IRS, he was in Tunisia for most of the filming of *Life of Brian,* and is the only person who captured every thoughtless remark, heated exchange, embarrassing detail, petty insult, and spiteful act of indifference.

So forgive me for not starting this book before writing the foreword, but I've got a chiropractor's appointment in twenty minutes.

I leave you in the highly capable hands of Howard, who, I know, will take very good care of you.

FOREWORD
BY ERIC IDLE

A Word About the "Author"

KIM "HOWARD" JOHNSON WAS INVENTED BY Graham Chapman during an idle moment on the set of *Life of Brian*. ▪ "Let's invent a person," he said. ▪ "An American!" said Cleese. ▪ "An American fan from the Midwest," chimed in Palin, "who keeps a daily diary of Python filming. And then doesn't publish it for years and years." ▪ "Who would believe that?" I remember muttering disgruntledly.

"Oh, you'd be surprised," said Terry Gilliam, helping himself to some more of my per diem. "Americans can be very naive. They'll buy almost anything."

Terry Jones was away checking out asses, and it was only later over dinner, after he had cast a slim young donkey, that we told him we had made up a character called Kim "Howard" Johnson. In fact it was he who added the quote marks.

How we laughed, and each day we'd make up stuff this "person" would write about us.

Indeed, so well was "Howard" written that he went on to have quite a successful career in America, and at one time he even "worked" for John Cleese as a tax dodge. So ridiculous has the Internet become that nowadays people take this character seriously, not only believing he is "real" but actually suggesting he worked with the late Del Close (a character clearly made up by Robin Williams during an improv night in Chicago).

But you and I know better about American "sources" and "reminiscences" and "Fox Newses" and will not easily be taken in by such an evident hoax.

As your American president [George W. Bush] might have said, if he could ever string enough words together: Just because something isn't true is no reason not to believe in it.

I think this might be a watchword for our times.

That and Always Look on the Bright Side . . .

FOREWORD
BY TERRY JONES

I USED TO PLAY A LOT of rugby football when I was at school. All I can remember about it was that it involved a lot of running around, falling in the mud, and shouting. I don't know what the shouting was for, but it seemed to go with the game. ▪ At the end of every match, we'd be in the showers and the other boys would be talking through the game:

▪ "You know that moment when Tim Hall got the ball

to Green and he beat two men before he was brought down . . ." etc., etc.

I would listen in disbelief. I couldn't remember a single event in the game—not even the moment when my nose got broken. It was just a blur of running around, falling in the mud, and shouting.

Well that's more or less how I feel about filming *Life of Brian*. There wasn't quite so much falling in the mud—in fact considering the weather conditions in Tunisia there was no falling in the mud at all—except at the end when there was a storm during the shooting of the dance routine on the crosses.

So it's wonderful to have Kim "Howard" Johnson's first-hand account of what was really happening behind the scenes, while I was running around, not falling in any mud, and shouting.

As far as I'm concerned Howard's diary is a treasure trove not only of forgotten things, but of things I didn't know in the first place. For instance I had no idea that Mike Palin shaved in the morning when he was playing a Roman but shaved the night before if he were playing a peasant.

This is a unique record of what it was like to participate in making a Python movie, and since there won't be any more, Howard's diaries are unrepeatable.

PREFACE

IT HAS LONG BEEN A TRADITION for American boys to dream of running away and joining the circus. I was fortunate enough to make that dream come true. In this case, however, I ran off to England and North Africa to join *Monty Python's Flying Circus*. Not what the traditionalists intended, perhaps, but working with Monty Python in Tunisia during the filming of *Life of Brian* offered more than could be fit into three rings.

I was front row center at a personal appearence by Graham Chapman
and Terry Jones at the Chicago opening of *Holy Grail*.

My interest in Python started innocently enough. One lazy Sunday
evening, I noted a listing for Chicago's public television station for a program called *Monty Python's Flying Circus* and turned to it with mild curiosity. Within five minutes, I had swallowed the hook. In the weeks that
followed, I delighted in transvestite lumberjacks, sheep that thought they
were birds, killer cars, the Spanish Inquisition, and a thousand and one
other brilliant bits of inspired lunacy far beyond the usual drivel on the
American networks. I eagerly devoured the scant information I could find
about Python and soon learned it was the product of five Englishmen,
Graham Chapman, John Cleese, Eric Idle, Terry Jones, and Michael Palin,
along with animator and lone American Terry Gilliam.

I naturally drove to Chicago for the opening of their first original film, *Monty Python and the Holy Grail,* when I discovered that Terry Jones and Graham Chapman would be appearing live at the theater. I was thrilled to meet them, albeit briefly, and resolved to keep in touch. I started a correspondence (admittedly mostly one-way) with Terry Jones, and in April of 1976 he invited me out to New York, where he and the rest of Python would be performing live at City Center. Even though I couldn't afford it and couldn't take the time off, I also couldn't let a chance like this go by. Terry seemed to remember me when I went backstage between shows, and he introduced me to all of the others, making for an evening I'd never forget.

Each patron at the Chicago premiere of *Holy Grail* received a free coconut
(seen in the crates behind Graham Chapman) while the supply lasted.

TOP: Flanked by Terry Jones and Terry Gilliam backstage at the City Center in 1976. Terry J gave me a personal tour of the backstage area. BOTTOM: Eric Idle, between Saturday night shows at the City Center, was nice enough to interrupt his dinner to sign autographs and pose with a fan.

FACING PAGE TOP: Michael Palin signs an autograph backstage while I sip a glass of wine. It was heady stuff for a young college student and Python fan. BOTTOM: Backstage at the City Center, I learned that, in the days before he gave up alcohol, Graham Chapman was seldom the quietest one in the room.

Becoming increasingly devoted to Python, I resolved to collect all the information that I could for a Monty Python fanzine. I planned to do an index to all the Python TV shows, records, books, and films, as well as any other Python projects, whether as a group or individually. Even though he wasn't terribly familiar with me, Michael Palin agreed to do a telephone interview when I tracked him down while he was hosting *Saturday Night Live*. Thanks to the interview, the first of the three volumes sold quite well, and I was encouraged enough to send copies to all of the Pythons; to say that I was overjoyed by their responses would be an understatement.

I had been considering a trip to London for some time but put it off due to issues of time and money, until I received a letter from Michael. In his closing comments, he told me to be sure to stop by if I did decide to make the trip. I booked the flight the next day.

It proved to be a most worthwhile week. I was able to meet and spend time with nearly all of the Pythons. I stayed much of the week at Graham's house, aside from an overnight trip to Wales to visit Terry Jones and his family while they were on vacation.

The Pythons were due to fly off to Tunisia the next month to shoot *Life of Brian,* so I heard a great deal about it, from talking both to them and to their manager, Anne Henshaw (now Anne James). Terry Jones had even given me the script and storyboards to read. After I arrived home in Illinois, I determined I would find a way to make it to Tunisia for the filming.

The results are in the following pages. They represent more than five weeks of Monty Python at work and at play, on location for the filming of *Life of Brian.* I've tried to include everything, just as it happened: the highs, the lows, and, most of all, the fun. If you can feel just some of the sense of excitement I felt at being a small part of the *Brian* experience, then I've succeeded.

My thanks go out to Anne James, the cast and crew of *Brian,* and my parents; to Laurie and Morgan, who, many years later, encouraged me to share my diary with the world; and, of course, to Graham Chapman, John Cleese, Terry Gilliam, Eric Idle, Terry Jones, and Michael Palin.

MONTY PYTHON'S
TUNISIAN HOLIDAY

LIFE OF BRIAN: A SYNOPSIS

A STAR LEADS THREE WISE MEN to Bethlehem, where they discover a ratbag mother and her newborn child. She seems quite interested in their gifts of gold and frankincense and is pleased to be told her son is the Messiah. But the Three Wise Men discover they are at the wrong stable, so they reclaim their gifts and go worship at the correct one. ▪ The opening credits are accompanied by a title song and lavish Terry Gilliam animation.

In Judea, A.D. 33, Jesus preaches to a large crowd. In the back, people are straining to hear, misinterpreting lines as "Blessed are the cheesemakers" and "Blessed are the Greek." When a fistfight breaks out, Brian and his ratbag mother, Mandy, leave, but not before Brian spots and is immediately smitten by Judith, who is part of a group of revolutionaries.

Brian and Mandy decide to go to a nearby stoning. They purchase stones and a false beard for Mandy, as women are not allowed at stonings. The crowd (most of whom are women in false beards) are to stone a man for saying the word "Jehovah," but it all goes awry when the charges against him are read.

As they leave, Brian and Mandy are accosted by an ungrateful ex-leper who lost his livelihood when he was cured by Jesus. Brian complains about the Romans, who occupy the country, only to learn that his own father was a Roman.

While selling snacks at the Coliseum, Brian encounters Judith, who is with the People's Front of Judea. He begs them to let him join the revolutionary group and is assigned to paint "Romans Go Home" on the wall of Pilate's palace.

That evening, he is caught painting the slogan by a centurion, who discovers his grammatical errors. As a punishment, he is ordered to write "Romans Go Home" on the wall one hundred times. This delights the revolutionaries.

The People's Front of Judea plots to rid their country of Romans, though asking "What have the Romans ever done for us?" proves counterproductive. The revolutionaries raid the palace to kidnap Pilate's wife, only to discover a rival group has the same idea. Brian is captured and thrown into a dungeon with a surprisingly cheerful prisoner called Ben.

Brian is brought before Pilate, who has an unfortunate speech impediment, and escapes while the soldiers are laughing at Pilate. Brian falls from a tower, takes a brief ride on a spaceship, and crashes near a marketplace. To escape the Roman soldiers, he tries to buy a beard, but has problems when he refuses to haggle.

Brian flees to the revolutionaries' headquarters. When soldiers arrive to search the building, Brian hides on a balcony. It collapses, and he falls onto a wall lined with prophets. He pretends to be one of the prophets speaking to the crowd but soon attracts a sizable following who won't leave him alone. He flees, and they are convinced he is the Messiah.

After Brian spends the night with Judith, he discovers a huge group of followers has gathered outside his window, which pleases neither Brian nor his mother. The revolutionaries are quick to exploit Brian's status as the Messiah for their own purposes, as are King Otto and his suicide squad.

Brian is arrested and sentenced to be crucified. Judith tries to rouse the revolutionaries to save him, but they are more concerned with his status as a martyr. Pilate and his friend Biggus Dickus address the crowd for Passover. The people roar at their speech impediments, but with the help of Judith, Pilate orders Brian to be released.

The centurion arrives at the scene of the crucifixions, but when all of the prisoners claim to be Brian, he releases the wrong man. As Brian hangs from the cross, the revolutionaries salute him, and his mother berates him, before all of them join in singing "Always Look on the Bright Side of Life."

The Journey to Monastir, in which I am immersed in all things Tunisian

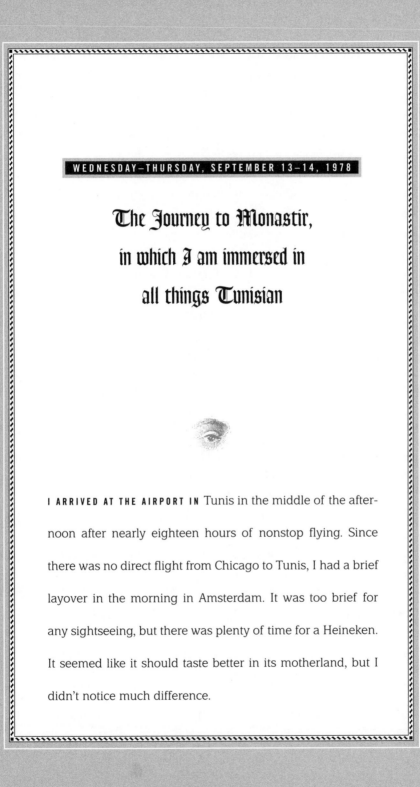

I ARRIVED AT THE AIRPORT IN Tunis in the middle of the afternoon after nearly eighteen hours of nonstop flying. Since there was no direct flight from Chicago to Tunis, I had a brief layover in the morning in Amsterdam. It was too brief for any sightseeing, but there was plenty of time for a Heineken. It seemed like it should taste better in its motherland, but I didn't notice much difference.

As I boarded my flight, I said a silent good-bye to Western civilization as I knew it. The KLM plane was only half full but seemed to be carrying a most varied assortment of passengers. There were Arab mothers with screaming babies, Frenchmen arguing with each other, excited English tourists, and businessmen of varying nationalities who seemed to regard the flight as an inconvenient if necessary part of the job.

The biggest adjustment for me was the lack of a common language, though everyone else on the plane seemed to take it all in stride. The pilot bravely attempted to struggle through the flight announcements in Arabic, French, Dutch, and English, and from the looks of the other passengers, he was barely understandable in any of them. "Le Alps is above us," he announced, prompting some of the English passengers to glance outside nervously.

No announcement was needed, however, when we reached the coastline of Africa. The sky and the sea were both perfect shades of blue, and there wasn't a cloud in sight. The sand along the shore was speckled with a few droppings of green. It was oppressively hot down there, no doubt, but from our vantage point there wasn't a photo in the world that could do it justice. We continued inland, and it wasn't long before we reached Tunis. In fact, we were nearly on top of it before anyone spotted it, largely due to the lack of skyscrapers and modern buildings. We circled the city once before touching down at the airport, which was a few miles from the city itself.

Tunis is the capital and largest city in Tunisia, located right on the Mediterranean across from Italy, and is, like most Tunisian cities, a curious mixture of the old and new. According to what I had read on the subject, Tunisia is considered to be the most modern of the North African countries, and its major industry is tourism.

Most of the Python filming would be done in the city of Monastir, about a four-hour drive along the coast south from Tunis. The Pythons were already down there preparing. I had arranged for a ride with a group flying in from London, but they would not be arriving until the next day, so it meant spending the night in Tunis.

I briefly contemplated spending the night in the airport until the next group arrived, deciding against it when it appeared the place would probably close up completely around nine that night.

The airport was far from any hotel, so I stopped at an office designated "Tunisian Tourist Information," a rather shabby room with three somewhat disheveled Tunisian men in it. After a bit of gesturing, one of them wrote out "Bus 35" and "Hotel Capitole." When the bus arrived, it was packed with Tunisians, and I felt slightly intimidated. Arabic is a harsh, guttural language, which sounds aggressive no matter what is being said, and it sounded a bit like everyone on the bus was arguing with someone else.

Thanks to the help of two boys who spoke English, I got off at the right stop for the Hotel Capitole, which was a couple of blocks ahead. I had still not noticed many tall buildings. Nearly all of the structures seemed to be either stone or cement, and the exterior of nearly every building was painted white or off-white, which I vaguely recalled as having a religious connotation. The outskirts of the city had been sparsely populated, but here in the center of town, more and more people crowded the streets. They made for an interesting picture; some were in traditional dress with white robes. Most of the older women still wore veils across their faces, but I occasionally spotted a younger girl in blue jeans and a sweater.

The Hotel Capitole was a small doorway hidden between larger buildings, which led into an old, run-down lobby badly in need of a coat of paint. I was so tired by that time, however, that if there hadn't been an open room, I would have gone outside and napped in the alley. I pried the desk clerk away from his card game, and he showed me into an ancient, creaking elevator that was nevertheless bigger than the lobby. He left, and I collapsed onto the bed for fourteen straight hours of sleep.

I rose around nine o'clock and found I had to fight the cockroaches for the shower, which was one of the filthiest I had ever seen. I was glad to pack my bags and wait for a bus to the airport.

As I walked down the street to the bus stop, I passed vendors and street peddlers pushing their wares. I was tempted by the smell of freshly baked bread and bits of fried dough, displayed appetizingly but unsanitarily on cracked Formica counters. Other merchants carried fruit, while another local businessman pushed along a cart full of fish that had undoubtedly been pulled from the sea this morning. I was a little leery of the health standards that were undoubtedly in effect, but out of necessity, I became a little more liberal, though I drew a line at drinking the water.

The bus pulled up shortly. It was much less crowded than yesterday, which made for a more relaxing ride to the airport. As the flight from London wasn't scheduled to arrive until midafternoon, I decided to sit back and read while I waited. I opened my pack and found *The Gulag Archipelago* sitting on top. I found the rather graphic descriptions of the Soviet police cells a little too unsettling, though, and decided to write a few postcards instead.

As the time of arrival drew closer, I wandered over to the gate. As I waited, a young, apparently European girl asked me a question in French; when I indicated my ignorance, she broke into a smile. "Oh, you speak English! I'm sorry, but I couldn't tell," she said in a distinctively American voice, the first I had heard in the past twenty-four hours. Her name was Carol, and she was originally from Connecticut. Now with the Peace Corps, she had been living in Tunis as an American teacher, but her two-year stint was almost up, and she would be returning to the States soon. Since the London plane was delayed, we had a nice chat in which she gave me a few helpful hints about living in Tunisia.

The plane touched down exactly an hour behind schedule, which seemed to be the accepted norm with Tunisair, so I began watching for arrivals. I had been informed to watch for a driver holding a MONTY PYTHON sign. The only person I knew who would be arriving was Bernard McKenna, a friend and writing partner of Graham Chapman, whom I had met the previous month in London. He had cowritten *The Odd Job,* a film Graham had produced and starred in. I had first encountered him in a pub where he was meeting with Graham about the film. At the time, Bernard explained that he had just returned from visiting his mother in Scotland.

"I had to go up and tell her about my divorce," explained Bernard. "My mother is a bit old-fashioned, and it didn't sit very well with her. Fortunately, though, I think I've probably dropped all the big bombshells on her that are possible by now." He went on to explain that his brother, a policeman, met him at the airport. "He offered to carry one of my bags, and as we were walking along, I asked him if it was illegal for a policeman to possess contraband. He said, 'Certainly.' We walked along farther, and then I stopped him and said, 'You're breaking the law,' and nodded to my bag. My brother, who is a bit nervous anyway, looked pale but carried on. Pretty soon he stopped and said, 'Yes, but I wasn't knowingly possessing contraband.' We started walking again, and as he was starting to calm down, I said, 'You are now knowingly possessing contraband.'"

A couple of days after that, Bernard had to stop by Graham's house for a bit of doctoring, as he had injured his arm when he slipped and fell in a public lavatory. I saw some of the passengers lining up at check-in from the London flight and spotted Bernard's bandaged arm, clutching a bag of duty-free cigarette cartons and bottles.

I heard a sound behind me and turned. One of the Tunisian drivers was holding up a sign reading MUNTY PYTON GRUP. It made an interesting sight in the midst of all the robes and veils, an incongruity grand enough to deserve a place on the Python TV series.

Bernard seemed startled to see me but quickly recovered and introduced me to Tania, a tanned, attractive brunette. I recalled that Anne Henshaw had mentioned that Eric Idle's girlfriend would be with the group. Tania told me she was originally from a suburb of Chicago, not terribly far from my own hometown. Small world indeed.

We wandered over to the rest of the group, where I was assigned to the Hotel Ruspina. The others headed downstairs to pick up luggage and equipment, and then we all stood waiting for the cars and van that would transport us to Monastir. As I introduced myself, I learned that most of the dozen or so people with the group were either crew members or makeup girls, though Bernard was one of the actors. I was assigned to the van, which was loaded with everyone who couldn't squeeze into the cars, and we started on the ride south.

I was talking with Kenteas, one of the makeup ladies, who was describing her work the previous week on the Sex Pistols film, when someone behind me called out, "Camels! Camels!" Another of the makeup crew, Susie Frear, visibly excited, pointed out a pair of camels in a field alongside the road, the first ones we had seen since our arrival. I was sure they wouldn't be the last, though deep down, I had to admit I was a little excited to see them. "Do you think there'll be lots of them down there?" Susie asked excitedly. Everyone shrugged, and she kept a vigil at the window.

We drove on past miles and miles of date trees, barren fields with the occasional donkey or camel, and even a few vineyards. Even though Tunisia is a Muslim country, it apparently has a fairly healthy wine industry.

As we continued, a few voices in the back began to urge our Tunisian driver to stop for tea. Even though we were seemingly in the middle of nowhere, he indicated that he knew of a place. A few minutes later, he pulled off the main highway and onto a dusty gravel road, which led to the only building in sight for miles. It was reminiscent of the kind of small gas station–general store usually found only in a rustic backwater town, but we all piled out and sat at some tables in front of the building while the driver ordered for us. There was no tea, so we had to settle for Tunisian coffee with goat's milk in place of cream. We sat outside as the sun fell and the temperature began to drop. In the distance we could see an occasional car or truck on the main road. "I wonder if we'll get to see any camels close up?" asked Susie.

The remainder of the drive was uneventful, and most of us either slept or tried to sleep. The bumpy roads and our driver's habits behind the wheel stopped me from dozing off, however. Our driver was fearless, passing cars casually and barely making it back to our lane in time. From what I have observed so far, Tunisian drivers seem to be a bit mad behind the wheel, and I find it amazing that the streets and highways aren't littered with casualties. The near-constant honking of horns is also unsettling. The natives seem to like the noise and lay on their horns at every opportunity. If a car is passing them, they honk. If they want a car to pass them, they honk. They honk when they're angry, but they also honk just to say hello.

At last we pulled up to the Hotel Ruspina, which would be my home for the next few weeks. A few of the other crew members who were also staying there piled out along with me, and I found out my luggage had been put on the other van, the one that had gone on into town. I received a halfhearted promise that it would be brought over from the other hotel, so I went in to register.

At the front desk, two of the unit electricians were trying to change rooms. The desk clerk was trying to explain in his broken English that he'd like them to share a room for the night until he could find another single. The two seemed strongly opposed to this suggestion, so he was attempting to pacify them at the same time he was trying to find the manager, who allegedly spoke much better English.

The Ruspina itself was a nice, modern hotel, and except for the staff of natives and local souvenirs, it looked much like any modern resort in

America. The lobby was small but still very nice, and at the moment it was populated by a group of older German tourists, animatedly chattering away on some topic of grave concern.

I was able to register without any problem, and wasn't asked to share my room, so I headed to the end of the hallway to room 145. I unlocked the door and found a closet full of clothes and a half-eaten watermelon. When I tried to explain to the allegedly English-speaking manager, things grew even more confusing. Through the protests of some of the crew members and some sort of minor miracle, they were able to realize that I needed another room. This time I was assigned to room 153, which was safely uninhabited. There was another plate of watermelon, this one un-eaten, waiting for me, so I ate a little and started preparing for bed.

Suddenly the phone rang. Who could be calling me here? Nobody even knew which room I was in. I answered and was immediately hit with an onslaught of French.

"Uh—could you say it in English, please? English?" I asked innocently.

"Ah, oui, monsieur," the voice replied, then hung up. As I tried to figure out what had just occurred, there was a knock on my door. I opened it somewhat cautiously, only to find a short, plump bellboy with a silly grin on his face and my bags under his arms. Amazed and relieved at their prompt arrival, I didn't ask any questions. I took them from the bellboy, and he remained there with the same sappy grin. With no comprehension of Tunisian currency, I handed him a few coins. He took on a rather pained expression, so I handed him a few more and indicated that that was all. He pasted on the grin again, thanked me, and left.

Final Rehearsal, in which the players are gathered

I HAD ARRANGED TO CATCH A ride into town with some of the grips and sparks (this is what the construction and electrical crews are called). I woke up at half past seven for an unsuccessful attempt at phoning home. I had been told that it was about a fifteen-minute ride into town (the Tunisian drivers usually seem to shave several minutes off that). Traveling the well-paved roads, we passed by a couple of other resort hotels on the way in. Not far from the Ruspina was the Monastir airport, which was rather small but looked shiny and brand-new from the road. Small clumps of grass and occasional palm trees dotted the roadside; the sandy soil didn't seem to allow a great variety of vegetation.

As I spotted the city of Monastir up ahead, one of the grips who had been here for a couple of weeks pointed out a long wall on our left. "The president of Tunisia has his summer house inside there," he informed us. "President Bourguiba is really old and sick right now. They've got him in a hospital in Paris, hooked up to some machine, but he always used to come here for a couple of weeks every summer. This is his hometown." We came to the end of the wall, and I looked inside the front gates but couldn't see anything but trees.

We drove into the town, and they dropped me off a couple of blocks away from the Hotel Sidi Mansour and continued on to the location. The Sidi Mansour is acting as the base of operations for the unit, as it is very near the principal location.

I had to walk through part of downtown Monastir, a curious combination of the old and new. It was slowly being modernized under President Bourguiba's direction, and he seems to want to make it a showplace. The local people seem to really care about him, not just because he's a hometown boy but also because he has really tried to help them. Tunisia was a French colony until 1956, when Bourguiba took over, and for many, he's the only ruler they've ever known. His presence is everywhere; there are pictures of him on all the currency, and posters of him in nearly every shop.

Across the street, I saw twenty-five or thirty tables in front of a café, most occupied by older men sipping the native coffee from tiny cups as they played dominoes or cards. I attracted a few mildly curious stares as I walked by. Around the corner, I spotted the Sidi Mansour, an ultramodern eight-story tourist hotel. I walked past the tennis courts and entered the lobby.

The lobby was probably five times larger than the lobby at the Ruspina and quite a bit busier. I looked for a familiar face and saw Susie, and she invited me to join her and another makeup girl, Diane, for a quick breakfast of tea and fresh rolls.

"They've decided to start shooting tomorrow, you know," Susie told me.

"What?!" I said in the middle of chewing on a roll. "I thought we weren't supposed to start until Monday. What happened?" I'd arrived in the nick of time.

"I guess they just have everything ready and don't want to waste any time. We'll be doing the stoning scene," she revealed, and the two of them excused themselves and left to go for a swim.

I decided that if the filming was to begin tomorrow, I'd better find someone who could tell me the whens and wheres of it. I went back into the lobby and spotted a couple of men who looked suspiciously like film people sitting in a corner. I approached them, and one of them introduced himself as Tim Hampton, the associate producer. He recommended that I go talk to John Goldstone, the producer, and gave me his room number.

John Goldstone had produced other Python projects in the past, but I had never met him. In fact, I had never met a film producer at all, so I felt a bit nervous about pounding on his door and introducing myself.

I needn't have worried. He was young, very friendly, and apparently genuinely happy to meet me—exactly the opposite of the vision I had feared. He invited me in and told me what was going to be happening.

The shooting schedule called for five weeks of filming in and around Monastir, then two weeks in the desert at Matmata, much farther south, and finally finishing at an old Roman coliseum in Carthage, near Tunis. Most of the filming in Monastir would be done in the Ribat, an ancient Muslim castle a few blocks away from the Sidi. John pointed it out to me from one of his windows. It was a rather odd sight in the center of the town, jutting out conspicuously from the more modern buildings.

Ribat actually means "castle," John explained, and this one was a national landmark. It was also a Muslim holy site (which meant no drinking was allowed) and was normally operated as a tourist attraction. The government had closed it off to the general public, however, so that Python was free to build sets and film there. The Ribat had been used in 1975 by Franco Zeffirelli for his *Jesus of Nazareth,* and one of his buildings was still standing next to it. Python was using it to store props and other materials, though one room was being prepared for use as Pontius Pilate's audience chamber. Many of the locals who had worked as extras for Zeffirelli would be used by our production, and some of the other locations would be the same.

John wasn't sure about what I should be doing but recommended that for the time being, I should observe everything and take notes, which would probably prove valuable at some point. He told me to come to the set at eight the next morning, then advised me that the Pythons would be rehearsing downstairs at noon today. He called downstairs to the production office and arranged for me to pick up a script and other relevant items, including my unit hat, as well as squaring me with the accountant's office for my living expenses.

Since I had a bit of time to kill before the rehearsal, I wandered up to the hotel pool to have a look at the script. Susie and Diane were already there, and we chatted until a few other people came up and joined us. Susie introduced me, and I learned they were all members of the repertory company, the group that would play most of the major parts not being handled by the Pythons. We were laughing and carrying on like old friends within moments, and when they found out I was there to help on a book about the film, they pounced on me playfully.

"Well then, you've certainly come to the right place," joked Terence Bayler, a tall, dark, middle-aged Englishman with a deep voice.

"Oh, yes, the rep company, as I see it, should certainly be the main focus of your book," Gwen Taylor assured me. "We shouldn't have much trouble freeing ourselves for interviews with you."

"Actually, we're all hard at work right now," Sue Jones-Davies assured me. She was short, dark, and Welsh, and indicated their sunbathing, explaining, "We must all look quite dark, as though we had been out in the sun for quite some time. Quite hard work, really."

"Oh, yes," agreed Terry as he sipped a cold drink. "I don't know how we put up with these harsh working conditions."

After a few more minutes, they went back inside to change clothes for the rehearsal. The cast and crew were spread around three different hotels. The Sidi Mansour was the location for the central core of the unit. Half of the Pythons were staying there—Terry Jones because he was directing, Terry Gilliam because he was the designer of the film, and Graham Chapman because he played Brian and was therefore in most of the scenes. All of the other personnel essential to the day-to-day shooting were there as well, including the makeup and costume people, the production and accounting offices, and the rep company.

Just outside of town, at the plush Hotel Meridien, were John Cleese, Eric Idle, and Michael Palin. Only two hundred yards away, though hidden by trees, was the Ruspina, which housed most of the grips and sparks, along with the remainder of the crew.

I started looking through my script and all the notes I had been given, inserting pages with the most recent script revisions in their proper places, distracted only by a pair of women who decided to take a distinctly non-American approach to their sunbathing. No one else seemed to take any interest in their lack of tops, so I likewise tried to ignore it.

I finished updating my script and was about to head to the lobby and kill more time when Graham and Bernard McKenna walked out poolside.

"Hello, Howard!" called Graham, and Bernard waved as I walked over to join them. Graham was carrying his ever-present pipe and had a newspaper under one arm. We all sat back in the deck chairs to catch up and catch some sun. When I had last seen Graham, a month ago in London, he had just started growing his beard for the film, and I saw that it had grown out well. He explained that while he was never that fond of beards, he felt it would be more comfortable and less painful to grow one of his own than to have a false one pasted on and taken off every day.

"I shall have to lose this, you know," said Bernard, indicating his full, bushy beard. "I've had it for several years now and don't quite know what it'll be like without it."

"It was a good thing you had it yesterday, or I'd never have recognized you at the airport," I told him. "Why do you have to lose it, anyway?"

"Roman soldiers can't have beards," he explained. "I suppose I'll have to do it today, if we're going to go tomorrow."

"Such a shame about Keith," said Graham quietly, and we all grew quiet. Graham had been a very good friend of Keith Moon, who had died just the week before. Graham had told me a number of stories about Keith and himself, and I'll always regret I never had the chance to see the two of them on a pub crawl, even one without alcohol (Graham was a recently recovered alcoholic).

Graham had told me the previous month that Keith was going to be coming to Tunisia to act in the film. Graham had wanted to feature him in his previous film, *The Odd Job,* but was forced to back down after studio executives claimed he would be "unmanageable." I'm sure Graham felt he could help make up for it with Keith in the Python film.

"How exactly did it happen?" I asked, as I had heard conflicting stories.

"Keith had been taking some pills to lessen his dependence on alcohol," Graham explained. "But at the same time, these pills would double the effect of any alcohol taken while they were in his system. In other words, if Keith had taken them and then had a quart of liquor, which he could handle, the pills would have given it the same effect as two quarts of liquor, which he couldn't."

Graham is a medical doctor and a Cambridge graduate, so he was well aware of the actual names for the medications Keith had taken.

"The thing that really makes me angry, though, is that now the press is going to get on the fact that it was a drug overdose. You know, 'He was a rock star so it had to be drugs,'" he said angrily. "Well, maybe it was a drug overdose, but it was the booze that killed him. Why don't they bring that out, so it may stop someone else from doing the same thing?!"

Meanwhile, Bernard had opened his script in an attempt to look at his lines, and a number of his papers began blowing away. We helped him collect them all, then decided it was probably time to head down to the small dining room where the rehearsal would be getting under way soon.

The tables in the room had all been pushed to one side, leaving a large open space in the center to stage the scenes. I didn't recognize anyone there, until Terry Gilliam burst in, followed by Terry Jones. They were carrying what appeared to be a strange suit of armor made of leather and straw, which they explained was a uniform for one of King Otto's men. They joined the costumers to discuss how the straw should be varnished, and whether or not the leather had the proper finish. I glanced at my script to see why King Otto sounded familiar and noted that he was the leader of a group of militant Teutonic Jews who had decided to help Brian. They intended to set up a Jewish state that would last a thousand years and have the Romans put away in little camps. Otto was the leader of a trained suicide squad that could kill themselves within twenty seconds. I looked at the costume more closely, and sure enough, there was a flap over the chest, which could be opened to allow the wearer to shove a knife through his heart. Sitting alongside the armor, I noticed a helmet, made of similar leather and straw, with an emblem that seemed to combine a Star of David and a swastika.

"Hello, Howard!"

I looked up to see Michael Palin's friendly face grinning at me. I rose to greet him, and he began telling me about the past week. All of the Pythons had arrived in Monastir the previous Sunday, so they could indulge in a bit of lounging about the pool, as well as a little rehearsing, before the filming began. Having a full week, he said, the Pythons had managed to do more rehearsing for *Brian* than they had ever done for any of their other shows. In fact, not much rehearsal was needed anyway, he explained, as there would probably be plenty of spare time while the scenes were set up.

Nearly everyone was filing in. While we were talking, I saw that John Cleese and Eric Idle had both materialized, as well as most of the rep company. I felt a slight sense of awe: For the first time ever, I was in the same room with all six members of Monty Python.

Terry Jones took stock of the situation and called everyone together to start the rehearsal. Whereas he had codirected *Holy Grail* with Terry Gilliam, Terry J was directing *Brian* by himself. When I talked to Terry G a month ago, he told me how he hated directing *Grail* and was determined not to direct *Brian*. He said the Pythons had just broken away from the BBC when they did *Grail*, and they found out they really had to do everything themselves.

"We really weren't working as happily as we normally did, and there was a lot more friction," he told me. "I think it developed also, that because Terry and I were suddenly the directors, rather than Ian MacNaughton [who directed the TV shows] . . . where Ian got all the shit before, you know, 'Let's pick on him' . . . Say [for example] you're [directing something] wrong. Suddenly there's Terry and me to be picked on because we were the ones who'd been doing it wrong, even though we knew we were doing it better than they could have done it.

"So there was that going on, and actually the group started splitting internally. I mean, we'd always argued and everything, but suddenly there were almost two groups. There was the group of the four that was just acting, and the other two that were running around doing ten million jobs. Working on a film is a reasonably boring thing if you're just an actor, 'cause you sit around all day waiting for the directors and the cameraman and everyone else to get their jobs together. So then you go out and do your bit, which only seems to take about a minute, whereas it seems to take about forty-five minutes to set up the shot for you to come out and do something for a minute. Everybody gets bored waiting, and I thought tempers went off a lot. And I think Terry and I were trying to prove something, that we could direct. Actually it was the first thing we had ever done, so we were very tense.

"There were great moments, I mean, it was a great hoot a lot of the time, but I still thought it was very rough. That's why I was absolutely determined not to be a director in the new one. I don't see the point of it. I think directing is a really shitty job, unless it's your own project. But when you're doing something that's sort of a group thing, and you're having to shout at people to get something done that they wrote, it gets a bit irritating. You're actually shouting and you get fed up with the whole thing, so I backed out.

"I feel really sorry for Terry on this new one. I think it's going to be very difficult. I think we're all capable of directing ourselves. We've all done our own projects as directors or being involved in that end of it. So to then come back to the group and have one of us being the one doing the directing . . . that's rough. But we don't have an alternative yet at the moment. Still, Terry's very keen to do it."

Indeed, Terry J seemed to be quite happy about going through with it all. He and Terry G were diverted by something on the costume, while everyone else shuffled around a few moments waiting.

I commented to Michael that Terry J seemed energetic and enthusiastic, very up for the project. "Yes, he's been looking forward to it very much," confirmed Michael. "It will be quite good for him really . . . This time he's on his own and won't have to share the credit. Or blame, as the case may be."

I saw Eric standing nearby and moved over to him. Eric was the only member of the group I hadn't had a chance to meet and talk with for any length of time, and I wanted to reintroduce myself at the first opportunity, but at that moment, Terry J started to organize everyone at the side of the room.

The first scene to be blocked—organizing the actors' movements and positions is called "blocking"—was the Sermon on the Mount. The Pythons and the rep company took their places, and Terry had the rest of us help to fill in the empty space.

In this scene, which occurs toward the beginning of the film, Brian and his mother, Mandy (played by Terry J in drag), join the crowd listening to Christ. No one in the back can hear the Beatitudes, and eventually a fight breaks out in the crowd. It involves several characters, and a number of run-throughs were needed. To make things easier, Terry J asked John to play Christ for the rehearsal, as he was the only actor not involved in the scene, and the actor playing Christ wouldn't arrive for weeks. John began improvising Beatitudes of his own in a quiet, steady monotone ("Blessed are the beekeepers . . .") until he finally started to run dry. At last someone found the real things, and John started up again.

When that scene proved satisfactory, we broke for lunch. A large table had been prepared for us, and the waiters began bringing in food. After lunch and several bottles of wine, Brian was led from his dungeon to be crucified. After that, we rolled into the scene in which Pontius Pilate addresses a crowd. Toward the conclusion, I noticed a group of English women lining up outside the door.

"They're part of a group here on holiday with Thomson's Tours," whispered Gwen. "I think they're going to be in this next scene."

Sure enough, as soon as Terry was satisfied with the next run-through, he called them in, arranging them in a semicircle around the room.

"Now, ladies, this is the stoning scene," he explained. "When we film this tomorrow, you will all be dressed as men, and all of you will be wearing false beards."

I suddenly recalled the scene. It was complicated, and Terry was trying to take his time to make sure all of them understood it. Even so, a couple of the older ladies were already looking puzzled.

"You see, in ancient times women were not allowed to go to stonings. Therefore, all of you are dressed as men so that you'll be allowed to participate. The man is being stoned because he committed blasphemy—he said the word 'Jehovah.' So in other words, whenever someone says 'Jehovah,' you throw your stones at them. We'll be providing you with stones made of polystyrene tomorrow, but right now we'll just have to carry on with what we have here," said Terry, gesturing toward the back of the room.

Someone was handing out paper, which the ladies were instructed to crumple up in the shape of stones, while John Young took his place at the center of the room. John was the senior member of the rep company, a Scottish actor who had first worked with Python in *Grail;* he had been living in Scotland while *Grail* was being filmed there, and the Pythons liked his work so much that they looked him up and brought him along to Tunisia.

John Cleese is the Jewish official in this scene who reads the charges against Matthias (Young), who is to be stoned to death. Naturally, the official says "Jehovah" numerous times as he reads the charges. There was a bit of confusion on the first few run-throughs as all the stones were not thrown on the first "Jehovah." The ladies seemed anxious to pelt both Johns with their paper balls, and after every flurry of paper-throwing, it took some time to recover all the bits of spent paper and get everyone ready for another try. Terry did his best, but as the afternoon went on, the ladies became more and more uncontrollable and silly, so he decided to call it a day.

Michael offered me a ride back to the Ruspina but got Terry to agree to one last rehearsal before we went back. This was to be a walk-through at the Ribat, which I was anxious to see. Michael, Terry J, Graham, and I rode down to the set, where some of the crew were finishing for the day. The three of them walked through the ex-leper scene, in which Brian and Mandy are approached by a cured leper who complains that Jesus, in curing him, has taken away his livelihood.

The Ribat itself is quite impressive, with a large courtyard, a smaller courtyard, a vast array of walkways, rooms tucked away everywhere, and even a tall tower. There were signs of Python activity throughout, from the Roman architectural bits made of polystyrene, to the decidedly Pythonesque naughty frescoes on the walls of Pilate's audience chamber and the back of Pilate's platform overlooking the large courtyard. The platform presently covered a long, sloping walkway where the ex-leper scene starts out. We all walked to the top of it, and they began to go through their dialogue as they started down.

Their projected path would take them down the walkway to the ground, at the other end of the wall, then left and all the way down that wall, under a passageway, and through the smaller courtyard. As they walked along, Terry took notes and tried to determine which lines of dialogue needed to be said at which point, so that everything would come out right at the end of their walk. Everyone seemed happy after only one full walk-through, so they decided to call it a day.

In the car—each of the Pythons has a rented car at his disposal; Michael, Terry J, and Terry G are driving themselves, while the others have drivers—Michael indicated he was very happy with the way things were going so far.

"Compared to *Grail*, working on *Brian* has almost been a holiday, at least up to now," he said. "The weather has been beautiful, whereas it was almost constantly raining at the locations in Scotland, and everything here is going as smoothly as can be. If this keeps up, I'll almost feel guilty about taking the money!"

As we pulled up at the Ruspina, he mentioned that some of the unit would be having dinner at the Sidi Mansour that evening and offered me a ride in. Delighted at the thought, I immediately accepted.

I cleaned up a bit when I got back to my room, unpacked a little more, and lay down to relax before dinner. I looked at some of the other papers I had been given with my script. One was a notice "To all guests at the Ruspina," informing us that members of the film unit would receive a 25 percent discount on all meals in the hotel restaurant. We would also receive a discount at another local restaurant, Le Coq, which was located near the Sidi Mansour. Unit discounts were also available to us at the Sidi Mansour and the Meridien.

I walked to the lobby to wait for Michael and noticed an odd sight. A large bulletin board with PYTHON across the top was in the rear of the lobby, in the same area as another chart listing desert excursions and volleyball games. Notes for the unit, call sheets, and other items would be posted there daily. I can imagine groups of older German or French tourists trying to make sense out of RUSHES TONIGHT AT 7:00 or the unbelievably complex call sheets, full of jargon and abbreviations, that told everyone when to be where.

Michael soon picked me up, and we found Terry J, John Goldstone, and a few others waiting in the bar just off the lobby of the Sidi Mansour.

John tried to arrange a table in the main dining room, until we discovered the floor show, which consisted of three Tunisian musicians playing native music. We were unable to appreciate the subtleties of the loud, shrill, piercing horns and the discordant tones, so we finally managed a smaller dining room to ourselves. The glass doors closed tightly enough to muffle the music, except for the blasts we received whenever a waiter would enter or leave.

We all crowded around one large table. I found myself sitting at one end next to John Goldstone, with Michael and Terry J just across from me. Eric and Tania were to my left; I really hadn't met the others at our table. After the waiters took our orders, Bernard, Kenteas, Susie, and Diane made their way to our dining room, taking a smaller table next to us.

At one point, we noticed that everyone in the entire place had gone quiet, though the music was blaring as loudly as ever. Looking into the main dining room through the large glass windows, we saw an old man dancing in a traditional costume, with two dozen beer bottles balanced on his head. His headgear consisted of two long boards, one on top of the other, with the beer bottles between and on top. Three pieces of pottery placed on the boards also remained stable during his gyrations.

"No, no, it's a trick," insisted Michael, as some of us grew suspicious. "They're all fastened on. Must be."

As we all agreed, the old man nodded his head slightly. One bottle on the end wobbled, then fell into his waiting hands. Slowly and meticulously, he let the rest of the bottles fall, one by one, into his hands. The audience in the other room, mostly older tourists, responded with an overwhelming ovation as our group tried to soak it all in.

We were jolted back to our present situation by the waiters, who brought us our wine after only a twenty-minute wait. Unfortunately, Terry J tested one of them and found it had become Tunisian vinegar. He grabbed a waiter and explained the situation in his best French. The waiter tasted it and, though he didn't appear to find anything amiss, shrugged, smiled, and begrudgingly brought another bottle.

Another commotion sprang up in the other room, and the music grew even louder. The tourists had formed a conga line and were drunkenly snake-dancing around the room. Our group got a few laughs out of the sight, especially when Michael called out, "There's John Young!" In the midst of it all, hands in the air and laughing, was our own Matthias.

As time went on, our dinner showed no signs of appearing, and to make matters worse, we hadn't seen any waiters in the past twenty minutes. John Goldstone, Michael, and Terry J had gotten into a lively discussion about Watergate, and Eric was grumbling about the service. He asked to borrow my pen and began writing on a napkin. When he had finished, he proudly displayed a makeshift certificate for "Absolutely the Worst Service in a Restaurant, Anywhere, Ever," signed it, and passed it around our table for all of us to verify and sign. Under Eric's watchful eye, I added my name to the list and passed it on to John Goldstone, who tried to ignore it.

"Go ahead, sign it," Eric urged. John tried to ignore him, but Eric refused to let the matter drop.

"I'm sorry, Eric, but I really don't think the service is all that bad," said John (who, it must be pointed out, was staying at the hotel and would probably have to endure many more meals at the restaurant). "After all, we did have a very nice soup already, and I'm afraid I don't have any complaints." Terry J and Mike looked over the controversial award and smiled but politely refused to sign as well. Undaunted, Eric obligingly forged their three signatures on the list, with John's name in a prominent spot at the top of the list.

"A very nice forgery," admired Terry, as they looked it over.

At last the food began arriving. The steaks came first, followed by the fish. Soon all of us but Eric had our food and began eating. After another fifteen minutes had gone by, he shook his head in disbelief.

"How can this be?" he asked incredulously. "I'm a vegetarian! They didn't even have to cook anything for me!"

Eventually, even Eric's dinner arrived, and Graham dropped in as well.

"You missed the floor show," Bernard noted.

"Yes, that's what I hear. Quite a pity," smiled Graham.

Things broke up soon afterward, though not everyone was ready to call it a night. Bernard, Graham, Michael, and I decided to stop in at the hotel disco. We were accompanied by Christine, the wife of our director of photography; she was born in Brazil, spoke seven languages, and was reputed to be a great dancer as well.

The disco craze has even spread to Tunisia, and there are supposed to be discos in all of the hotels, although this one could be considered a disco in only the most generous possible interpretation of the word. It looked like a converted bar with an area cleared out of the middle for dancing. For some strange, slightly unsettling reason, the door was locked after each guest entered, requiring a doorman to stand there with a key.

Once inside, Christine immediately grabbed Michael and pulled him onto the dance floor while the rest of us went to the bar and ordered a round of drinks. Bernard and I got the local beer, Celtia; it came in a small green bottle and was surprisingly good. They also carried Tuborg, which was a pleasant surprise.

After Christine tired out Michael, she tried to drag Bernard out to dance. He attempted to resist, claiming his arm wasn't well enough, but she finally coaxed him out. Despite his earlier protests, his left arm seemed to be more mobile now that he was on the dance floor, I thought. We all had a couple more drinks, and Michael gave me a ride back to the Ruspina.

Eric had earlier announced his intention to watch the Ali-Spinks re-match on a special live broadcast feed at three o'clock in the morning. I debated the question and decided to set my alarm for half past two. I dragged myself over to the Meridien, where a television set was glowing in a far corner. A couple of tourists and several locals were gathered in front of the set, but no sign of Eric. The fight was apparently being broadcast as a direct feed from ABC-TV; the announcers were French, but the title cards ("Coming up—the Ali dressing room!") were all in English. As the commentators were winding up, I saw Eric walking over in his robe and slippers, still looking awfully tired.

"Have they started yet?" he asked groggily.

I assured him it was just getting under way. He took a seat, starting to talk a bit more as he woke up.

"I've seen him fight a couple of times. He's really incredible," he recalled. "Once was in New York. I was sitting with Mick Jagger and the Stones. I don't know how it happened, but our group was sitting right next to Henry Kissinger. Ron Wood did a really great job of humiliating his bodyguards!"

We tried to interpret the results of each round with little success, as neither of us was fully awake at any time. There was no doubt of Ali's victory, though, and as soon as the bout ended, we all began dragging ourselves away slowly.

"Damn it," I muttered as I prepared to walk back to the Ruspina. "I'll have to be getting up in another hour and a half. It hardly seems worth going back to sleep."

"That's exactly where I'm going right now," noted Eric, trudging toward the elevators, "And I don't think I'll have any trouble falling asleep."

The Stoning Scene, in which Brian and his mother, Mandy, join a crowd that is ready to stone Matthias to death for blasphemy because he uttered the word "Jehovah"

I WOKE AT A QUARTER TO six, ruing my decision to watch the Ali-Spinks fight a couple of hours earlier. Grabbing my notebook, camera, and tape recorder, I caught a ride to the set with some grips and camera crew. The first people started arriving on the set around 6:30 for makeup, wardrobe fittings, and general preparation. ▪ Today would indeed be the stoning scene, and the unit was setting up next to the wall where Matthias was to be stoned. I felt a rush of excitement at my first real experience in filming.

It was a fairly short, not too complicated scene, but it would take the entire day to shoot. Terry J and Terry G were the first Pythons to arrive on the set, Terry J because he was directing, and Terry G because, as art director, he would have to oversee everything relating to the look of the film. He began busying himself with the polystyrene boulder that would be dropped on John Cleese, touching up the paint in a few spots. Terry J studied the viewfinder of the camera, making some final decisions on shots. The stoning would be filmed against a wall just outside of the Ribat, apparently on the same spot that Zeffirelli shot his own stoning scene.

John Cleese drifted onto the set, looking relaxed and enthusiastic. He settled into one of the folding chairs, waiting to be called for makeup and his costume. Bernard and Andrew MacLachlan, another member of the rep company, had also arrived and were being dressed in their Roman soldier outfits. Their job would be to stand on either side of Matthias, trying to look serious and solemn as they sweated inside their costumes.

I heard a group approaching and turned to find three dozen women in men's robes, all wearing obviously phony beards. That was the idea, of course, as they were supposed to be trying to disguise themselves as men to attend the stoning. A few of the women were connected with members of the cast and crew, others were the English ladies snatched from a Thomson's Tour, and still others were locals or foreign tourists who didn't understand a word of English and whose direction had to be issued through a translator.

The sky looked a bit cloudy at first, but fortunately for the crew (though less fortunately for the cast in the heavy costumes), the sun soon burned away any chance of a cloud cover. The women who had attended yesterday's rehearsal did their best to instruct the newcomers, while a costumed John Cleese paged through George Burns's autobiography.

At last the cameras, lights, and screens were in place, and several walk-throughs seemed to reinforce the blocking, despite a few stones thrown prematurely by the crowd. Matthias was led to the wall by the pair of soldiers, the Jewish official read the charges against him, and he was struck by an unexpected stone.

At long last, after more than three years of development, the camera turned. Exactly as rehearsed, Matthias is led to his place against the wall, to the jeers and threats of the mob. The charges against him are read, and, right on cue, the unexpected stone is cast, catching him squarely in the crotch.

Even though the rocks were only chunks of painted polystyrene, they could still pack a wallop. John Young was apparently unscathed and carried on to the end of the scene none the worse for wear.

Bernard had already shaved off his beard before reporting in, and he looked naked without it. A full cast had been made of it, ironically, so that the makeup crew could fashion another one for him. He couldn't wear a beard while a Roman soldier, but he would need a false beard for some different scenes. Gwen told me, "At first he only shaved half of it off and then wandered around the hotel. You should have seen the looks the locals gave him!"

I had been warned that filmmaking was not a very glamorous, exciting job, and I quickly learned that wasn't a great exaggeration. It seemed to consist largely of waiting around on the set and shooting the same scene over and over again from countless different angles, with different blocking and different shots. Luckily, with the Pythons around, it was impossible to get too bored. It was my first experience ever on a movie set, and it is amazing to think of all of the work that goes on to produce just a minute or two of screen time. (Some of the crew here also worked on *Superman: The Movie,* and they told me that it wasn't uncommon to work all day long and wind up with maybe twelve seconds of usable footage.)

John Cleese told me that friends often asked to accompany him to the studio when he was filming. He said that every time he agreed, they wound up being disappointed and bored. "They always sit around saying, 'When is something going to happen? When are they going to *do* something?' I explain to them that yes, we'll be filming in just a bit after they move the lights around, or check out the sound again. But actually, filming is just a little bit of acting and a lot of sitting around and waiting."

As I stood watching, Terry J noticed the Minolta hanging around my neck and approached me. "Howard, our regular still photographer, David Appleby, doesn't arrive until tomorrow. If I get you a supply of film, do you think you might sort of act as still photographer for the day?"

The Ribat in Monastir, more than any other location, would be the home of *Life of Brian*. At least two-thirds of the filming took place in or around this magnificent Muslim landmark, and, at last glance, it was still standing afterward.

I immediately agreed, happy to help; then I realized I hadn't the faintest idea of how a still photographer worked. In addition, I didn't have the heart to tell Terry that I had just bought the camera a couple of weeks earlier and hadn't ever operated a 35 mm camera before. Tim Hampton found me a few rolls of film and told me to shoot whatever looked interesting. I followed his instructions the rest of the day, as I tried to stay out of everyone's way.

The rest of the day continued to involve the stoning sequence, shot with different close-ups, from different angles, and in a seemingly infinite number of variations. We only used one camera, though there was a smaller 16 mm camera standing by.

Michael arrived fairly early, and Eric, despite the late evening/early morning, made it out by ten thirty. They slipped into costumes and makeup, even though they wouldn't have to step in front of a camera until after lunch. The morning was mostly long shots and close-ups of John, Bernard, Andrew, and John Young, but each shot required the scene to be redone in its entirety.

Occasional takes were spoiled for any number of reasons: A muffed line, a premature stone, a camera or lighting problem, and a stray cloud rolling across the sun were all contributing factors. There was an additional problem with the shooting, as we were filming outside of the Ribat next to a fairly well traveled road. There were a few local policemen on the set to help us out; they stopped traffic a short distance away when we were ready to roll. One of the Tunisians with our unit, Habib, used a bullhorn to bark out an order in Arabic whenever something needed to be done, and someone would invariably jump to it. Habib is in charge of the Tunisians on the film and speaks English quite well.

We will apparently be taking a break every day about midmorning ("elevenses," as it is called) for tea or Coke, accompanied by cheese or tuna rolls. The midafternoon break for tea and biscuits is, appropriately, teatime. Very civilized.

Graham, who wasn't needed until midafternoon, stopped by about half past twelve, just in time for lunch. We lined up just outside the Memmo's truck (that's what was painted on it, so everyone assumes that is the name of the caterer), walked through, and filled our plates. Several tables and chairs had been set up in one of the larger upstairs rooms at the Ribat, and nearly everyone ate there. The grips and sparks began carrying trays to their working area and sat back in the shade, several of them catching a quick nap before filming resumed.

The Pythons had been assigned to three trailers (or caravans, as the Brits refer to them), where they could take their meals in air-conditioned comfort. Terry J and Mike shared one, John and Graham another, and Terry G and Eric the third. A fourth, parked in back of the others, was assigned to Sue Jones-Davies, Gwen, and, when she arrives, Carol Cleveland. It seemed to be turning into a popular spot to apply makeup and a lounge area for the rest of the rep company. In addition, the restrooms were vastly preferable to those in the Ribat—using the facilities will undoubtedly pose a problem, due to some of the complicated costumes.

We had an hour and a half for lunch today, plenty of time for everyone to be fed. Afterward, we drifted leisurely back to the set. The hottest part of the day in Tunisia is usually just after lunchtime, when the sun is high enough to destroy the last remnants of a morning breeze. The rise in temperature caught many unaware; they had dressed too heavily, fooled by the cool air early in the morning. When I was given my unit hat (a white sailor's cap with the brim down, and a Python sticker across the front), I was told it was a good idea to wear some sort of hat whenever I was out in the sun, because of the heat. A few of the grips and sparks seem to have formed a splinter group, having torn the Python stickers off their hats and replaced it by scrawling, with thick black marker, COBRA.

John Cleese was talking with some of the admiring women from the British tour group and offered his autograph in exchange for some suntan oil. After a bit of searching, he located some tanning cream, but I don't know if he was able to get rid of the autograph. Several of the women asked him to do a silly walk, but he begged off as politely as he could, explaining that it had been years since he had last done it. He looked a bit uncomfortable, and I remembered he had told me that he constantly gets requests for the same thing whenever he is recognized.

"Being recognized is a bit of a problem occasionally, though I suppose it would be a bigger problem if I were never recognized," he explained. "I was in Harrod's one day trying to choose between two items, when I noticed two older women standing a short distance away, whispering and pointing at me discreetly. I tried to ignore them and concentrate on what I was doing. Finally, one of them approached me and asked if I would sign an autograph for her daughter. Now, I don't mind doing autographs. Actually, it's quite easy, just writing down your name, so I signed one very politely and gave it to her. She thanked me and walked away. A few moments later, I noticed her standing with her accomplice and watching me. Again, I tried to ignore them, until the same lady approached me and said, 'Do you think I could have an autograph for my grandson?' So I wrote another one. She went back and joined her friend in staring some more, until I noticed she was moving in again. So I quickly left to try to lose her before I became caught in a trap. I didn't know how many relatives she could have had!"

The afternoon's filming began with shots of the crowd of women dressed as men, with close-ups of Michael, Eric, and Terry G (dressed as women dressed as men). The camera was placed in front of them as they ran through the scene a number of times. Everyone threw their stones during each take, narrowly missing the camera operators, the crew, and even the still photographer du jour. Eric, in particular, took great delight in throwing the stones as hard as he could against the stone wall just in front of him. But his enthusiasm had its drawback: Whenever one of his stones hit the wall, it would break off tiny pieces of the painted outer layer, exposing the polystyrene. One stone even broke completely into two chunks.

By midafternoon, the heat seemed to be affecting everybody. John Cleese and Michael Palin had some time off. After finishing a cup of water, Mike, relaxing in a folding chair in the shade, became very keen on the idea of throwing small rocks into the cup from a distance. His first few attempts were unsuccessful, and John led in the jeers, after which he grabbed a handful of rocks to try it himself.

Two cups were set up, and Terry G joined in, delighted at this new diversion. He sank the first two rocks he attempted, so John and Mike insisted that he move the cup farther back. Eric joined in, and a powerful competitive spirit soon developed. They were taking it all much more seriously. When someone unknowingly walked past in front of a cup, knocking it over, he was admonished by loud irate protests. Competition was keen, and cups were stacked on each other and placed in various designs. As they were throwing, John and Mike decided that they might have accidentally hit upon the historical basis for actual stonings.

"You know, this would be a lot more fun if the cup emitted screams of pain when struck by a stone," offered John.

"My mother emits screams of pain when struck by stones," offered Mike.

"Well, then, let's do her next," said John, as their improvisation drew to a close. "And immediately after that, the first actual stoning was held."

By this time, Terry J had noticed that his actors were missing, and after a bit of searching, he found them all intent on throwing rocks into small cups. He looked quite interested and would probably have liked to join in for a few rounds, but duty called, and he was forced to break it up.

The stoning scene ended with a large boulder dropped on the Jewish official by the members of the crowd. By this time, the character played by Michael has already been stoned to death, so that meant that during the next sequence, Michael was forced to lie motionless on the muddy ground, covered with the mock stones, while the irritating Tunisian flies made him even more uncomfortable. After a couple of takes, he picked himself up, his face and costume covered with dirt and mud. Adding insult to injury, he discovered that he wouldn't be visible in the shots anyway, as he was flat on the ground. He looked at it optimistically.

"Well, hopefully this is the worst indignity I'll have to face during the filming," he said. "They always like to crush your spirit, crumble your last remaining bits of pride and self-respect, right at the start, just to keep the actors in line."

John Young must have felt much the same way, as his head, shins, and groin had been struck repeatedly with the mock stones, all in an attempt to hit his knee for one shot.

The sun began hanging low, and it became a race against time to finish everything today before the light gave out. If we couldn't, it would mean calling back all of the tourist ladies for another day of filming. Naturally, as soon as we tried to hurry things up, the camera broke down. A couple of operators started tearing it apart while another camera was set up in case they failed.

Terry J was now in his Mandy costume, ready to do his bit as Brian's screechy, domineering mother. Though all of the Pythons do a masterful job in elderly drag, Terry can break me up with the raising of an eyebrow. He was strapped into a harness that gave him enormous sagging breasts and buttocks and a potbelly, all of which fit under Mandy's dress. It suggested a medieval torture device, but when I mentioned it to Terry, he said it was still more comfortable than the Sir Bedevere costume he had to wear in *Grail*. It was wonderful to watch Terry directing everyone while walking around in this ridiculous outfit—it seemed to add just the right element of the absurd.

At last the camera problems were resolved, so there were a few shots of Mandy and Brian walking up. Most of the women from the tour group looked like they were ready to get back to their hotels; for them, filmmaking may have lost just a little bit of glamour. Nevertheless, they carried on well, and Terry called a wrap to the first day of filming.

The cast changed out of their costumes and cleaned up a bit, then headed back to their hotels. Michael offered me a ride back to the Ruspina and explained to me that the shooting schedule gave us every Sunday and every other Saturday free. All of the hotels are on the sea, but if the shooting schedule keeps up at this rate, the only chance I'll have to make it to the beach will be on those days off.

Back at the hotel, I went for a run along the beach, where I encountered a few of the sparks who had the same idea. After I finished, I showered and had dinner in the restaurant at the Ruspina; some British tourists invited me to join them. The restaurant overlooked the pool, where some sort of Tunisian wedding was to take place. We could see a large tent set up in front of several dozen rows of chairs. Going outside, I learned that the bride was a personal secretary to President Bourguiba, and the owner of the Ruspina was a friend of someone or another. I joined with a large contingent of tourists in watching the ceremony, which was rather anticlimactic. In fact, I didn't even realize that it had concluded until crowds of Tunisians in formal dress began streaming away from the tent.

I relaxed in anticipation of a day off. Even though we'd only filmed for one day, it seemed like we'd been at it all week.

A Day Off, in which there is much resting by the pool

I FORGOT TO SET MY ALARM, so I finally rolled out of bed today at the embarrassingly decadent time of half past two in the afternoon. I must be more jet-lagged than I had realized. ▪ I decided to go for a walk along the beach. John Cleese had the same idea, and we walked together for a while. As we headed toward the Ruspina, he revealed that he had spent much of the morning writing.

"I'm not entirely happy with the ending of the stoning scene," he said. "You know, as it stands now, it ends with Bernard inadvertently saying 'Jehovah' and being chased off by the crowd. I'm not completely comfortable with it. I think we may be trying to get too much out of the 'Jehovah' joke."

As we walked along, he explained that he planned to spend most of his free time writing at his hotel; he has to script a fifth and come up with an idea for a sixth *Fawlty Towers* episode for the show's second series. He said it was slow going so far and asked if I'd ever had an interesting experience in a hotel. "I need some good hotel stories," he noted.

It sounds like the other Pythons are going to be keeping busy as well. Graham and Bernard mentioned that they planned to do some writing together during the filming, and Michael said he hoped to turn out another *Ripping Yarns,* even though the atmosphere here didn't seem too conducive to working.

John hadn't been to the Ruspina yet, so we headed down the pathway to the hotel and joined some of the grips and sparks, who were having tea at the poolside. John went for a quick swim. He looked around as he joined us back at our table.

"This has a much better atmosphere than the Meridien," he noted. "That place is much too big and spread out—I don't feel awfully comfortable in it. You never see anybody there." He went into the lobby and made an appointment for a massage, then returned.

"Quite a big deal over here last night," noted Reg Parsons, one of the crew members I spotted observing the wedding last night. He described the ceremony.

"Ah, yes, so you were taken in by that, eh? Actually, that's all put on for the tourists, you see, twice a week," John teased. "I took my dinner at the Meridien last night, ordering a 'genuine Tunisian dinner,' as they called it. They served me some type of lasagna, prawn salad, and some Norwegian fish."

John was called in for his massage, and the others began drifting away. I decided to put in for a phone call to the United States, and I let my parents know that I had arrived safely and was still alive, at a cost of just twelve dollars for six minutes.

The Latin Lesson, in which Brian attempts to paint "Romans Go Home" on a wall of the palace

EVERYONE SEEMS TO HAVE HAD A quiet day off, although I heard a few scattered comments about Bernard in the Sidi Mansour disco Saturday night . . . Michael spent much of the time trying to write, and Graham said that he spent Sunday morning doing minor medical work for a few of the more unfortunate members of the cast but later found time to do a bit of writing while lounging alongside the pool.

Filming this morning involved the scene in which Brian is apprehended for painting anti-Roman graffiti on a wall, with John as the Roman centurion who catches him. The scene is supposed to take place at night. Naturally, it was the brightest, sunniest day yet, so the camera operators used a darker filter in order to shoot "day for night."

The scene was filmed in the large courtyard, fairly safe from the noises of the cars and donkeys on the road outside. Most of the locals were kept out as well, leaving it to the various cast and crew members to spoil the occasional shots today. Problems with the sunlight were never really big enough to qualify as major, though there were some delays. Skies were clear most of the time; there were a few scattered clouds rolling past, and even a brief bank of clouds that covered the sky. Strangely enough, a heavy cloud cover that remains for a time is not as problematic to the filming as occasional clouds that briefly cover the sun. The important thing is that the light stay constant. If the clouds remain heavy, they can compensate for it, but when the lighting changes every couple of minutes, it can ruin a shot. It was the latter sort of weather that prevailed early in the day and spoiled any chance of turning a camera before our midmorning break, so the first part of the morning was spent rehearsing.

John did the first rehearsals in his centurion costume while wearing his wristwatch. He noted that he rather fancied doing the part of the centurion throughout the film while wearing his watch but was afraid the audience would then spend the first few scenes whispering, "He's forgotten to take his wristwatch off!" Determined to salvage some sort of victory from it all, he decided to leave his watch on underneath his centurion wristbands for a few run-throughs.

As soon as we broke for tea at midmorning, the sky naturally cleared. This time, though, it appeared as though it would hold, so as soon as everyone finished their rolls, they carried their tea back to their places so that we could get an early start.

I met David Appleby, the still photographer, a young, likable, quiet man who arrived here yesterday. That meant I could concentrate on taking notes of the proceedings.

The first few takes failed for various reasons. More clouds rolled in on the first take. The sound of a plane overhead drowned out the sound track of the second attempt, and just as we began the third take, John's costume started coming undone. By this time, a few people began to feel a bit frustrated, though helpless. John was getting tired of the walk toward Brian at the beginning of the sequence. This was compounded by the fact that his costume included a number of clanking metal objects and leather straps, and the slightest movement on his part was clearly audible to Garth Marshall, our sound man. As a result, John had to stand quite a ways away and walk up to Brian as he painted the wall.

On the next take, John approached Graham right on cue and they went into a Latin lesson, a marvelous bit in which they are transformed from a soldier arresting a revolutionary to a stern schoolmaster instructing a rather dim student. It started out perfectly, with both of them hitting their lines with incredible timing, right up to the point at which a wrong answer by Brian infuriates the centurion so much that he draws his sword. On this take, John reached for his sword, only to find it hanging upside down in his belt, quite out of reach. For a split second, he appeared poised between anger and laughter, but quickly let out a good-natured chuckle, and the rest of the crew joined in. I noticed that throughout the rest of the day's takes John kept his hand carefully but unobtrusively to his side to steady the sword.

There were a few problems inherent in the scene itself, due to the fact that Brian did actually have to paint on the wall. No matter how water soluble the bright red paint, the Tunisian government simply would not allow us to paint on their walls—a definite problem, in that we needed to cover the entire wall with "Romans Go Home" painted one hundred times. Terry G and his crew somehow managed to cover the entire wall with some sort of plaster/papier-mâché shell, and it looked perfect. If I had not been told, I would have sworn that the wall was the real thing, instead of a model covering the actual stones, sticking out about two inches.

The paint was applied in one take, and there was no real problem in removing the paint from the wall for a second as it simply came off with a squirt of water. The biggest delay was in waiting for it to dry, though that didn't take long in the hot Tunisian sun. If Graham had started painting on it while it was still moist, however, it would begin to run. During the subsequent takes, Graham didn't actually have to paint on the wall since the camera wouldn't show it from that angle, though he did get some red paint from the paint pot on his fingers, which had to be cleaned before the next take.

I noticed Graham sitting under a large umbrella after one take, lounging in a folding chair. Susie was scrubbing the paint from one hand and almost looked like she was giving him a manicure. Diane was fanning him and holding an icepack to his head, while Graham held a small electric fan in his other hand. All he needed was a handmaiden feeding him grapes, I thought.

"You must have some great contract," I said to him.

"Ah, yes," he laughed. "Well, it's actually not all as frivolous as it looks. You see, we're doing close-ups of me painting, so I can't be sweating a great deal or the shots won't match."

Earlier in the day, before the sun had gotten really hot, no one was perspiring noticeably, but now, just standing in the sun for a few minutes was enough to set anyone off. In a typically Hollywood touch, Susie carefully applied a few drops of cosmetic perspiration to his brow as he rose to continue the scene.

The actual painting of the wall by Graham took a bit of doing. The first attempt at "Romanes Eunt Domus" saw the entire thing off center. That portion of the wall was then sprayed down and allowed to dry, while everyone stood by waiting. Graham almost got by in the next take, but ended with "domum" instead of "domus," so a spray and a dry then followed as everyone stood by patiently. We didn't wait long enough, though, as the paint began running almost immediately on the next try. The next attempt finally succeeded, though, and we were able to film John doing his corrections. We broke for lunch shortly after that, while the courtyard was watered down to make it suitable for the rest of the day-for-night filming in the afternoon.

Insects haven't yet become a source of major discomfort. There are really no mosquitoes, but the flies are making up for their absence. These Tunisian flies are no larger than the average American housefly; they make their presence known through their numbers and have even annoyed some of the actors while filming. The ants aren't as much of a problem, though they are incredibly large, leading John to quip that *Them!* may have been filmed on location here.

As we sat around waiting for the filming to commence, Graham and I started talking about the medical problems he had been running across.

"Most really aren't too serious," he reflected. "There has been quite a bit of diarrhea and a few upset stomachs, all easy to treat. The main problem seems to be making sure that everyone gets enough salt. The heat and sweating while working seems to make people feel quite weak and unwell, and they need to replace the salt in their system. Oh, I also faced an infected arm—not too serious—plus a few other problems best not talked about. One woman who came to me wanted to talk about something she couldn't talk about, but I felt she didn't have what she thought she had, so I didn't give her anything for treatment until I saw the result of the tests. Actually, though, now she's gone back to Italy, so it really doesn't make any difference anyway."

I had to concur with Michael, who noted earlier that Graham had a practice going on location that any doctor in London would give his right arm for.

Christine and a girl I didn't recognize were walking around the set with a large jar of salt tablets and a few quarts of bottled water, in line with Dr. Chapman's instructions. These were being handed out each day to all crew members who wanted them.

"Yeah, give me some of those," bellowed Roy Rodehouse, a large, good-natured, bearlike spark, and as he reached for them he called to Graham, "How many of 'em should I take?"

"Well, I don't know," puzzled Graham. "Perhaps you should just forgo some of the tablets, and we could arrange that a salt lick be installed for you."

"Yes, right next to your watering hole," suggested John. "Something you could just sort of go to instinctually."

After lunch was Brian's run across the courtyard as he creeps up to paint the wall. The first few shots were from Brian's point of view, in which two drunken soldiers stagger by as Brian hides, and a small dog wanders by. The Tunisian dog handler had two small dogs, which he claimed could walk across the courtyard easily enough, so he turned one loose. To the delight of all, as the camera rolled, the dog wandered about for a few seconds, then stopped and sniffed at the base of a statue of Caesar, lifted his leg, and peed. This bit of improvisation won him the first standing ovation of the film. He was then collected by his trainer, and, amazingly enough, repeated his feat for a second take. Terry J was so delighted by this that he suggested, only half joking, that the soldiers walk by again, following suit at the same corner of the statue. He was outvoted, even after pointing out that after a night of drinking, the soldiers would certainly need to relieve themselves.

Next, Graham had to make several mad dashes across the courtyard in the heat of the midday sun. Fortunately for the crew, but less fortunately for Graham, there were no clouds in the sky, so the day-for-night effect will be much easier to apply effectively, despite the heat. Terry J remained off-camera, relaying instructions.

"Go on now, Graham, look, they're all behind you. Peer about . . . now look, they've all left you . . . look about and have a run for the next statue. Have a look over your shoulder . . . look over that way . . . look back again . . . look all around."

Getting the close-ups of Graham in this scene proved to be more difficult than anticipated. When he was actually running, the cameraman had a hard time keeping him in shot due to his jerky, quasi-stealthy movements. If he just stood there or tried running in place, there would be no change of light or shadows to indicate movement. In a burst of inspiration, four of the crew members were assigned to hold small squares of canvas high enough so the shadows would fall against Graham, and they began running next to him. Just as hoped, when the shadows fell against Graham as he ran in place, it gave the perfect illusion of running through the courtyard at night while keeping Graham's face in shot.

"You wouldn't see something like this on a Zeffirelli set," Terry G commented as he watched the men with the canvases over their heads running in a circle next to Graham.

It apparently worked quite well, and Graham soon discovered that he didn't even need to run in place. He seemed rather disappointed when the shots were finished and was quite keen to keep at it. In fact, he indicated that he was willing to try it while in a chair with a cup of tea.

It began to grow late, and the crew was about to wrap things up when we heard a report of a poisonous snake residing on one of the top floors of the Ribat.

"It lives in a crevice of some sort, and the only time anyone ever sees it is when it pokes its head out to catch itself a bird," one of the makeup girls reported. "Every evening at half past six the snake comes out, catches a bird for dinner, and then pops back in."

"A lot more entertaining than a wristwatch," noted Bernard. "Sort of a daily ritual, is it?"

"No, really, that's what one of the locals told us," she said, wide-eyed.

Filming had to wrap a bit earlier than we had hoped. The shadow of the west wall grew long, and so we finished before it caught up to us. Just as everyone started to head back to their hotels, a huge, modern Tunisian fire truck pulled up outside the Ribat. Perhaps in response to the snake? I wondered. Two men got out; one wore a plain green work uniform, while the other, clearly his superior, wore the same type of uniform but with a more impressive military cut to it, with several colorful campaign ribbons across his chest.

They pulled out an enormous section of ladder, leaned it against the top of a wall, and proceeded to free a bird that had gotten itself caught near one of the upper windows (perhaps while trying to flee the snake?). An impressive exhibition, undoubtedly staged for our benefit, as I doubt they haul out the fire truck every time a bird is in trouble. Maybe the fire chief wanted a part in the film.

Coincidentally, two of the assistant directors, Matthew Binns and Melvin Lind (or "Binns and Lind," as John Cleese liked to refer to them individually and collectively), asked whether I might be available tomorrow to serve as a palace guard. I agreed, and Matthew noted in passing, "Oh, you'll have to lose the mustache, though." A small price to pay for immortality, I suppose. Matthew and Melvin are young, no more than their midtwenties, but do their jobs very well. They are assigned to organize all of the things no one else wanted to organize, including the transportation, the extras, and keeping an eye on the cast. They are easy to spot, as they always carry walkie-talkies. They have to remember to turn them down while filming to prevent a squawking "Matthew or Melvin, come in!" in the midst of a crucial take.

John gave me a lift back to the Ruspina, where I decided to go for a quick swim and do a little letter writing before dinner. I had dinner at the

Ruspina, where every meal seems to be an adventure and it is proving impossible to get anything quickly. Service seems to be slow everywhere I eat here, proving my first dinner at the Sidi Mansour was no fluke. I wonder if it has to do with the general mood in the country. They seem to attach little importance to time and seldom feel the need to rush about anything.

Most of the food so far, though, has been surprisingly good. Many of the dishes are French; though the French left more than twenty years ago, their influence is still strong. We've been surprised at the beef dishes offered, since we saw very few cows in the countryside. There is always quite a bit of chicken, fish, and mutton on the menus, so there hasn't been much to get used to insofar as the food.

Ordering is quite an adventure. The hotel menu is printed in several languages, none of which is English. I've made a few feeble attempts to translate, using my phrasebooks, with no success, and usually end up pointing to whatever looks most palatable. There have been a few surprises, though all have been edible. I had planned to try learning a bit of French while I was here. I think I'll begin by learning the names on the menu.

Ladders and Tunnels, in which the last slogan is painted and the revolutionaries make their first entrance into the sewer tunnels

SOMEONE HAS BEEN BUSY SINCE WE left yesterday. The front wall of Pilate's palace overlooking the forum was covered with "Romani Ite Domum" in various shapes and sizes, totaling nearly a hundred in all. I don't know who did it or when, but it must have taken all night to finish it. The area above the walkway was left blank, but Terry J said that will be matted in during postproduction, so it will look like the entire wall has been covered.

Michael was back on the set today after having Monday off, and he reported spending it lying in the sun, writing, and rehearsing.

"I found an isolated spot on the beach near the Meridien, which is ideal for rehearsing some of my things, as I can be as loud as I want to," Michael told me. "I was apparently all alone when I went into one of my Pontius Pilate speeches. Just as I shouted 'This man wanks as high as any in Wome,' a man on a bicycle rode past. He stared, then sped off as fast as I've ever seen anyone ride."

Bernard had quite an exciting evening. I don't think anyone in the unit is enjoying themselves more, while at the same time suffering as many mishaps, as Bernard. Somehow he became locked in his hotel room last night, unable to get out. He did his best to call and get a key sent up, but to no avail. He began pounding on the door and yelling, but no one else was around to hear (or else they were afraid to interfere). Finally, Bernard heard someone coming down the hallway and started yelling again. Fortunately, it was Terry J, and, through the door, Bernard explained his problem. Through Terry's efforts, a key was finally sent up, by which time Bernard had fallen asleep. He went directly downstairs to dinner and was told the restaurant had stopped serving. That was apparently the wrong thing to tell Bernard at that time.

"What do you mean it's closed?! I've been locked in my bloody room for the last three hours trying to get a bloody key, and now you're telling me I'm too late for dinner?!" He was soon ushered to a table by a rather frightened-looking waiter.

The first shot of the day was Brian standing on top of a ladder, brush in hand, as though he had just finished painting the last slogan. Terry J expressed doubts that Graham would enjoy standing on the top of the creaky wooden ladder, but even though it was shaky, and appeared to be held together with only twine lashings, it held together sufficiently well. Despite his initial uneasiness, Graham was soon scurrying up and down as though it were a steel-reinforced staircase.

There was a little uncertainty as to the start of the scene. It was supposed to occur the next morning, with the guards assigned to Brian asleep at their posts, though they have a line as soon as he's done painting.

"How are we supposed to wake up for our line?" asked Bernard.

"Yes, I see . . ." puzzled Terry J, then called to the top of the ladder. "Graham, when you're done, call out 'Finished!' to the guards so they wake up. That should also let us cut away to a wide shot of the wall."

"Right," said Graham, and the camera started to roll. He put a few dabs of paint on the nearest slogan, dropped his brush back into the paint pot, and obediently called out, "Finished!"

"Right," said Bernard, as he and Andrew rubbed the sleep from their eyes. "Now don't do it again!"

"Let's print that one!" Terry said proudly after Brian had completed his run away from the guards. While the next shot was set up, Terry and Graham discussed the lack of problems encountered so far with *Brian,* as opposed to the first two days of *Grail,* which Terry called "atrocities."

"Things are going so much better than I expected, I can hardly believe it," noted Terry. "The writing on the wall looks much better than I had dreamed of in my sketches."

"I had anticipated finding a few things to grumble about, but I've really been disappointed in that so far," said Graham. "Everything is going so much smoother than I had anticipated. It worries me slightly that I'm actually enjoying myself. I usually find it necessary to grumble a bit. If I don't, then people will think I'm having a good time and won't want to pay me.

"Even so," Graham added as Terry walked away, "there is one thing that plagues Python, it seems. Everything in our films seems to be covered with dust or dirt, to make it look either old or rotten. Whenever one picks it up, the dust gets all over, making one's hands very dirty by the end of the day. Aside from that minor point, I really have no complaints so far."

Everyone I've talked to up to this point who had also worked on *Grail* seemed to be amazed at the smoothness of filming here. Nearly all I could get about the filming of *Grail* was horror stories, how the weather was terrible and it rained nearly every day.

This morning, as seems to be the case most mornings here, there was a slight cloud cover early. It had burned off by the time we were ready to shoot, though, and remained sunny and hot the rest of the day. It was also the stillest day so far, with no breeze, even in the morning, to cool things off.

Once we got started, there were very few spoiled takes. We were far enough away from the street noises so that most of the spoiled takes were due to mistakes on our part for various reasons. Nearly all of the painting scenes had been completed by lunchtime, so we broke for a fairly lengthy lunch. After he finished, John lounged around finishing his grapes, amusing himself by throwing grape skins at various passersby.

"That's something to put in your book," he noted after taking a successful shot at Bernard. "Cleese proves deadly with used grape skins at five feet."

He started playing a finger game in which he appeared to be removing his thumb from his hand, amusing a few locals with some curious facial expressions.

I ran into Eric, who described a few scenes that didn't make it into the shooting script. "We did have a Last Supper scene that didn't quite make it," he recalled. "Also, we ended up dropping quite a few jokes about virgin birth."

Talk turned to the evolution of the film. *Life of Brian* could be traced back to a joke Eric came up with shortly after they had completed *Grail*. He claimed the title of their next film would be *Jesus Christ, Lust for Glory,* and the Pythons eventually decided to do a spoof of biblical epics. They soon found they couldn't do a spoof of the life of Christ, as they found him to be very good, very decent, and therefore difficult to satirize. It then became *The Gospel According to St. Brian,* the story of a thirteenth apostle, not as well known as the others because he spent most of his time at home taking care of the books.

The film was all set to go when EMI backed out of it, withdrawing the money that had been promised to the Pythons. Apparently, someone had shown EMI head Lord Bernard Delfont certain portions of the script that, when taken out of context, seemed to him to be objectionable. While another backer was being sought, the group went off to Barbados on holiday in January of 1978 to rework the script again. It underwent a major change, becoming more or less the current script for *Brian.* (For a time, it had also been called simply *Monty Python's New Film,* because, as Michael explained it, "We didn't particularly want to draw attention to the fact that it's a religious film.")

I headed back to the large courtyard and noticed Graham withdrawing a packet of tobacco and his omnipresent pipe from a small pouch attached to his belt as he sat in his Brian costume.

"Well, you know [regular costumer] Hazel Pethig designed the costumes for this, of course," Graham explained. "She's always nice enough to give me some way to carry my pipe."

Closer to the set, John greeted me with what sounded like "Eo posso mataar moseguscum oma coliairteo."

"Christine taught it to me," he explained. "It's Brazilian Portuguese, and it means 'I can kill bats with an egg spoon.' Auf deutsch ich kann mich eine io lo fo fliedermoiseturtain. That's it in German. It's the only Portuguese I know."

"Can you say it in Arabic yet?"

"No, not yet. I shall have to work on that." He looked around to Habib, the Tunisian who was working with the unit and also serving as a translator. Habib quickly taught him to say the phrase in French, which proved little challenge, before attempting the more challenging Arabic translation.

"Let me see . . ." Habib said thoughtfully. "I can kill . . . neshum noctul . . ."

"Neshum noctul . . ."

"Let's see . . . we have to translate it in some precise form, there are so many words for different types of bats."

"Little ones."

"Dbsria . . ."

"Neshum noctul dbsria . . ."

"No, wait . . . dbsria is a word little children use. It is hard because it is a silly phrase," explained Habib. "Neshum noctul edebeya . . . dim rafa . . . with a spoon."

"Dim rafa . . ."

"Ita cauwa. We have to use coffee spoon, okay?"

"Oh, yes, that's fine. Neshum noctul edebeya dim rafa ita cauwa," said John proudly. "Okay, we'll do some more tomorrow."

He proudly approached a group of locals with the phrase and was met by a curious combination of laughter and the caution usually reserved for the deranged.

According to the day's call sheet, it was to be an extended day, perhaps accounting for the lengthy lunch hour. When filming finally did resume, it was to finish one last bit of the morning's scene, and everyone then packed and moved to another wall of the Ribat. I had noticed a sewer tunnel there earlier, constructed by our crew and covered with a

Costume designer Hazel Pethig devised a small pouch for his belt that would allow Graham to carry his pipe and tobacco throughout the day.

heavy black tarp to prevent light from seeping in. A false perspective was attached to one end.

This would be one of the scenes in which the Judean revolutionaries climb into the sewer and crawl through on their way to raid Pilate's palace. The prop men began to pump smoke into the tunnel with small charcoal burners. Although the outside of the tunnel was unfinished plywood, the inside looked exactly like a decaying, slimy brick tunnel, with fungus and mold caking it in all directions, and the smoke adding just the right touch of haziness.

The costumes for the revolutionaries while on their commando raid consisted of loose-fitting black robes, which the actors found very comfortable, perhaps to compensate for having to crawl through the tunnel. Their comfort was short-lived when they saw what Terry G had in store for them. Each of them would be carrying a large coil of heavy rope slung over one shoulder and a coil of equally heavy netting over the other. In addition, each of them was assigned a particular weapon, either a knife, a club, wooden handcuffs, or some other heavy, clumsy sort of object that Andrew charged was deliberately designed to impede them. Bernard just kept looking warily at his props and at the tunnel.

For most of them, the worst part of the costume was the handheld lanterns they had to carry. Actually small electric lights, they were powered by a power pack strapped to the actor's back. An electric cord was strung from the power pack along the arm, concealed by the sleeve, and connected to the light. This meant that once they were wired, they couldn't put their lanterns down until they were disconnected.

"All of this electricity forces one to be very careful when having a pee," confided Michael, and he went off to join several of the other commandos who were similarly dreading the trip into the tunnel.

When the camera started to roll, the first shots were of the commandos dropping down into the sewer tunnel. The actors were rounded up, and more smoke was pumped in. One by one, they dropped into the dark hole, and I could hear their muffled thumps as they crawled around. At last, all of them were inside, and part of the canvas was pulled away to let them out. The commandos all staggered out as quickly as they were able.

"That is absolutely the worst scene I have had to do, ever," swore

Michael, as he collapsed into a chair. "Dropping into a smoke-filled tunnel which I didn't know the depth of, with all of my gear and a light that doesn't work. That was the worst scene I have ever shot anywhere. But I refuse to complain about it."

A section of sewer tunnels was constructed under a heavy tarp, which would allow filming of the commandos crawling even in the bright midday sun.

The tunnel claimed its first casualty, with Bernard rubbing his bad elbow and showing it to Dr. Chapman.

"Yes, it looks as though perhaps we'd better call off your tunnel-crawling adventures," Graham advised, as he tried moving the arm about.

Bernard looked as pleased as he dared at this reprieve from further stumbling around in the sewer.

Just as the commandos were about to go again, we heard a blast of something that sounded like the Tunisian musicians from a few nights ago. It was apparently a very scratchy record being played and broadcast through the town on loudspeakers. An old mosque was located right next to the Ribat, not twenty yards from the sewer set, and the speakers were going full blast. It was a strange, discordant sound that the locals told us was prayer music, and it was played every day around this time. Andrew noted that perhaps the prayer, which was a particularly long one, was meant to wish them good luck in the sewer. After several minutes, the commandos took their places and began descending.

I was called away by Susie for a quick Roman soldier haircut; just as she was finishing, Melvin approached to inform me that my services as a Roman soldier would not be required that day. "But tomorrow, for sure," he assured me.

When I returned to the set, everyone not directly involved with the commando scene stood by watching. Michael was not in that particular shot, and so he sat back and gathered his strength. "You know," he pondered, noting the crowd staring at the canvas-covered tunnel, "if a flying saucer were to land here right now, the occupants would probably think this large black thing was some sort of shrine, and we were all just sort of sitting around worshipping it."

Charles McKeown, another member of the rep company, wriggled free of his gear and collapsed next to Michael. He stared at a half-eaten sandwich left over from an earlier break, now lying in the dust after it had apparently been stepped on.

"Is that yours?" he asked Michael innocently.

"Why, yes, actually. I'm hoping someone will kick it about in the dirt a bit more before I eat it, though," deadpanned Michael. "I noticed a few cigarette butts lying about, and I'm starting to feel a bit peckish for a fag sandwich."

The "extended day" warning on the call sheet was apparently true, as the shooting in the sewer lasted long after the sun had gone down. The commandos were finally released, and a few of the Tunisians in Roman armor were brought around, ready to act as palace guards. Matthew had been drilling and marching with them near the mosque. They were placed in position and then marched by the top of the tunnel for a couple of takes. Even though they didn't seem to be able to march in formation, they looked good enough to pass in the shots, so we were able to wrap for the day.

Matthew and Melvin passed out the call sheets for the next day as everyone started to disperse. It looked as though it would be a big day, as we were set to start filming the crowd scene outside Pilate's palace. Besides the regular crowd, there will be about 450 locals working as extras. They are going to have to react to Michael's speeches as Pilate with fits of laughter, and several people are worried about the potential for disaster, as we will be working with that many people, most of whom don't understand English and probably won't take direction awfully well. The call sheet even lists a Tunisian comedian on call, just in case we can't get the proper responses from the crowd.

Back at the Ruspina, I joined some of the grips and sparks for drinks and dinner at the restaurant next to the pool, as it was supposed to be quicker than the indoor version (I didn't see how it could be any slower). The only real drawback to eating outside was the hordes of wild cats that flock around the customers, looking for handouts. Around the Ribat, there are likewise dozens of wild cats constantly in the background, too wild to be petted or held, but always lurking about when someone is eating.

Some of the tourists, particularly the older German women, enjoy feeding the cats, which only compounds the problem. The waiters seem to accept it all as a matter of course. When the cats get a little too bold, the waiters simply walk toward them menacingly with a loud hiss. I decided the best thing to do was defend my own food as well as I could and leave the German tourists to fend for themselves.

Pilate's Address, in which hundreds of non-English-speaking Tunisians must be trained to laugh on cue

I MADE MY DEBUT ON-CAMERA, thus getting to watch the entire impressive proceedings from the best seat in the house—Pilate's platform overlooking the crowds in the forum. ▪ The day started out a bit earlier than usual, as I had to pick up my Roman soldier costume and get to the set for an early call. I arrived at the Sidi Mansour around 7:00 A.M., where I saw a huge mob of locals in front of the crowd wardrobe house. They were loud and quite unruly, despite the orders barked out by several policemen who were standing by for crowd control.

I was thankful to be reporting to the artists' makeup house instead, which was much more sedate. The soldiers' costumes were all basically the same. I wore a red felt tunic underneath it all. My dagger was then strapped on, followed by the heavy leather chest plate, which covered me front and back. I had a sword hung at my side and a red cape fastened to my shoulders. The costume was topped off with knee-high sandals and a helmet. I had to have my hair pinned up a bit beneath the helmet, but the overall effect seemed satisfactory. It wasn't as uncomfortable as it might have been, but the chest plate made it impossible to really relax. Whenever my torso sank too low, my neck got caught in the opening for the head. As I experimented throughout the day, I figured out how to slip in and out of the chest plate, so I only had to wear it when shots with the Roman soldiers were imminent.

As I waited in the makeup house for the rest of the soldiers to dress for the ride to the Ribat, another wardrobe man entered, looking as though he had been in battle.

"You won't believe what it's like over there!" gasped Charles. "There are over seven hundred locals queued up, and we can only use four hundred and fifty at the most. I don't know what's going to happen. They're impossible as it is now!" He huddled with another wardrobe man to discuss strategy, shaking his head nervously all the time.

"You should see it. There are policemen down there beating the people with sticks. A few fights had broken out, and the policemen were trying to stop them as best they could. Apparently, it's almost become a game to some of the young people, to see how close they can come without actually being struck." He shook his head. "Well, perhaps the police here are better able to handle their own people than we are. You know, you can't really say to them 'I'm sorry, but we haven't any more work today, could you please come back tomorrow?' I mean, it just doesn't work!"

"What sort of money do they make as extras?" I asked.

"That's another thing. They get paid about three pounds a day, but to them, I suppose it's as much money as they make in a month, so it's no wonder they fight over the jobs."

I was herded onto the bus with the rest of the Roman soldiers, and we were driven to the Ribat. All of the Pythons and the rep company had to report to the set early today, and they sleepily stepped into their costumes and had makeup applied. The mob of Tunisians were led down the street to the Ribat, where they sat and waited for their big scene.

Today would be the ambitious sequence in which Pontius Pilate addresses the crowd, asking them who they want released for Passover. Michael's Pilate, however, has a very pronounced speech impediment, which breaks up everyone who hears him. Even the crowd that he addresses falls down in waves of convulsive laughter. The reactions of the crowd are essential to the scene, so everyone is a bit nervous about the reaction of the locals.

The first shots were of Pilate and his entourage and guards as they step out onto the platform, with only a few people shouting out the crowd reactions in order to give the actors the appropriate cues. Michael, as Pilate, was accompanied by Graham, who plays Biggus Dickus, his friend from Rome, and John, Eric, and Terry G were all Roman soldiers. The rep company and a few others joined in with the crowd reactions and lines; the Tunisians all sat outside the Ribat during the first part of the morning.

Michael quickly began to get into the role, and I heard him joking with the others up on the platform. "Ni! Ni! Ni!" he called out between scenes as he strutted around the platform. "We are the Knights Who Appear in Other Films!"

After the group shots were completed, each of the group received his individual close-ups. The two soldiers in the back, Eric and Terry G, had little to do in the scene except to try to conceal their laughter at Pilate's lisp, so the close-ups for those two consisted mostly of laughter.

During Terry G's close-ups, I noticed Michael crawling just below camera range, about knee-high. I later learned that Michael and John were making obscene threats in order to keep Terry laughing. Then, to facilitate Eric's laughter during his close-ups, Michael carefully inserted a spear up his tunic.

Close-ups were finished by late morning, and we broke for tea. When we prepared to resume, Terry J learned that Eric had been called away. Rather than hold up filming, Terry asked me to double for Eric during the long shots, as I was already dressed as a Roman soldier. I clambered up to the platform and informed the others.

The Pythons rehearse on the platform overlooking the courtyard for Pilate's address to the crowd.

"Very good," noted John. "They're so far away, I don't even think you'll need to worry about looking away from the camera."

"All you'll need to do is . . . well, just watch me," instructed Terry G, who was my counterpart on the opposite side of the platform. "First we march out, make a sharp turn, and stand still. Then watch me, and start laughing and cracking up when I do."

He demonstrated, and we ran through it a few times. Since all of the close-ups had been completed, there was little to worry about. The camera was so far off in one corner that we would only be seen as distant figures in the background.

As we waited, the crowd of locals were ushered into the courtyard and scattered throughout the area. On the platform above, we watched, apprehensive yet impressed, as they kept coming in.

"I hear Zeffirelli used more than seven hundred in here," noted John. "I don't really know why, as we can make this place look like it's overflowing with less than five hundred."

As we watched from above, Terry J began to coach the crowd with their reactions, aided by some interpreters. He demonstrated how they should laugh, doubling over and falling down, kicking up his heels, from his perch on top of the camera platform alongside the camera crew. Every eye was on him as he demonstrated. There were a few tense, silent moments. Would they get it? Then, slowly, the locals began laughing, hearty belly laughs. It was infectious. Soon gales of laughter rang throughout the courtyard. From on high, Terry G, Mike, John, Graham, and I marveled at the crowd's performance.

"Most of them probably worked with Zeffirelli," noted John. "They must think this is great. In *Jesus of Nazareth,* about all they could do was stand around, with maybe some occasional shouting. But look at them now. They all really seem to be enjoying themselves."

Michael was taking full advantage of the receptive audience as he strutted about, noting, "This is a comedian's dream! What a sense of power. They respond to every line!" He looked out into the masses, pretending to call to someone in the back. "Oh, Mr. Brando! Marlon, dear, I'm afraid we won't be able to use you today. Sorry!"

Habib and Terry J began to run the crowd through their lines, which they were theoretically learning phonetically. Michael couldn't resist taking advantage.

"Is there anyone here who hasn't slept with Zeffirelli?" he asked the crowd.

Nearly five hundred Tunisians shouted "No!"

The camera finally started to roll, and I followed Terry G's lead, breaking up at the appropriate moments. John, in character as the Roman centurion, turned to Terry and me and barked, "Get hold of yourselves, men!" and other intimidating ad libs.

Before long, Terry J decided we had gotten some terrific footage of the crowd, so we broke for a luncheon with 550. The Tunisian extras were all given sack lunches and retreated to eat on their own. This was not due to any sort of prejudice on anyone's part, but apparently because of orders from the Tunisian government, a sort of separate-but-equal edict that I didn't really understand.

The scene continued immediately after lunch, and the crowd resumed their places. I was demoted back down to the crowd, as the camera wouldn't be aimed toward the platform. Michael stayed on high, however, in order to feed cues to the crowd, and also, I suspect, because he rather enjoyed it all. He continued to stand very close to the front edge of the platform (during the morning, Mike, John, and Graham had all stood close to the edge, next to a fifty-foot drop below). It all made me a little nervous, especially considering the way the platform had been creaking earlier in the day.

I stood in the middle of the crowd for the remainder of the afternoon, looking like a Roman guard and breaking into raucous laughter on cue. Michael eventually tired of giving cues, and Jonathan Benson took over for the rest of the day. Jonathan is our very capable first assistant director; he does most of the shouting for Terry J, and just before each take, it is his voice that booms, "Turn the camera!"

The crowd remained marvelous throughout the afternoon, reacting perfectly and even learning how to say "Welease Woger" and "Welease Wodewick" phonetically. Terry J was enormously pleased with the crowd, as was everyone, and it meant that we might be able to finish early tomorrow.

Pilate's Address Redux, in which there are close-ups, quacking, and problems with trumpets

TRANSPORTATION TO THE SET SEEMS TO be my biggest obstacle so far, but I've been able to make it each morning, either bumming rides from the crew members staying at the Ruspina or taking a not always reliable minibus or even a taxi.

■ When I finally did make it to the set this morning, I found that today would be more of the same as yesterday, though on a smaller scale. It would involve the reactions of Terry J and the rep company to Pilate's speech, as they were the first ones to begin ridiculing the Romans. Only about eighty locals were needed today, and those just to surround the rep company to make them look like part of a bigger crowd. A large number of locals had to be turned away today. The makeup and wardrobe departments were relieved, as it had taken them all more than three hours to get all of the extras ready yesterday.

Although I was a Roman soldier again today, there wasn't much to do, since none of the soldiers were in the shots with the rep company. The locals used today were once again very good, particularly in the shots in which they had to roll on the ground and quack like a duck.

The close-ups of the trumpeters and the trumpet-carriers also had to be done this morning, and those almost ended up being more troublesome than the crowd scenes. There were four locals in Roman uniforms lined up on a narrow ledge near the top of the wall, holding six-foot horns with large, heavy banners draped from them. Immediately below them on the ground were four accompanying locals, also in costume, with long forked sticks of varying lengths, which they would use to prop up the trumpets from below.

Terry wanted a shot of the trumpets being raised, seemingly a simple enough task. The trumpets were quite heavy, though, and very hard to raise by themselves, let alone raising all four of them simultaneously. It became harder and harder for the trumpet-carriers to keep the horns raised to the same height as the rehearsing progressed. To compound the problem, the banner on one of them began to bunch up. Each time that happened, it had to be pulled back in, a prop man had to straighten it out, and the trumpet had to be carefully placed back in the fork of the stick, all of which was at least a three-man job. To make things even more difficult, one of the trumpets began falling apart and had to be replaced entirely.

At last, everything appeared to be ready to go, when a few scattered clouds rolled in. Rather than take the chance of spoiling a shot, Terry decided to wait. Unfortunately, the clouds began to grow in number and density, so rather than keep everyone in place, we broke until the sky cleared.

John, Mike, Eric, and Graham arrived during the delay and began getting into costume. The trumpet shot resumed after a half-hour wait. Eric brought his cricket bat out of his trailer, and he and John amused themselves in the road between the Ribat and the mosque by playing a bit of cricket, bouncing the ball off several cars unlucky enough to get in their way.

They were soon chased back inside with the others to do more individual close-ups for Pilate's address, and they slipped into the armor and robes before taking their places. Again the two guards, played by Eric and Terry G, were supposed to suppress their laughter, and again Mike, Graham, and John helped out by making farting sounds and sexual threats. At one point, I noticed Mike on his hands and knees, beginning to climb up Terry G's leg.

All but ten of the extras were released just before lunch to make conditions less crowded for the afternoon, and John and Eric got in a bit more cricket just before lunch. When filming resumed after lunch, the morning's clouds had all but disappeared, making way for another scorching Tunisian afternoon. Since we had finished up the crowd scenes so quickly, Terry J had promised everyone a short afternoon, planning only a brief scene with Brian and a shot of Sue Jones-Davies releasing pigeons as a signal to the revolutionaries.

I sat waiting with another Roman soldier called Clive, an aspiring young British filmmaker who, like me, had hopes of working on the Python film. The Roman soldiers actually had a rather easy day of it. Another soldier and I were placed at different levels on the sloping walkway for the shots of the trumpeters, but after standing in for a time, it became apparent that we wouldn't be seen in the shot, so we were released.

The two of us were the only soldiers to see even that much action today. The other soldiers had been costumed and on the set fairly early and spent the day sitting on the sidelines watching the filming. Some were occasionally interrupted by a wardrobe or makeup person, who would stop and tidy them up, even though it was quickly becoming apparent that none of them would be used. Finally, Melvin announced to the soldiers that none of us would be needed today, and we could go back to the Sidi and collect our pay.

Another crowd scene is planned for tomorrow, this time outside of Mandy's house. Most of the crowd scenes are being filmed as early in the production as possible, and all are exteriors. The thinking is that if things grind to a halt because of bad weather, it's better to have two or three actors

The second day of Pilate's address.

sitting around grumbling while they wait for it to blow over, rather than three or four hundred extras as well.

I returned my costume at the Sidi Mansour and looked in vain for a ride back to the Ribat; even though it was only a quick, minor shot of the pigeons being released, I wanted to be there. When it became apparent that there were no rides forthcoming, I walked up to the pool. Bernard, Andrew, and John Young were relaxing in the sun, soon joined by Graham. I noticed a sign claiming that rushes were scheduled for tonight, though this was nothing new. We had been expecting rushes to arrive for the past several nights. I finally decided to give up on trying to make it back to the Ribat, as Graham assured me that they would probably already be finished. I eventually walked downstairs, where the remaining cast and crew members were straggling in, and caught a ride back to my hotel with John Cleese.

"So you're playing Roman soldiers now, eh, Johnson?" he teased. "Actually, that's good, it gives you a more complete picture of what the filming is really like.

"When we were filming *Grail* in Scotland, I had a driver that took me to the set each day. One day I said to him, 'You'd ought to talk to one of the assistant directors. Perhaps they can find something for you to do in the film.' He told me, 'Actually, I've already done six parts.' I was amazed. Before we had finished, he played something like a dozen roles."

Brian appeared to be turning into a similar situation, with most of the crew and passersby being allotted various roles. It seems to be a safe bet that before filming ends, everyone will appear before the camera in some capacity, as English-speaking bodies appear to be at a premium.

I decided to forgo the rushes and spend the evening writing. Michael Palin had offered me the use of his typewriter, so I decided to take advantage and pick it up at his hotel. He appeared to be getting ready to leave for the rushes.

"What scene is tomorrow?" he asked. "What am I playing?"

I explained that it would be the crowd scene outside Mandy's house, though I wasn't sure what role he would play.

"Oh, yes, I think I'm a peasant," he recalled. "I always try to check the call sheet the night before to see what I'm playing. Whenever I'm a Roman, I always shave in the morning. When I'm a revolutionary or a peasant, I always make it a point to shave the night before, so by morning I'm a bit rough. I really have quite a few clean roles in this film, which is unusual. I enjoy playing Pilate and Romans because they're all so neat and clean!"

The Morning After, in which Mandy and Brian address the multitude

EARLY THIS MORNING, I CORNERED TERRY J in his trailer, just as he was getting into his Mandy costume, and asked about the rushes the night before. ▪ "Oh, they were just disastrous!" He shook his head, sighing. "Nothing could be seen, everybody was out of shot, and everything was out of focus." ▪ "Really?" I asked. ▪ "Yes! I may have to end up using my 8 mm camera," he joked. "No, actually, they were fine. They looked very beautiful and very funny. We'll need to shoot a few short pickups on the stoning scene, shooting some of the crowd with actual women in beards. We'll also need to shoot Brian and Mandy in the background in order to establish them at the stoning a bit better.

"The only other problem was a close-up of the writing on the wall. The close-up of the actual writing has to be done a bit differently. Graham was writing rather frantically in the wide shot but was writing rather slowly in the close-up. Also, John was holding his paintbrush a bit differently, which looked rather awkward."

Terry seemed happy with his first look at the footage, and the continuity problems sounded minor and very fixable. *Life of Brian* seems to be off to a good start.

Terry continued to squeeze into his Mandy costume as I left. I walked onto the set dressed as a peasant, wearing two robes, a turban, and my cutoff shorts underneath—all in all, a much more comfortable costume than my suit of armor.

Mandy's house was in a smaller courtyard, built in the corner of the large courtyard. In the scene, Brian is spending the night with Judith, unaware that a large crowd has followed him to his mother's house and is waiting for him to address the throng. The courtyard was to be filled with people, though it took fewer than two hundred to fill this area. Again, a Thomson's tour group was brought in. English-speaking extras were strongly preferred, as the crowd had a number of responses to be delivered in unison, including one good-sized paragraph. Very few locals were needed, and I heard that there had been a few scuffles this morning at the crowd house when nearly everyone was turned away.

Today was also Graham's nude scene. He was a bit apprehensive about it, as it involved standing completely naked in front of nearly two hundred people. Before the filming began, a couple of older Thomson's ladies were walking around the dressing caravans, apparently looking for autographs. They stuck their heads into Graham's quarters, only to find him standing there stark naked. Both of the women grew pale and were completely at a loss.

"It's all right, I'm a doctor," Graham reassured them.

"Oh, of course," they replied, looking relieved, and they calmly left.

Finally, everyone was ushered into the courtyard and carefully positioned. The members of the rep company, Michael, and John were just below me near the top of the stairs. Michael stood on a very precarious stone wall, while Eric was placed off to one side; everyone else was appointed to fill in the empty space. We were each given sticks with either gourds or sandals tied to them, depending on which sect we followed.

The shooting began with close-ups of Brian, Mandy, and Judith. Graham was a bit reluctant to drop his shorts but was resigned to his fate. He threw open the shutters of the window for all to see, and the crowd started chanting, "The Messiah!" right on cue. Apparently, some of the women didn't know what the scene was about and were rather shocked to see Graham standing there in the raw. It didn't faze Mike, John, or Eric, though. "Is he really Jewish?" called Eric, and he was quickly followed by a barrage of circumcision jokes between takes.

The speeches by Brian, Mandy, and Judith were all accompanied by appropriate responses from the crowd, which hailed Brian as the Messiah. (Mandy responded, "There's no Messiah in here. There's a mess, all right, but no Messiah!") The crowd spoke all of their lines in unison. The locals had to learn their lines phonetically, through repetition. Habib and Terry J took turns on the bullhorn pronouncing the words. The locals managed to pick up the words quickly, just as they had learned to say "Welease Woger" and "Welease Wodewick" earlier this week. Assisted by the Thomson's tourists who were scattered around the crowd with them, they were soon whipped into fine shape.

The locals really seemed to love taking direction from Terry, and his enthusiasm was infectious. Even dressed as Mandy, Terry put everything he had into getting the crowd stirred up. Considering that most of the locals had probably worked with Zeffirelli, it was probably quite a shock to see the director of the film rolling on the ground laughing. It undoubtedly loosened up the Tunisians. As one of the locals told Terry after a take: "Zeffirelli is good—but you are better."

We broke for a quick lunch after a few more close-ups. When we returned, we were missing a few bodies. To help fill the courtyard, Terry had to have several more locals called in. Scattered Tunisians brandished their poles with the gourds and sandals, while Habib, Terry, and Jonathan Benson did their best to convey instructions to the crowd. The camera would be looking from the window down at the crowd, so it was essential for the crowd to respond as well as possible.

The afternoon scenes were a bit more difficult, due to the relative complexity of the crowd's dialogue, but the efforts of Habib, Terry, and Jonathan seemed to pay off, as the throng repeated the dialogue line for line. It was a time-consuming process, but the crowd eventually became quite skillful at repeating their lines. Terry became so confident that he decided to shoot whole stretches of dialogue, rather than the line-by-line parroting he had planned, and we were soon able to go through nearly the entire scene.

The steps toward the top that the actors were kneeling on were becoming ever harder and more uncomfortable, so we all bunched up portions of our robes to serve as knee pads. The view of the crowd from our vantage point on high was spectacular. There were people hanging everywhere. The rep company and some of the Pythons needed close-ups for some of their individual dialogue. I noticed Michael standing up straight to deliver his lines on the crumbling wall, even though it was a twenty-five-foot drop to the ground. I could hardly bear to watch, but he made it through fine, helped on and off the wall by some of the others.

There was only one accident during the shooting today. One of the Thomson's men who was sitting on a ledge above the wall near Eric slipped down an arch to the ground, about twelve feet below. Graham rushed over and had a look, but fortunately he was only shaken a little and not seriously injured.

Despite the crowded conditions, filming inside the smaller courtyard proved a pleasant change. The entire courtyard was covered over with a large white cloth, apparently to help even out the light for filming, but while it allowed enough light for the camera, it seemed to stop much of the heat. Michael feigned disappointment that he wouldn't get a chance to work on his suntan.

The Thomson's people had to leave at the end of the day to return to London, but they all seemed to enjoy the filming (with the possible exception of the man who fell) and collected autographs before leaving.

"Our initial thoughts had been to suppress all publicity about the film until after it was put together, to prevent any fanatical religious groups from mounting an attack against the film before it's released," explained Michael. "Then we hoped to carefully control the amount of publicity that came out in a slow, carefully paced campaign.

"However, in just half a dozen days of shooting, we've already had two groups of tourists from London here at the location, and doubtless they're marching back to London filled with all sorts of stories and holiday photographs—" Before he could finish his thoughts, he was snatched away by a middle-aged woman who wanted her picture taken with him.

The call sheets were handed out at the end of the day. A small paragraph at the bottom invited everyone to a spaghetti-tasting competition that evening between Mr. Memmo, our caterer, and a Tunisian chef, to determine which style of spaghetti was better. Everyone would sample both kinds, and an international jury selected from the cast and crew would determine the winner. I decided to attend and arranged with a couple of sparks for a ride from the Ruspina to the tasting, not realizing that tonight we would almost touch off an international incident.

It all began simply enough, as everyone stood at the hotel bar, waiting and making small talk before dinner. The head table was apparently reserved for the "international jury." Terry G represented America, makeup girl Elaine Carew was Australian, Christine sat in for Brazil, and Terry J and John Goldstone would represent Britain, while others filled in various slots for Tunisia, Italy, and France. It wasn't particularly well organized, but no one seemed to care. The first dish was calamari in tomato sauce, followed by a few others before the two huge bowls of spaghetti. There was little difference in the taste, though the Tunisian pasta was more like macaroni than spaghetti. The Italian version apparently won, though by that time, none of us really cared.

Carol Cleveland and her husband, Peter Brett, arrived just as we were finishing our dinner, and were delighted to see everyone. Carol is considered by Python fans to be "the first lady of Python" and is much admired by the group for her comedic skills in the female roles not played by them. They had arrived for a week's filming, as Carol was only doing a few smaller roles; she would return for the final week in Gabes. They both settled in for some spaghetti, just as a commotion erupted from a pair of tables in the back, where some of the grips and sparks were apparently imbibing.

As our plates were cleared away, the Tunisian chef brought in a huge, intricately decorated cake, covered with fruit rings, cherries, and complicated designs. He had obviously labored long and hard over it and made quite a show of displaying it to us. After the unveiling and applause, he went off to find someone to cut and serve it.

In retrospect, perhaps making such an elaborate presentation may have called undue attention, because the next thing I knew, I heard a collective gasp arise from several of our group. One of the young sparks had picked up the massive cake and was dancing around the room, holding it above his head, balanced on one hand. Some of the group tried to ignore him and hoped for the best, even though it proved difficult to ignore someone walking past with a large cake precariously perched over their heads.

The only tables that had not tensed up at this point were those filled with grips and sparks, and so the cake-bearer approached them with a crazed look in his eye. They were all laughing like mad when he threw the cake.

A few shrieks erupted, the grips and sparks were splitting their sides, and everyone else watched with reactions ranging from a bemused tolerance to stunned disbelief. His intended target had jumped away at the last second, so the cake landed halfway on the table. The horror-stricken chef looked on, wondering if this was some sort of normal English custom. The room remained silent for what seemed like an eternity, and then a low rumbling began as people started to take it all in.

"Well, at least that livened things up," said Graham quietly.

John Goldstone and Tim Hampton, both attempting to remain calm, walked over and began speaking with the chef. Our continuity girl just shook her head and kept repeating, "Oh my God, how could you?"

Several others were staring menacingly at the cake hurler, while he turned several different shades of red, trying to laugh it off. Eventually, things settled down, and the waiters tried to salvage and serve the remnants of the cake. Graham took a bite, then murmured, "No great loss anyway . . ."

The Ex-Leper Scene, another Morning After, and more Stoning, in which there are retakes, close-ups, and the Tunisian Department of Tourism

THE COURTYARD OUTSIDE OF MANDY'S HOUSE was sparsely populated for this morning's filming. Michael was dressed as the ex-leper for the scene in which he attempts to beg from Brian and Mandy, following them through the marketplace as he complains of losing his livelihood because he was healed. ■ Most of the scene consists of a long tracking shot—this is the scene that Terry walked them through on the final day of rehearsal. The sequence finishes just outside Mandy's house, and only the ending would be filmed today. A number of locals had been placed around the courtyard to serve as set dressing and would walk, sit, or otherwise occupy themselves in what was supposed to represent their daily routine. The adult extras were joined by children, sheep, chickens, and a donkey. Only the donkey was an inconvenience, in part because of his size, and in part due to his propensity for relieving himself in the small doorway through which the cast and crew had to pass (attracting swarms of houseflies as well).

Michael, Graham, and Terry J were all in costume, waiting while Terry dealt with a few last-minute details. As they stood by, the cake-hurling spark, much more sedate, approached Michael.

"Hello, Michael." He smiled tentatively. "You, uh, weren't there last night to, uh, see everything, were you?"

"Ah, no," he responded pleasantly. "I missed it last night, but I did read about it this morning in one of the local papers."

The cake-hurling spark was apparently seeking allies, hoping that he wouldn't be sent home in the aftermath of the incident. Most of us were mercifully oblivious to any behind-the-scenes discussions regarding his fate, but the uproar had died down considerably overnight.

The actors soon took their places, and Jonathan tried to set the background action. One of the chickens that had been placed on a balcony was flapping about, however, disrupting things in general. "Somebody do something about that chicken!" Jonathan ordered.

One of the Tunisian crew members cornered the uncooperative chicken and grabbed it by its feet, then started swinging it around in a circle.

"No! Wait, stop!" Jonathan protested, disturbed by what he perceived as cruelty to the chicken. The local indicated for him to wait a moment and stopped swinging the chicken. He placed it carefully at its spot on the balcony, where it sat quietly for the rest of the morning.

"Oh, well, very good!" Jonathan praised him. "Do that anytime you need to!"

The camera was soon rolling. The ex-leper tails Brian and Mandy as he explains how he is still trying to maintain his begging. Mandy leaves in disgust, but Brian finally gives him a coin.

The first attempts failed for various reasons. During one take, Graham tried to throw a coin in his begging cup but missed. "Half a dinari for me bloody life story," ad-libbed Michael, "and you can't even hit my bloody cup!"

After a couple of usable takes, someone noticed that Mandy didn't have her beard. She is supposed to be holding it in her hand as she returns from the stoning.

"Shit! I left it at the hotel," recalled Terry J.

A quick conference determined that they would just carry on without it. Mandy would keep one hand out of sight of the camera, and the shooting would continue.

Terry Bayler's false mustache kept falling off between shots, and he did his best to reaffix it. One of the locals approached him, going to great pains to point out the faulty mustache. "Ah, yes, thank you, thank you very much," he said politely, even though reaffixing the mustache had long since become a routine.

"Everyone around here is so helpful, especially about mustaches and beards coming loose," noted Michael. "I've had people cross through a very crowded courtyard and go to a great deal of trouble and inconvenience to point it out, even though I was long aware of it."

Most of the shots were soon finished, and the camera was being set to film the reverse shots from on high of Brian, Mandy, and the ex-leper coming through the archway into the courtyard. Part of the larger courtyard was visible through the archway, though, so it had to be blocked off.

"They seem to be sealing all of the actors inside here for use at some future date," observed Michael. "You know, if something like Pompeii were to happen here at this very minute, with all of us in these costumes, could you imagine the people who would uncover us in the future? 'My God, did they really live like this?!'"

Outside, the larger courtyard was being prepared for a later scene. The huge polystyrene statue of Caesar that had previously stood in the courtyard was laid on its side. It appeared a little worse for wear, but we were apparently almost finished with it. Its left index finger had somehow broken off, and someone had placed an empty Coke bottle in its hand.

All of the actors playing revolutionaries were happy to see that the sewer tunnel had been dismantled, which meant that there would be no more crawling around, at least for the time being.

As I surveyed the activity, I was called for the next shot, which involved more close-ups of John, Eric, Michael, and the rep company from yesterday's scene. The filming of the individual close-ups at the top of the steps took about an hour, the rep company finishing their lines first, followed by Eric's lines asking Mandy if she was a virgin. Then John climbed a shaky ladder and crawled into a tiny room overlooking the small courtyard. He was to stick his head out the small window and speak to Judith during her address to the crowd.

John was apparently finding it difficult to concentrate, and the more times that he went through his lengthy speech, the longer it seemed to grow.

"This is an extremely uncomfortable position, you know," he informed all of us between takes. "I'm forced to take a position closely akin to that of a giraffe drinking water."

After a few more takes, John came up with a new simile. "Actually, this room is very reminiscent of the type of cell used to confine Greek political prisoners, in which one is unable to completely stand up or sit down, that being the purpose . . ."

John Young was meandering around the courtyard with his Super 8 movie camera, shooting people and things of interest, when he was spotted by John.

"I want a clause in that man's contract," teased John, pointing down at John Young, "that we be allowed to release our film before John Young comes out with his. It wouldn't do to have him rushing his version to the theaters ahead of ours."

Filming was continuing on schedule; some scenes were going quicker than expected, so there were opportunities to do some retakes. Terry J decided that after lunch, we would reshoot the stoning and wall-painting sequences. As I was still dressed as a peasant, I was placed in the middle of a group of women, all of whom were wearing obviously false beards, for a shot of Brian and Mandy arriving. We were given polystyrene stones and told to look menacing. Mandy gave me a rather violent push out of her way as she and Brian took their places in the crowd, stones in hand. After a few more similar takes, Terry decided there really wasn't time for the wall painting today. Instead, the crew laid down sections of aluminum rods for the camera to allow a tracking shot of the crowd approaching the stoning. It meant that the camera, which was placed low to the ground, had to point upward at the crowd, because just a short distance behind were the streets of Monastir.

Matthew and Melvin began handing out the familiar yellow call sheets for Monday's filming, a sure sign that we were almost finished. There was another handbill as well, this one on green paper, inviting us to a cocktail party in our honor, sponsored by the Tunisian tourism director. The expected jokes about cakes began to circulate, but John Goldstone had been quite worried that the Department of Tourism might actually cancel tonight's party due to the cake incident.

As it was Saturday night, and Sunday was our only day off this week, everyone seemed ready to unwind. I decided to walk to the Skanes Palace Hotel, about a mile away, where the party was being held. There was an impressive array of snacks and hors d'oeuvres, including the only potato chips I have seen so far in Tunisia, and most of the unit gathered near the food and the drinks. Everyone made small talk; although the grips and sparks had been invited, they failed to turn up, apparently gun-shy after last night. Some of them were apparently going into Sousse, about fifteen miles north of Monastir, for a night in the big city.

The conversations were brought to a halt by the entertainment, which turned out to be more Tunisian musicians. They were soon joined by a trio of belly dancers, which proved to be a popular diversion. But people began drifting away, and I found myself talking with Carol Cleveland and Peter Brett as we all stood outside the Skanes Palace in hopes of getting a car to the Ruspina. The few that stopped were already booked. At last we decided to walk, and so we began hiking alongside the road under the bright light of the full moon, with Carol dressed to kill in a long dress and heels.

A Day Off, in which there are camels and beaches

I DECIDED TO SPEND AT LEAST part of my free afternoon on the beach. When I arrived, I saw Peter sunning himself on one of the hotel's straw mats, and he invited me to join him. I sat down and started reading, then suddenly asked, "Where's Carol?" ■ "Oh, she's out in the water somewhere," he said, then scanned the bodies along the shore and pointed her out. I noticed that she had shed the top of her bathing suit, as had most of the other women there. Peter must have immediately guessed what I was thinking. "It's funny, isn't it? This topless thing? I mean, everybody makes such a big thing of it at other places." I agreed, trying to act as blasé as I could, and we both agreed, very maturely and sensibly, that we were all in favor of it.

Carol soon joined us, and we all stretched out in the sun reading. After a while, I looked up and noticed two local boys leading one large camel and two smaller ones down the beach. Carol looked up in excitement.

"Look, camels! Look at them," she alerted us.

They were led down to the edge of the beach and paused. A few of the tourists flocked over to have their pictures taken on the animals. Carol went back to her reading but kept one eye on the group at all times. When the crowd began to thin, she searched through her bag and found her camera, and I agreed to take her picture.

She covered up with a scarf, and we approached them. The local boys helped her into the saddle behind the hump and instructed her to hold on tight. They tapped at the camel's legs with small switches, and it rose slowly. Carol hung on as it grew steadier and finally stood still. She nevertheless had a queasy look on her face as I tried to focus the camera. After I snapped a couple of shots, she signaled to the boy holding the reins, who tapped the camel's legs; it slowly unfolded them and lowered her to the ground. She staggered away after giving one of the boys some coins.

"Kind of a rough ride?" I asked. "You know, I'm pretty sure we have a camel back in our animal compound near the Ribat. You could probably have waited and ridden the camel there next week."

"That's all right. I don't think I'll want to ride any more camels for a while," she assured me, with no small measure of relief.

We settled back onto our straw mats and resumed reading. A few minutes later, Carol spotted John walking along the beach. She waved him over to say hi, and he had a seat next to us. At the moment, he was between writing and taking a break, he explained.

"I'm having an awful time writing the fifth show," he said, referring to the second series of *Fawlty Towers*. "Do any of you have any interesting stories about things that have happened to you in hotels? I'm absolutely stuck on an idea for a sixth show. Connie will be coming down in a couple of weeks, so hopefully we can figure something out and write it then." Connie is Connie Booth, John's former wife; and they remain very friendly and still cowrite *Fawlty Towers* together.

John declined an invitation for lunch, noting that he tried to avoid lunch on weekends because he was trying to cut down, and continued down the beach to his hotel. I went back to my room and called home and was floored to discover that the eight-minute call was fifty dollars. It's a good thing I'm not feeling homesick!

After I finished some typing, I carried Michael's typewriter back to the Meridien, but as he was out, I left it with Eric to avoid lugging it back. After a quick dinner, I decided to turn in early. It was going to be a busy week.

The Bedroom Scene and Commandos in the Corridors, in which the set is cleared, the commandos raid again, and Cleese speaks

I RODE TO THE SET WITH Carol and Peter; even though they weren't in any scenes, they were getting bored lying on the beach and decided to watch some of the filming. This was the scene of the morning after Brian and Judith have spent the night together, an interior scene in Brian's bedroom, when they are discovered by Mandy and discover the mob of followers outside the window. Since Graham and Sue were both nude, it was a closed set. Of course, it was being shot in such a small room in an upper corner of the Ribat that it would have probably been a closed set even without the nudity.

Before the set was cleared, I sat around the outskirts of the set with a notebook and pen, trying to gather material. There were still a number of people gathered outside the room, people not quite important enough to be in the room but still required to stand nearby.

One of the grips struggled to nail in the window frames more securely. This would be the interior of the scene we shot last week, when Brian throws the windows open and is spotted by the crowd below in Mandy's courtyard. The two rooms were different and the windows didn't seem to match up, but with it all edited together, I doubted anyone would notice.

The grip asked me to help him operate the windows from the outside of the room, because they wouldn't stay closed. It was necessary for the two of us to squat down out of sight on either side of the windows and reach up carefully to hold the window shutters closed after Mandy, Brian, and Judith pulled them shut. It was trickier than it seemed, as I had to pull my fingers away just as the actors would push the window open again, or else I'd have gotten them smashed. I also had to reach up to hold the shutter closed at just the right moment—too slowly and the window would fly open, too quickly and my hand would be seen in the shot. In addition, I had to squat to the side in a particularly uncomfortable position. I'm not sure if the onlookers realized just how difficult it all was.

The small room grew very warm, in part due to the large lights needed for the scene, as well as the number of persons crowded into the small room. The underdressed Graham and Sue may have been comfortable, but Terry J in his Mandy costume must have been sweltering. Some of the sparks aimed a large fan next to the window to cool it off between takes, but the motor burned out within minutes of turning it on, and a replacement had to be sought. One additional side effect of the heat was an unpleasant smell that began to drift across the set. One of Terry G's duties was dressing the sets, and here he had draped several small dried octopi on a nail near the window. The heat was obviously affecting them.

As the scene involved Mandy in full costume, John Cleese stood inside to help with the direction while Terry J was in front of the camera. From all reports, it was apparently a very uncomfortable scene to film. The door to Brian's bedroom was only four feet tall, so Mandy nearly had to crawl through it to enter. Terry got caught several times, once bumping his head on a piece of wood, which almost knocked his headdress off, and he was in a bit of pain.

Everyone who emerged from the room sounded rather miserable, and the short break for tea was welcomed. As Terry had almost finished his shots as Mandy, John decided to get out and cool down.

"Would you like to get my reactions to the first week of filming?" he asked me on his way out. Not only was I happy to chat with him, I was equally delighted for an excuse to get out of working the window shutter after more than two hours of squatting.

As we stepped out into the sun and walked toward the mosque, John offered to tell me how the scene came about.

"It was originally written for Graham and me, by Graham and me," he explained as we sat down on the steps of the mosque. "When Brian woke up, he had two girls in bed with him called Cheryl and Karen. When Mandy came knocking on the door, he sort of hid them, and they went behind a curtain. Eventually, they giggled, because they didn't think this was quite the behavior of a man who was likely to lead them out of captivity. They giggled a bit, and when Mandy found them, she asked Brian who they were. Brian said, 'They're two of my disciples, Mum.' She said, 'Disciples? They haven't got a stitch on! What are they doing here?' And Brian said 'We were discussing eternal life, and it got a bit late, so they stayed.'

"And then in the next draft, we decided to take that out, because we took a whole big section out of the middle of the film—I think this was when we were in Barbados—so all the girls went. Then, of course, it struck us in the next stage that it was very sensible to put Judith in there. In fact, Judith disappears from the story from about the time Brian goes on the raid and all his escapes and that kind of thing. We do get a glimpse of Judith in the marketplace, but she's rather disappeared from the story, and we wanted to get her right back in there just as soon as we could, and this was the first time we could really get her back into the story. It's interesting, it went through about three different stages."

The first day of filming had an unusual feel to it, he explained.

"The thing about the first day, there was an odd atmosphere, and I couldn't work out what it was," he explained. "Then I suddenly realized that there was absolutely no sense of occasion. I think if anybody had walked on the set, they could have thought it had been about the Monday of the fifth week. It was a lovely feeling; everybody knew just what they were doing, because everybody, in a very efficient, unhurried way, was going about their task. And I think that's been characteristic so far."

He rearranged himself on the concrete steps and continued searching his memory of the past week.

"The only really bad time I've had so far was on the Wednesday morning, when we were up on the projection where Pilate stood. There I found it extremely trying, because the light was so bright that the tears were literally coming down my cheeks during the take and it was almost impossible to act. Most looks of innocence and surprise involve widening the eyes a bit, and you can't do that when it simply causes you more pain than you can cope with. Thank God we were able to shoot it again the next day, Peter [Biziou, the cinematographer] put up a canopy made of white nylon and did the whole thing in a rather pleasant, diffused light, which is apparently bright enough for his purposes and which was very nice to act in. It was very interesting. We completely redid all of the takes, and they were far funnier than they had been the first day.

"The extras, of course, were sensational, the four hundred and fifty Tunisian extras. When they first fell to the ground laughing, nearly five hundred of them, it was one of the funniest sights I had ever seen, because they just sort of fell to the ground in waves, like something out of a land-based Esther Williams movie!

"We've had a problem with one of the shots in the stoning sequence that is quite interesting. We've got a very complicated convention going there. It starts out simple, in that women aren't allowed to go to stoning, so they have to put on beards to go there as men to be allowed to go at all. But then the complicated thing was, two of the women were being played by Michael and Eric, and Charles and Terry Bayler were playing two of the other women, so we had a picture in which I think four out of the nine faces were men pretending to be women pretending to be men, and I suspect that's too difficult for the audience. I just don't think the convention's clear enough. I rather hope that we're going to be able to reshoot it with at least three more obvious girls between Eric and Mike, just to help the clarity of it.

"Otherwise, one of the few bits of inefficiency that we've had is that the projector was rather bad when we were watching rushes on the first day. The focus kept going in and out, and I know it upset poor old Mike, the focus puller, who's got his heart in his job, and it makes it look like he's cocked it all up. I know he was a bit upset, but hopefully that's been put right. Otherwise, everything is going along in a very clear and quiet and orderly way, and I think it feels good because we're a bit ahead of schedule."

John admitted that he was feeling more confident about it all now, after the successes of the first two weeks.

"We've shot those two big crowd scenes, which could have been real buggers. We've got them under our belts," he explained, "and I'm almost sure that they all worked. We did each of them in a day and a half rather than two days, and some of that involved quite a bit of reshooting. I feel that we can get most of it right.

"The scene this morning, which is Mandy arriving and finding Judith in Brian's room, they've just done some very, very good takes on it, and I think we've done everything we really need there. This afternoon, it's just people running around in passages, which is time-consuming, but you can't really get it wrong. So I feel very confident about it, and I think it's in the cards that we're going to have that little bit of extra time to reshoot the odd thing that'll enable us to give the movie a really good gloss. The only thing is, one's always got one caveat, which is I still don't know quite how, naturally, Terry is thinking of cutting it in his mind. So one is always one stage removed from what's going on. Still, you can have a pretty fair guess."

I recalled John's presence in the room this morning, overseeing the direction while Terry J was in front of the camera, so I asked how it came about.

"I only do this because I know how, as an actor, I need two things from a director. Obviously, helpful suggestions and criticisms are fine, but what I really need is faster or slower, and bigger or smaller. If I get that, I basically get it right. I was in there today—Graham was a little bit too big at the start, and so I brought his performance down, and he really was performing beautifully after that. Terry was a little tight, which sometimes happens. Quite interesting, but sometimes it happens that when you're not a hundred percent confident in what you're doing, you tighten up a little, like a cricketer who goes in to bat after making a couple of low scores, or a footballer when the crowd's getting after him. You tighten up a little bit, play a little defensively, and you don't have that loose expansiveness which you actually need to make a comedy scene work at its best. Terry was getting that in the second half of the scene, but it took him a long time to loosen up in the first half. Very much like me on the opening day as the Jewish official at the stoning. I really took several takes to get going. I was quite tight at the start. Sometimes it creeps up on you without you knowing it, and it was not helped this morning by the fact that Terry's entrance was through an extremely small door, and in his second entrance, he caught his foot in a most unfortunate way and skinned his instep. All this kind of thing builds up a pressure on you and makes it difficult to relax and build up the really good flowing timing that makes it funny. But we got a really good take just at the end of the beginning of that scene, and I reckon we're there now."

The second day of filming, involving the Latin lesson, was also encouraging, he noted.

"We saw the rushes, and I was very struck, in that here we were, shooting the scene in the Roman Forum at midnight, in very real colors, just as though it were a proper adventure story, and the audience would be on the edge of their seat. I got a little bit of a kick out of it and thought how I'd never seen a comedy scene played in this sort of slightly forbidding, slightly cool blue light. It's much more like something out of a drama, although I think, conceivably, we may lose a laugh or two because it is shot, as it were, at night. I think the overall effect is to enhance its quality. It's rather interesting."

John looked to the week ahead but did not foresee any serious difficulties.

"I've got a very easy week this week. I've got a real pushover, actually. I've just got to go away and look at three scenes I think the dialogue might be slightly improved in. It's only minor changes. Then I've got a fairly heavy week the following week, then a very light one, then a heavy one. And then when I go to Gabes, I'm hardly in the movie again. It's marvelous—I can just go and read. I come into it again when we go up to Carthage, but I do almost nothing in Gabes!"

We walked back to the large courtyard, where a number of the unit were lounging around in the canvas chairs. Only a handful were outside of Brian's bedroom, where the filming was continuing. It was a slow, leisurely morning. Terry G and some of his crew were building a marketplace, and currently focusing on a long row of shops. A number of upcoming scenes were set in the marketplace, so more than two rows of shops were being constructed. They seemed amazingly strong. Constructed primarily of sticks and straw, they were still sturdy enough to allow crew members to nap in them, away from the midday sun.

As was often the case, lunch was the best meal of the day. Memmo's catering truck and his Italian chefs always serve good food and plenty of it, though it is a mystery how they manage in their crowded little trailer. In addition to fresh fruits and vegetables, meat, and fish, we have had some sort of pasta every day as well, including an incredible lasagna.

After lunch, the commandos had been called, as the afternoon filming involved them all creeping through the corridors beneath Pilate's palace. One long corridor on the second floor of the Ribat had to be sealed off completely, so that no light from the outside could be allowed to penetrate. It became especially hot and stuffy when rows of torches hanging along the walls were lit. The commandos climbed into their costumes and gear and lined up along one end of the corridor with the usual amount of grumbling. No one could blame them today. Everyone was feeling the heat and stuffiness, and we all got some idea of what it must have been like in the tunnels.

As the camera rolled, the commandos would creep along, electric torches in hand, down the corridor. They are almost discovered by a Roman general, played by Bernard, until he lecherously discovers Lucillus, the young eunuch for whom he had been searching. Lucillus was played by Matthew in a very effeminate-looking wig and makeup; he was even required to give emit a little giggle and swish away. For the rest of the day, everyone tried to rattle Matthew with Bernard's sing-songy lines: "Lucillus, where are you? I'm coming to find you . . ."

The corridor we were using had been our original lunchroom; the tables

and chairs had been moved around the corner to a smaller hallway. I was
dressed as a Roman soldier in preparation for some possible shooting, along
with three others, but I soon shed everything but my tunic. All four of us
piled our gear along a wall for use as pillows for a quick nap until it was time
for our shots. Unlike the others, I couldn't fall asleep, however, so I sat back
and watched the commandos creep along.

With interior filming scheduled for the day, and with the crowd scene in the courtyard completed, art director Terry Gilliam (right) supervised the erection of a marketplace in its place.

The corridor was lit by torches, but since torchlight by itself wasn't sufficient, we had to improvise. Just adding more lights would wash out the flickering of the torches. Then one of the crew hit upon another idea. Pieces of black cardboard were rolled into tubes and taped to the front of each spotlight, and a piece of orange gel was held in front of the opening of the tube. The light was then focused on a screen made of thin white cloth, to diffuse the strong white light. When it was time for the filming, the sparks in charge of the devices would move the end of each tube, squeezing it in and out to give a convincing illusion of flickering torchlight.

More than a half dozen of the devices had been constructed, and they seemed to work well for the first few takes. But even though they were unplugged between takes, they still began to grow warmer. Finally, in the middle of one take, one piece of cardboard caught fire. The commandos continued down the corridor, and the burning cardboard was pulled to the floor and calmly, quietly stamped out. Another tube was created for that light, and all of the cardboard was soaked in water. This still didn't seem to matter, though, as on the very next take, two more tubes burst into flames. Finally admitting defeat, the sparks ended up waving their arms in front of their lights, none of which burst into flames.

Melvin released all four of us soldiers. It was becoming routine for us to dress, sit around all day, and finish without being used. I felt just a little disappointed that I wouldn't be used that day, as Maggie Weston had given me a drastic haircut that morning, and she guaranteed that it wouldn't hang out of my helmet.

There was a notice on the call sheets announcing the organization of a tennis tournament for the Python championships, along with a notice that a great deal of laundry seemed to be going astray. Those who had gotten someone else's laundry were asked to bring it to the production office, where a grand drawing would be held.

The second set of rushes came in today but will not be shown until tomorrow night. They are trying to get a new film projector, or at least have the other one fixed so that it will focus properly.

I got a ride back to the Ruspina with Michael and had a quick run before dinner. Carol and Peter were eating with another couple, and I stopped to say hello; I was introduced to June and John Case, a British couple here with the film. John was to play Pilate's wife, as well as a shopkeeper. John was easily six feet nine inches but despite his intimidating appearance couldn't have been nicer.

After dinner, we all headed poolside. A belly dancer was scheduled to appear with a band, but as the dancer was running late, the band had been asked to perform some sort of cabaret.

One of the band members wrapped a turban around his head and performed a comic mentalist act. Then he made an announcement in French that caused quite a commotion among those who could understand him.

As we looked on, bewildered, he removed his eyeglasses slowly and carefully. Then very slowly, very precisely, he held the tip of the left arm of his glasses up to his nostril. Dramatically, he slid it in up to the bend and appeared to be concentrating.

Carol was going into hysterics and had trouble keeping her seat, and the rest of our group was cracking up. The rest of the crowd were staring at the spectacle—literally—with mouths hanging open. Apparently, he had told everyone in French that he was going to snort his glasses, and everyone had a good laugh, but no one took him seriously.

The glasses continued their ascent up his nostril until finally the whole arm, a good six inches, had been lodged up his nose. Our group responded with a standing ovation, while most of the others looked stunned. Carol was laughing so hard she could barely stand.

The rest of the night could only seem anticlimactic after that, so we left shortly after the belly dancer arrived. She may have been good, but for sheer presentation, she couldn't touch the glasses-snorter.

The Haggling Scene, in which Brian buys a beard

WHEN WE ARRIVED THIS MORNING, PILATE'S Forum had nearly completed its transformation into a marketplace, with rows of stalls lining the huge courtyard. Each of the stalls had been set up and stocked just as it must have been two thousand years ago, authentic to the last detail. Today's filming would center on a shop that sells beards to women so that they can attend stonings.

In a typically Terry G touch, the stall next to it was decorated with hundreds of tiny fish, octopi, squid, and other types of aromatic seafood. Directly across was a stall featuring several freshly plucked chickens, which were also roasting in the sun.

This was Eric's first big scene after a week and a half of filming; he had very little to do up to this point and was getting very bored. Today he was quite happy to have a chance to do some acting. He noted that we had been filming for about ten days and said that all he had to say was "Are you a virgin?"

"I'm sure you've been asking that, but was it during the filming?" teased Terry J.

There was a longer than usual delay to the morning's shooting as the finishing touches were put on the set. When it appeared as though there would be quite a wait, Graham took off his heavy shirt. "I have found," he observed, "that the quickest way to get things started is to not be ready for them." Sure enough, as soon as Graham got comfortable, they called for him.

In the morning's scene, Brian hides from the soldiers in the marketplace and decides to buy a beard to disguise himself. The shopkeeper, played by Eric, won't let him pay the full price of twenty shekels, insisting that he haggle with him to lower the price. John Case portrayed Burt, the massive assistant who enforces Eric's demand to haggle. Despite a few muffed lines, technical problems, and miscellaneous interruptions, there were no serious problems. (Though at one point, when a low-flying plane started to drown out the voice track, Eric changed his "Four for the gourd" line to "Four for the plane?")

It was a particularly long scene, and they tried to get it all in a single take without breaking it into smaller bits. A number of locals were costumed and loaded with props, then instructed to walk around in the background, to contribute to the feel of the marketplace. They acquitted themselves well. Eric was quite pleased with the morning's filming, and particularly happy that he could remain so comfortable; because his feet weren't visible in any shots, he was able to wear his sneakers beneath his robes.

The haggling scene was completed before lunch, and the rest of the day was to be spent doing various shots of people wandering through the marketplace. There were background shots of the general bustle and crowds passing through, followed by shots of Judith passing out handbills and a petition. That was followed by Brian running through the marketplace and hiding from the Roman soldiers. Toward the end of the day, Melvin alerted the squad of Roman soldier extras, and we slipped into our armor.

We assembled in the corner of the courtyard that last week had served as the area outside Mandy's house and lined up in two columns. I was on one end as I had been given a promotion—a helmet with a fancy feathered plume. I was instructed to drill the troops, which were mostly non-English-speaking Tunisian locals, and soon had them marching in step.

John Cleese and Bernard joined us; I took my place at the head of the line next to Bernard, and John stood in front to lead us out. We began by marching in place to keep in step, staying out of view in the archway until we were called. I felt some tiny sense of accomplishment at having gotten them all marching in step, until we began moving and I realized that we would have to climb up three steps. Naturally, they broke step to climb the stairs, shattering their military precision and any hopes I had of becoming a drill instructor. We marched toward the camera in the marketplace, looking for Brian with swords drawn. As the aisle narrowed, I walked single file behind John and Bernard, poking through a pile of cloth in a stall.

We tried a couple of run-throughs to keep everyone in step while going up the stairs, but John marched us along too rapidly. We did two more takes which satisfied John and Terry J, so the Roman soldiers were released.

A few minutes later, John, Bernard, and I were talking in the marketplace, still in uniform, when David Appleby starting snapping pictures. A few of the Tunisian soldiers then gathered around us, anxious to have their pictures taken, as David kept shooting. Then John started camping it up, with a limp wrist and a silly, swishy grin, and Bernard and I followed suit. We apparently provided a nice contrast to the deadly serious, military poses of the Tunisians, and David seemed very pleased.

Everyone rode back to the Sidi Mansour to change clothes. The scheduled showing of the second set of rushes was postponed again due to the broken projector, so I decided to go back to the Ruspina. As I inquired in the production office, John offered me a lift. "I should be leaving shortly, I hope—I have a massage at six," he explained. "Come on, let's play a little Ping-Pong until then."

The Ping-Pong table was near the production office; he handed me a paddle, and we began. He was quite good, but I managed to keep him from getting too far ahead. After a couple of games, we walked into the office but were told we might have to wait.

"What?" he asked with concern. "There are no cars or drivers? I have an appointment for a massage at six. How am I going to get back there?"

Habib scratched his head for a moment and then led us outside. "Aha!" he exclaimed and pointed triumphantly to the large bus used to transport extras. He had a word with the driver, then waved us in. John and I sprawled out amidst the empty seats and rode back to the hotel, alone except for the driver.

Brian Speaks, in which Brian becomes a prophet and begins to attract a following

I STARTED OUT EARLY THIS MORNING getting into costume as a Roman soldier. No sooner had I finished than Matthew decided I would make a better stand-in for Terry Bayler. As soon as I had wriggled out of my armor and into Terry's costume, Melvin approached me. "I think we'll make you into a double for Michael instead." Three roles in only ten minutes—at this rate, I was bound to pass up John Cleese's *Grail* driver.

After I changed into Michael's robes, I was fitted with his wig and beard for the part of a very old, tedious prophet. It was the first time I had ever worn any artificial hair, and I quickly understood why everyone always avoided it. The beard loosened with every movement of my mouth (and came off several times before I had even reached the Ribat). For a finishing touch, I was covered with potter's earth (the filmmaker's version of dirt), as I apparently looked a little too hygienic.

I would be standing in for Michael in the role of the Boring Prophet, a character that vaguely resembles the "It's Man" on the *Flying Circus* shows. The character stands on a wall alongside a group of more flamboyant, blood-and-thunder prophets, all of whom are preaching to the passersby, until Michael is knocked from his spot when Brian falls on him from above.

Michael saw me in costume and had a hearty laugh; it was the first time he had a look at the costume he would eventually be wearing. He then gave me a few tips on how to play the character when the camera rolled: "When you're up on the wall, make very tiny gestures, because you're very tedious, and insignificant, and boring."

Filming began with shots of Brian hiding in the marketplace as Roman soldiers searched for him, more or less doing the things that didn't get finished yesterday. There were doubles on hand for all of the prophets, but none of us were used since the wall couldn't be seen during any of the shots.

When those were finished, we started filming shots of Brian preaching to the crowd while standing on the wall as he begins to attract a following. During a break, I noticed a long, tall man covered with filth walking past me. He stopped and looked at me, rolling his eyes. "Do you believe this shit, Howard?" he asked.

"Clive?!" I gasped. The aspiring young filmmaker was covered from head to toe with a thick crust of mud, which was gradually drying and flaking off. He wore a stringy, braided wig suggesting dreadlocks, though it was difficult to tell under the mud. Around his waist was a brief, dirty loincloth that barely covered him. "I'm doubling for Terry G," he explained. It suddenly made perfect sense; Terry Gilliam was rarely interested in playing a role unless it involved filth or extremes of some kind. "Do you believe this shit?" he asked again, looking at himself incredulously, and attracting

I was prepared to double Michael Palin (sans beard) as the Boring Prophet, but ultimately, I was not needed for any of the shots that day.

the stares of everyone else as well. I suddenly had a new appreciation for the opportunity to double for Michael.

All of the doubles were summoned by Jonathan, as long shots of Brian preaching were being readied. "Clive, I don't think you'll be seen in this shot," Jonathan told him sympathetically. "You can just go and lie down or something for now."

I prepared to take Michael's place on the wall, until someone pointed out that the Boring Prophet had already been knocked off the wall and into a large vase. Whenever Brian was on the wall, Michael could not be. Instead, one of the locals agreed to lie headfirst in the large vase with his feet sticking out, for twice his normal day's pay. Since I was now out of a job, I was recruited to stand in for Graham while the lights and camera were set.

Graham had arrived on set in a very good mood this morning. There had been a Royal Premiere in London last night for *The Odd Job,* the film he had cowritten with Bernard and starred in, he explained. "I talked to London about half past two this morning, and apparently the premiere went extremely well. This now means that Columbia, which has already done a great deal of promotion for the film, will probably do even more promotion before it goes into general release next week and the general public and the critics get a look at it."

Last week, Graham had entertained hopes that he might be able to jet back to London for the premiere, but he gave up on that when he discovered the hectic filming schedule. Bernard, on the other hand, fancied an overnight flight to Malta but had no interest at all in the Royal Premiere, professing a general disdain for royalty.

Filming finally resumed about midmorning, with Brian preaching to the crowds. Today was Carol Cleveland's first day of work. Apparently, she was told to be ready two days ago and was told the same thing yesterday. She didn't mind hanging around the set, but she was glad to finally get started after the previous false alarms.

Carol was part of a group with Terry J, Michael, John, and Terry G, along with several other people who were to observe Brian from the crowd. As the morning scenes were all shot from the crowd's perspective, with the camera looking up at Brian, the crowd members only needed to give their lines at the correct time, without worrying about their positions. It all went well, despite a few spoiled takes mostly due to outside interference, including yet another airplane, some hammering in the distance, and a braying donkey.

There was a notice on today's call sheet from Jonathan, warning that on some days the lunch breaks would have to be reduced to one hour, due to the loss of sunlight and the shortening of the afternoon shooting time. He wasn't joking. The hour-and-a-half lunch was becoming extinct, being replaced by the hour lunch (and even a half-hour lunch on busy days is apparently a possibility). Still, an hour is plenty of time to eat, though it didn't leave time for a swim at the Sidi Mansour.

The same scene continued after lunch, this time from Brian's point of view, with the camera pointing down into the crowd. Everyone anticipated a relatively simple, straightforward scene that could be finished quickly, but a number of minor annoyances resulted in ten takes before Terry was satisfied. Terry J was playing a character who walks through the crowd and exchanges a few words with Brian; then he had to climb behind the camera each time he finished his dialogue and stepped out of shot. By the time we had gotten the last take, Terry was pretty well exhausted. I sat along one end of the wall, out of shot, and gave him a hand as he scurried up the wall in time to get behind the camera for the remainder of the scene. The usual small problems continued to plague various takes, including animal noises, traffic, and odd items that no one had anticipated.

After the third take, Carol tried to tell Terry very discreetly that she needed to slip away and use the ladies' room between takes. She tried to be as quiet and tasteful about it as possible, so naturally, when some of the Pythons found out, they did their best to bring the matter to everyone's attention.

Terry J asked if she could hold out for a couple more takes, and Carol gamely agreed. A few of the actors then booed Terry, and Bernard suggested that she just use one of the assorted receptacles dangling from Terry G's costume. Michael immediately dubbed one of them "the Thespo-Squat," and the group began delivering flowery testimonials as to its effectiveness for all actors who had to go during an important scene.

"I got through all of *Hamlet* with a severe case of diarrhea," boasted Terry G.

"I went fourteen times during *The Lady's Not for Burning* and got rave reviews," testified Michael.

Carol was finally allowed to use the restroom and got a healthy round of applause on her embarrassed return. Nevertheless, as the afternoon dragged on, around the eighth or ninth take, tempers began to grow short. The sun was hotter than it had been for several days, and all of the actors had been standing in it with little respite. There always seemed to be a short delay between takes, as all modern footprints had to be swept away without disturbing the actors' marks. A donkey brayed to disrupt another take, and he was threatened with being sent to Tunis. Somehow, Terry managed to get everything that was needed in ten takes, and we were able to move on.

By this time, though, the afternoon was nearly gone, and there wasn't time for much else. There was barely enough time for some shots of Brian climbing down off the wall and starting through the marketplace, followed by the crowd that had gathered. For a scene with that many people—there were at least fifty in the crowd—it went rather well. Fortunately, only a few people had lines. As the sun started sinking low, it turned into a race against time to finish the scene while we still had enough light, but Terry seemed satisfied.

I left my costume in Michael's trailer, not having done anything all day except for standing in for Graham on a couple of occasions. (Clive had not been used today either, despite his coating of mud, so I could scarcely complain.) I went back to the Sidi Mansour and had a drink. Sue's husband, Chris, and their baby had arrived that day. Carol and Peter were there as well, and we all walked down to Le Coq for dinner. It was a small local restaurant, just a hundred yards or so down from the Sidi. Not a fancy place by any stretch of the imagination, it was a small, wallpaper-peeling-from-the-wall type of place, but the food was excellent, and most of the unit loved it better than the hotel restaurants. It consisted of two very small rooms with three tables each, which we always pushed together whenever we ate there. It seemed to be the best place to go in Monastir for very acceptable wine, a fantastic fish soup, and overall fine authentic Tunisian food.

I did become a little concerned because the second batch of rushes was to be shown at half past eight, and as it grew close to that time our food still hadn't arrived. I decided to relax. Terry J was still eating; if he wasn't worried, neither would I be.

We arrived at the Sidi in time to view the second half of the rushes. The reaction from all was very positive, though the projector was still out of focus and the sound was abysmal. Still, everyone seemed very happy, particularly with the 450 Tunisians rolling on their backs laughing, and everyone was still laughing as they walked away from the viewing room.

Brian Speaks Redux, in which he falls in with an odd group of prophets

ALTHOUGH WE STILL SEEM TO FINISH each day's scheduled shooting, it is taking increasingly longer to get it all done. Filming has become more of a routine, and the initial excitement has settled into just another working day. Nevertheless, as working days go, they are fascinating, and today was no exception. ■ Everyone seemed to be moving at a leisurely pace this morning, setting up several possible camera positions to film a brief long shot looking across the top of the marketplace to the wall, where all of the prophets were standing. All of the actors playing prophets were in full costume, with no doubles needed. Terry G was covered with mud, decked out in the same loincloth and wig that Clive had worn yesterday. The cool early morning air and a moderate breeze inside the Ribat combined with the effects of drying mud to produce a bone-chilling cold effect on Terry. He borrowed a cape from one of the Roman soldiers and wrapped it around his body to provide some warmth.

The marketplace set was still standing from the previous day. The dead chickens and sheep carcasses had been wrapped in plastic bags overnight, which made things slightly more bearable. The usual small animals, including sheep, chickens, and donkeys, were placed about the set, along with our first camel. It was initially an object of curiosity, but the novelty wore off quickly. We had been warned that camels could be vicious and vile tempered, and this one did not disappoint. It seemed to take a dislike to being led about and even to standing; it would only remain quiet when it was allowed to lie on the ground. All of the other occupants of the animal compound, in unison, couldn't match the braying of our camel, which sounded slightly lower in pitch than a cow, and three times as loud.

The camera was placed on the platform overlooking Pilate's Forum for the long shots of the marketplace and the prophets. Fortunately, there was no audio needed, as our camel bellowed throughout. Each of the stalls in the marketplace was occupied by one or two extras acting as shopkeepers, and we had created a startlingly authentic business district. Bernard even tried haggling with one of the extras over a dish of rice and got him to drop his rate down to half of his original asking price.

Haggling is an accepted part of life in Tunisia, one that the cast and crew had learned to accept and master out of necessity. The haggling scene between Graham and Eric is quite authentic, as nearly everything could be brought down in price by at least one-third by haggling with shopkeepers.

"My only other experience in haggling turned out to be a rather humiliating failure in Spain," admitted Bernard. "I asked a shopkeeper how much she was asking for a belt, and she told me it was 125 pesetas. I told her, 'Sixty,' and she immediately began counting out sixty belts."

After the long shots, the prophets were positioned on the wall for some closer shots. The crew began laying down the aluminum rails for a tracking shot, so the camera could be pulled along slowly. The shot pans from Terry G to Charles to Michael as they give their heartfelt speeches, all displaying great passion except for Michael. While we waited, Terry G's dirt began to dry and crumble off as the sun grew hotter. He had to have potter's earth thrown on him several times, because he tended to jump about and flail his arms while preaching.

Even though Monastir is not a large town, the airport seems to be astonishingly busy. Planes passed overhead at an amazing rate, holding up several takes, though spoiling only a few.

After those takes were finished, there was a short break for tea. Terry G remained on his arch on the wall and had a Coke handed to him, posing for a few photos in all of his filth, in hopes of a job in a Coca-Cola advertisement. Coke seems to have permeated Tunisia as thoroughly as it has the Western world.

"I took a ride down south, into the desert, towards Gabes and Matmata, where we'll be shooting later," Michael related. "I was gone all day Sunday, driving through some of the most primitive, backward, remote villages I've ever seen. No matter where I was, though, if I looked around a little, I could always find an old Coca-Cola sign somewhere."

After the break, the five prophets were positioned on the wall for their close-ups, which would be shot with a handheld camera. The rails were removed, and each prophet except for Michael (the Boring Prophet) was apportioned a number of followers. Fires were lit in the charcoal burners to get the area looking appropriately dusty. Some takes involved all five prophets preaching simultaneously. Then each went through his blood-and-thunder rant, describing the terrible fates awaiting those who didn't repent and the terrible demons that would punish them. All except for Michael, of course.

As the Boring Prophet, Michael was in top form, like Arthur Putey in rags. He told the parable of a man who would someday lose his neighbor's hammer, and would not remember where he had put things that he had used only the day before, droning on and on in the most brilliantly dull monotone. Terry J urged him to continue even after he had reached the end of his scripted monologue, and so he improvised superbly, completely unrehearsed, as the crew tried not to laugh out loud.

"And verily, there shall come a day when a man shall not know where lieth the things possessed by their fathers, that their fathers had put there only just the night before . . . and yea, in the words of the prophet Nehemiah, son of Zebediah, as vouchsafed through Malachi through the prophet Anariah, there shall be rumors of things going astray . . ." Michael improvised brilliantly as the camera rolled. The cast and crew marveled at his performance as he rattled off line after wonderfully inane line for several minutes, finally drifting to a rambling close, to a burst of applause. We were all able to laugh at last, and laugh we did.

The next scene required more of a setup, though Brian's fall onto the Boring Prophet was surprisingly easy to film. Graham hung on to an apparatus on the end of a rope, and a large, fluffy mattress was placed at Michael's feet. Graham climbed up a few steps on a ladder to reach the apparatus and grabbed hold, then on cue dropped about four feet to the ground. Before he landed, though, he pushed Michael forward with his feet, onto the mattress, as he fell. It seemed to go smoothly enough, so after a run-through, Terry was ready to film it.

There was only one hitch. Graham was supposed to be holding a gourd in his hand, as he would need it while he was speaking to the crowd. He had to hang on to the apparatus with both hands, so he experimented, holding the gourd first in one hand, then holding it in his mouth. Although it only required a few takes for the close-ups and long shots, the sun was already getting quite hot, and by the last takes, it was becoming difficult for Graham to hang on for any length of time.

Next, the Boring Prophet was to be knocked into a large vase after Brian falls on him. Michael gamely refused to use a double for this shot. (In fact, none of the Pythons have used doubles for any stunts so far.) When he was ready, prop man Peter Grant and big Roy Rodehouse picked up Michael by his ankles. As the camera rolled, they dropped him carefully into the vase. Although it was well padded, and he didn't have to stay inside very long, it must have been very unpleasant, but he didn't complain a bit. It required several takes, but Michael held up very well, and Terry J said the end result was excellent.

We broke for an abbreviated lunch at twelve thirty. Even though it was just an hour, it seemed to be the hottest part of the day. People took advantage of it by going for a swim, reading, or just sitting around and being silly. The locals found a shady spot of rock and napped before we resumed.

Everything has taken on a more relaxed feeling lately. The crew has begun sitting on the huge polystyrene statue of Caesar as it lies on its side, even though it doesn't appear to be too solid. The left index finger has been reattached by a helpful unit member, even though it will almost certainly come off again if it is moved. In the past several days, people have hung shirts and bags on the left hand, and there is almost always an empty Coke bottle in one of the hands.

This afternoon's filming turned into a race against time, trying to finish before we lost the sun, which usually happened sooner in the Ribat than anywhere else. The first afternoon sequence was another hazardous one for Michael, though no other actors were needed. Brian's fall down onto the Boring Prophet was shot from Brian's point of view. The camera was fastened onto Graham's rope apparatus, which hung from the rope and a pulley device at the very top of the large wall. Rather than being dropped from the top of the wall, though, the camera was pulled up from just above Michael's head to the top of the wall quickly, with the film to be run in reverse. In order for the shot to work, the locals walking in front of the prophets had to walk backward. When the sequence was run in reverse, Brian would appear to be falling down while all of the passersby would be walking forward.

It was nevertheless a risky shot. If the rope broke or the camera fell, it would certainly ruin the camera when it hit. It would almost certainly ruin Michael if it hit him, but he continued to preach despite his uneasiness. Four crew members were stationed at the very top of the wall to pull the camera up quickly and smoothly. It was difficult to focus the camera as it hung in that position, and it also had to be stopped and started before and after it was pulled up. It looked like there might be some problems when it was tested, as the rope with the camera began swinging slightly, threatening to dash the camera against the stone wall. The crew members were advised to try it again, pulling it up a bit more smoothly, and that seemed to eliminate the problem. The only difficulty remaining was that we wouldn't know how it looked until the rushes came back.

ABOVE: The Boring Prophet in action, just before being struck by a falling Brian. RIGHT: Terry G's Blood-and-Thunder Prophet between takes.

The marketplace was being taken apart slowly, with the more valuable items in the stalls being carried away first with appropriate care. One of the locals in the stall selling jewelery actually operated a jewelery store in town. He brought with him a number of interesting items, including some beautiful amber, and had built up a respectable clientele among the cast and crew.

The dismantling continued, and the dead chickens and two sheep carcasses were knocked into a cart next to the rotting fish and octopi, while the leather armor was carefully stacked next to the fine rugs. If they kept up the demolition, the marketplace would be down by morning.

The end of the afternoon was taken up with a few brief shots, including Judith running to the crowd that was watching the prophets, followed

Special effects, Tunisian-style.
Brian steps onto a balcony to hide from
the Roman soldiers . . .

. . . but it collapses beneath him and sends
him down onto the Boring Prophet . . .

. who is knocked into a large vase. The balcony scene was actually shot after Brian's collision with the Boring Prophet and in a different part of the Ribat.

by individual close-ups of all the other prophets and the crowds watching them. This was typical. Whenever the sun started to dip low in the sky, Terry usually came up with several short, miscellaneous scenes that could be done quickly. And, more often than not, they were finished.

Graham had a theory about this, which I have dubbed Chapman's Law. "The amount of time necessary to shoot a scene directly corresponds to the amount of time available," he explained. "In other words, if there is only half an hour left to shoot a complicated or troublesome scene, more often than not, it gets done. On the other hand, if there is a relatively simple scene, but all afternoon to shoot it, the scene generally expands enough somehow to fill up most of the afternoon."

It was already after five, and shadows covered the west side of the courtyard, but there was one scene left to shoot. Nearly everyone had been released, and the crew moved into the smaller courtyard, where Graham would have to take a fall from a balcony that collapses beneath him. By the end of the afternoon, the wind had picked up considerably in the narrow courtyard and raised enough dust and sand to cause everyone discomfort. The balcony itself was quite small and made largely of sticks, with a few heavier pieces of wood propping it up from below.

The area beneath the balcony was lined with large mattresses on platforms, so that Graham would actually only fall three or four feet. He needed to take care that pieces of wood from the balcony didn't fall on him and also had to make sure that he didn't fall off the mattresses. To further complicate matters, it was all to be attempted in a single take.

Two cameras were turning when he stepped onto the precarious balcony. For a moment, it looked as though it wasn't going to fall, but it obediently collapsed right on cue. Despite all of the potential problems, the scene came off beautifully, and we wrapped for the day.

The call sheet indicated that tomorrow would be an extended day of filming, which no one seemed to mind as we would have Saturday and Sunday off. Another note on the call sheet advised that if we completed both the matte shot and the night shot in Pilate's Forum tomorrow, then we would be shooting in Sousse next Monday. A third note informed us that a BBC television crew would be down for a week, starting tomorrow, and we were asked to cooperate with them as much as possible.

Sousse, about twenty minutes north of Monastir, is one of the largest cities in Tunisia; some of the cast and crew have driven up there, usually for dinner. I rode back to the Ruspina with Mimoun, one of the drivers, who usually drove for Eric. His English was better than most drivers', though his pronunciations were challenging.

"That Monsieur Iddle! He always go to Sousse—every night!" he said, finding this quite witty and laughing enthusiastically at the very thought of it.

The Hypocaust and the Ex-Leper, in which there are more commandos crawling in tunnels, a shorter wig, and wall washing

TODAY WAS SET ASIDE FOR A number of miscellaneous shots.

■ The marketplace had been almost entirely dismantled overnight. All of the stalls were down, and the wood and other debris covered at least half the courtyard. ■ Due to the mess in the courtyard, the first scenes would be shot in a small, scaled-down version of the Ribat, located about half a block from the real thing. It was actually only one story high and had been serving as the animal compound for the unit. It consisted of a fairly good-sized courtyard surrounded by four walls, and little else.

I shed my Roman solder costume once I got a look at the inside of the small courtyard, as it was obvious the soldiers wouldn't be used for a while. The sewer tunnels had been set up here, larger than ever, and covered with black canvas and plastic. In addition to two large lengths of tunnel, an open section of the palace underground had been constructed as well. This was the hypocaust, an open section held up by small archways, which was just big enough to permit the commandos to crawl around inside.

The commandos all understandably despised the tunnels. They were claustrophobic, filled with smoke, and poorly ventilated, and the actors all had to step out between takes for fresh air. The costumes weighed them down and limited their mobility, making it even more difficult to maneuver in such a small space.

"Terry G seems to enjoy hanging things on people," Michael noted as the wires for his lantern were run along the length of his arm. "I always try to avoid him when I'm in this costume, for fear he'll think of something else to put on me."

The BBC film crew was walking around the set, observing the festivities. They even climbed inside the hypocaust to film some of the commandos crawling about but spent most of the morning sifting through the rubble at the Ribat, watching sets being torn down and erected. Terry G granted them an impromptu interview in which a great many of the questions centered on the naughty statues and frescoes.

Many of the morning's shots were tracking shots that required quite a bit of time to set up; this allowed the commandos to spend much of the morning lounging around the set in costumes. By half past ten, the last bit of shade was gone from the smaller courtyard, and there was really no place to hide from the sun. It was obvious that we would face another long, hot Tunisian day.

By lunchtime, most of the tunnel shots were completed, so we would be starting up in the Ribat in the afternoon. As it was an extended day, the remaining tunnel filming would be finished tonight.

A load of mail arrived from London just before lunch, which cheered up those who got letters and disappointed those who didn't. Bernard noted that he received a nice letter from his wife's lawyer pertaining to their divorce proceedings, which seemed to lift his spirits a bit.

Communications here are not exactly the best. Despite the unit's constant contact with London, most of us feel rather cut off from the outside world. Incoming letters take much time to arrive, and outgoing letters even longer. The few English-language papers I've seen at the Ruspina are always several days old. I have occasionally found the international edition of *Time* or *Newsweek* at the Meridien, and when I take them to the set, they are always enthusiastically received. English-language radio broadcasts are quite rare, and the television networks seem to rely on thirty- or forty-year-old films of Tunisian culture, which are, of course, in Arabic or French. And any telephone call is an adventure.

Fortunately, outgoing mail could always be dropped off in the production office, from whence it would be carried to London and mailed from there, speeding things up considerably. Luckily, I discovered this shortly after arriving and did not have to rely on the postal system in place at the Ruspina, which consisted of a small white birdcage of the type usually sold to tourists, sitting on the front desk in the lobby, to which a small handwritten sign reading MAIL had been affixed. I noticed the same postcards and letters had been sitting inside ever since my arrival two weeks ago; they undoubtedly would be delivered weeks or even months after their senders had arrived home.

After lunch, work in the Ribat had apparently been completed. The entire marketplace had been torn apart and shoved into one corner, and workers were finishing the demolition of the large wall. All of the columns and statues had been reerected in the courtyard, and the huge statue of Caesar was standing once again, its index finger intact.

The outside wall of Pilate's palace had been repainted with "Romani Ite Domum," looking just as it had before, for matting purposes and for the reshoot of Brian's run away from the soldiers after he had finished painting. Graham and the soldiers walked through it a few times; then Terry rolled the camera. The original intent was for the soldiers to trip over an old ragpicker and his huge bundle. As the soldiers ran along after Brian, however, they took a couple of rough spills. Terry Bayler scraped his leg, and Bernard nearly hurt his bad arm. Fortunately, neither injury was serious, but they briefly held up the shooting.

Next was the conclusion of the ex-leper scene.

"After looking at the rushes, we decided my original costume made me look too much like an Indian," explained Michael (he meant the American kind), "so we had to get one that was more appropriate for an ex-leper."

The new wig was much shorter and unkempt, and his clothes were even more tattered and torn. "This is a bit of a hard scene for me to get the feeling of, as it's the end of a longer scene which hasn't been shot yet," he explained. In order to shoot this portion of the scene, which is in the small courtyard just outside Mandy's house, a large white silk screen had to cover the entire courtyard again, which was very time-consuming.

There were apparently some worries over another of the ex-leper's lines. In referring to his cure by Jesus, he says, "He cured me, the bastard."

"It's very much in character for the ex-leper to say that," explained Michael, "but not entirely essential to the scene. I think the feeling is now that it would probably prove more trouble than it's worth. We may change it to simply 'He cured me,' or some less risky equivalent."

The BBC crew has been shooting some of today's scenes. While the reverses of the ex-leper scene were being set up, they were able to grab Graham and Mike for interviews. The crew is being headed up by Iain Johnstone, who explained that they were here to do either a program on the making of *Brian* or else an overview of ten years of Monty Python.

By the time the wall-painting and the ex-leper sequences were finished, it was growing dark, but since it was an extended day, there was still plenty left to do. Everyone then packed and moved over across the street once again to the mini-Ribat for more tunnel filming.

Darkness had fallen by the time the crew was ready to resume. It had gotten colder very quickly, and the commandos pulled their costumes closer in an attempt to keep warm. As hot as it had gotten earlier in the day, it became quite chilly when the cool breezes started to blow. The caterers set up a table in the corner of the courtyard; commandos climbed through the hypocaust and emerged to discover a hot dinner waiting for them. Everyone not necessary to the scene had long since returned to the hotels.

After the short dinner break, it was back in the tunnels for the commandos to finish their crawling. They didn't seem to do nearly as much complaining tonight, as the chilly breeze outside made the tunnels themselves feel more comfy, cozy, and warm. The only drawback remained the smoke that was being pumped inside with the charcoal burners, which smelled rather unpleasant even from a distance.

For the fifth time, Jonathan Benson shouted, "One last time!" It looked as though we would wrap shortly, so I began slipping out of my Roman soldier costume. Then Matthew announced that the Roman soldiers were needed.

It was after 10:00 P.M. when we all moved back to the large courtyard of the Ribat across the street and took our places in the deck chairs as we waited for the lights and camera to be set. Several long brushes and buckets were brought in for workmen, played by locals dressed in rags. The commandos had gathered here as well, but I was still unsure what the next scene would involve.

Then I remembered some comments Michael had made during a drive back to the Ruspina the day after the wall-painting scene, when he expressed his disappointment that the wall had been washed clean. "I had an idea for a nice sight gag, one that might have been a little trouble and not essential to the plot, but would still be a nice touch," he explained. "After Brian has painted the wall with the slogan a hundred times, I thought it would be nice to show him, or someone else, walking past the wall much later, with a crew of workmen in the background furiously trying to scrub off all the slogans. It's not essential, but it would have been a nice little thing to have done, just as a flourish."

At the time Michael described it, I agreed that it would have been a wonderful throwaway sight gag, but since the wall had been cleaned, I didn't think it would happen. I found out tonight that I was wrong. I loved the idea of the gag, and once I learned what we would be shooting, I stopped grumbling about the lateness. In fact, I would have stayed several more hours just to get it filmed.

As I waited for the shooting to commence, I sat next to a local playing a soldier who was not quite as devoted to the film. "This is bullshit," he whined. "Zeffirelli always paid us more than this, and tonight we stay out here so late!"

I was a little surprised to find the Tunisians were starting to go Hollywood on us. He just shook his head, annoyed. It puzzled me, as I knew all of the extras were being paid more for working the long hours tonight. He seemed talkative and told me in excellent English that he was attending college out of town. He was very keen to lecture me about the girls in his country.

"Tunisian women are very strict, very religious. You must go out with them for two, three months before you can even kiss them. And that is all they let you do," he complained. Suddenly, his face brightened with a new thought. "But sometimes, you do find one. And when you do, she is the best. None better. Their mothers teach them before they marry, and they are fantastic!" His face lit up, apparently with a past memory.

Terry J and Jonathan began to place the workmen, scattering them along the wall at various spots, giving them brushes and buckets, and instructing them in how to clean. None of them were allowed to scrub very hard, as the slogans had to last through several takes. One of the workmen was given the job of scrubbing down the area of the wall that was blank, with the slogan to be matted on later. He couldn't quite understand why everyone else was scrubbing paint off the wall while he was scrubbing on a bare area. Jonathan explained that they would put something up there later so that it would look like he was washing off writing, but the local just shook his head and laughed. He was obviously thinking, "These crazy Englishmen," as he turned and started scrubbing the bare wall. He occasionally shook his head and laughed to himself, that these people were so stupid that they thought they could add some paint later to the bare wall.

The Roman soldiers were lined up behind the workmen, except for another local and myself. There were two statues at either end of the courtyard, and we were to march between them, standing guard. We had to drill a bit to keep it symmetrical, each of us reaching the opposite statue at the same time, then turning and marching back. Once all of the soldiers and workmen were ready, the commandos ran from the far end of the courtyard, past the camera, trying to avoid soldiers as they set out on their raid. It seemed to go well, so a couple of takes were enough, and we finally wrapped for the day.

A Day Off, in which there is shopping and real-world haggling

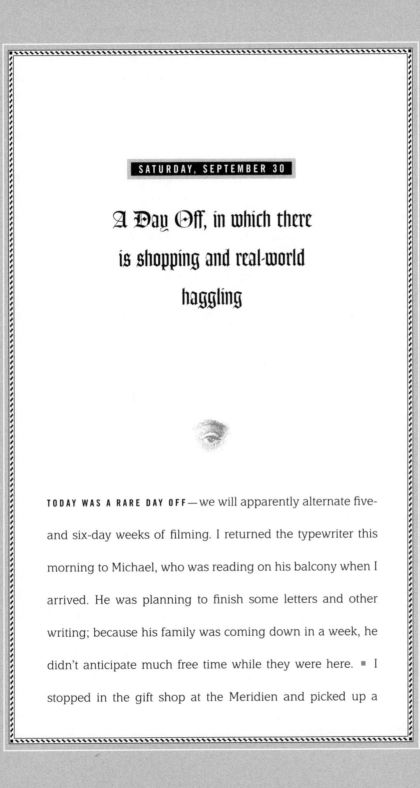

TODAY WAS A RARE DAY OFF—we will apparently alternate five- and six-day weeks of filming. I returned the typewriter this morning to Michael, who was reading on his balcony when I arrived. He was planning to finish some letters and other writing; because his family was coming down in a week, he didn't anticipate much free time while they were here. ■ I stopped in the gift shop at the Meridien and picked up a

Newsweek. The cover feature was "The Avedon Look," which seemed to have little to do with our life in Tunisia, so I paged through it when I got back to my room. Following Michael's example, I did some reading on my first-floor balcony, which was surrounded by a dense growth of palms, date trees, and shrubbery. There wasn't much of a view, and the sky was cloudy and gray as well.

I picked up some mail at the front desk, where I saw John and June Case. They had been stuck in the hotel for the past couple of days, and since it was too overcast for the beach, we decided to share a taxi into town. As we waited for the car to arrive, he told me about his career in show business.

"It was really because of my size," he explained. "Everyone had always been telling me I ought to get into it, and I wanted to do it, but I didn't really know how. It was hard for me in the beginning, because whenever I'd get a part, it was usually just for a day or two, and I had another job at the time. Finally I went into business for myself, the insurance business, so I could get away anytime I needed to.

"I got some work. Probably the best-known thing I've done before this was an ad for British Airways. I was one of three different customers that they had to accommodate. My agency puts out a book each year, and someone saw my picture in it. That's how I got the job with the Pythons here."

Our driver dropped us off downtown, about half a dozen blocks from the Sidi Mansour. Our first stop was the Monoprix, which seemed to be a Tunisian Woolworth's. It was a modern building with modern items, everything from school supplies to a small grocery section with a liquor store. The prices for hard liquor were outrageous—close to twenty dollars for a bottle of scotch—perhaps to discourage drinking in the Muslim country. The hotel bars were much cheaper. I bought shampoo and some cookies and chocolate for snacking.

We then walked across the street to the authentic local marketplace. The center of town and the actual markets were located inside a huge wall that once undoubtedly enclosed the entire town, an area several blocks square. This was where the locals traded and haggled, what we had tried to re-create with the film unit. It was an area not seen by most tourists on their packaged holidays. There were few frills at these shops, all of which were quite small and stood right next to each other. Huge baskets of grain were displayed outside some of the shops; vendors roamed the aisles, and there were several beggars calling to us. There were a number of unsavory, suspicious-looking characters skulking about the alleyways. I hadn't heard of anyone in the unit having trouble with them, but we had all been warned about pickpockets. Probably because I was accompanied by all six feet nine inches of John Case, none of them seemed to think it was worth a try, and no one came near us.

Some of the shops didn't even look like shops. We passed one open doorway that contained a weaving loom, with an old man bent over it. He obviously lived there and sold his weaving from his home. We walked on a bit farther and found a somewhat wider selection of clothing. June looked at some native shirts, and, after a few minutes of haggling, they brought the price down to an agreeable level and she bought a couple of them.

As it was growing late, I decided to walk down to the Sidi, where I encountered Terry J and Peter Biziou discussing next week's filming. Graham and Bernard came down to the hotel bar as well, and it began to grow crowded with cast and crew. The weather didn't really allow much sunning or swimming; the most popular alternative appeared to be drinking and socializing.

Michael arrived and mentioned that rushes would be shown later that afternoon, so I decided to stay around. Python manager Anne Henshaw and her daughter Rachel had just arrived for a weeklong stay, and she was warmly greeted. The rushes were soon under way, and everyone watched appreciatively. There was a general feeling of overall satisfaction with them, and all seems well with *Life of Brian.*

A Second Day Off, in which there is a rainstorm and a chat with Carol

AFTER SLEEPING IN AND SPENDING A leisurely morning off reading *Fear and Loathing on the Campaign Trail*, I took a walk along the beach, where I encountered Carol and Peter and, a few minutes later, Anne and Rachel Henshaw. Anne seemed to be worried about Graham, which came as a surprise to me. ▪ "Graham is really keeping long hours, I'm afraid," she explained. "He hasn't had a day off since the filming started, and I'm afraid it's beginning to wear on him."

I remembered all of the doctoring Graham was doing at night after he finished performing, in addition to the writing he was trying to finish, and sympathized.

"I'm almost surprised that the two Terrys are carrying on so well. Both of them are on the set every day and work when they get back to their hotels every night," I added.

"I know, but Terry J just seems to thrive on it," noted Anne. "He's really happy doing it all. The one I really feel for is Eric. Of all the Pythons, the one with the lowest level for boredom is probably Eric, and he's had almost nothing to do in the first two weeks. He's so terribly bored right now, and you really can't blame him."

I walked back to the beach at the Ruspina and joined Carol and Peter for a few minutes, but thick black clouds were covering the sky, and we all decided to call it quits just before it started spitting raindrops. It looked like it could develop into quite a storm, so we hurried along the path and made it to the Ruspina just as the sky let loose.

The Ruspina bar was jammed with people seeking refuge from the storm, despite the signs banning swimsuits from the bar. I had been wanting to interview Carol for some time, and she suggested this might be an opportune moment. As the lobby was so crowded, we walked up to the second floor and sat on a bench near the landing. I started by asking her how she first became involved with the Pythons.

"It was right at the beginning, about nine years ago," she explained. "I'm not quite sure who it was that introduced me to the whole setup. Someone sort of suggested my name when they were looking for a female. They'd only written five episodes, so there wasn't an awful lot to do, but they wanted someone. I didn't know any of the lads, I'd never met or worked with any of them, but someone put my name forth as a sort of possible choice. I was interviewed by the producer, who at the time was also going to direct the first four episodes. He's the one who actually cast me, and I was only supposed to do the five and that was it, the end of my contract. But by that time, the fellows decided they liked me, and I seemed to fit in with what they were doing. I must admit that the first couple of episodes, I didn't understand what the hell was going on! I didn't understand what it was all about, but they liked me, and I seemed to fit in after a

The torrential rains had driven everyone from the beaches into the bar at the Ruspina.

bit, and they kept me on as their regular female. It was really the fellows who decided they wanted me around, so that was really very nice."

Once she became attuned to their ideas, Carol explained, she enjoyed the process a great deal.

"I loved it once I got used to it. I was baffled to begin with, but I think everyone was rather baffled to begin with, for the first couple of episodes. But once I loosened up and decided, 'Well, whatever this is all about, I'll just enjoy it,' I got into the zaniness of it all. I thought it was splendid and

I loved doing it. I loved working with them, it was one of the happiest experiences I've ever had. Little did anyone know at the time, at the beginning, what a great fantastic success it was going to be! I had no idea. I just thought, 'Well, this is fun,' but I've never loved anything quite so much."

I asked her what sort of experience she'd had before she started with the group that might have caused them to bring up her name in the first place.

"I'd already been doing a fair amount of comedy, a sort of 'glamour stooge,' in various television comedy shows, working with various comedy stars—the Two Ronnies, Spike Milligan, Peter Sellers. I suppose someone had taken note of all that and my name came up. I'd been doing mainly television work, doing some drama as well, but somehow early on I did get into this comedy thing."

Once *Flying Circus* ended in 1974, however, Carol started doing much more theater and much less television. "I found myself longing to do more proper theater, really get in there and do it. Eventually I did, and about two years ago, I decided I was absolutely going to concentrate on theater, even if it meant working out of town, repertory, fringe, whatever—I wanted to do theater work. And having put my mind to it, one thing led to another, and for the last two and a half years, that's practically all I've been doing. In fact, I want to get back to television now. I had a couple of rather unfortunate experiences in the theater doing some fringe work. The plays were good, but the rest of the production wasn't really up to scratch, and I was a bit disillusioned with it. I thought, 'My goodness, I think I'd better just go back to television, where people can't afford to muck around, where they have to cast properly because they can't afford to make mistakes with their casting, or they can't afford to waste time during rehearsals.' And therefore, you know the end result is going to be worth it. I feel now I'd really like to do a nice play on television. That will possibly be my next venture."

Carol explained that she had wanted to go into performing ever since she was a child. "I wanted to be a dancer to begin with. I was born in England but brought up in America—I'm half American. I got started right at the beginning, because my parents were in the business. My mom and dad met on a film set, so it was in the blood, obviously, from the word go. My mother wasn't a pushy, theatrical mom at all, but I think she was delighted that I went that way. It's always made her happy and very proud, but she didn't push me into it by any means. She did get me into dancing at a very early age. At five, I started taking ballet lessons. When I was thirteen or fourteen, I decided that instead of being a dancer, I would be an actress. I was given a part in an amateur production where I was the leading dancer, and I played Cinderella at the last minute because the girl that was supposed to do it broke her leg. That was a great turning point for me. I decided acting is a lot of fun, and from that moment on, I've never really wanted to do anything else. This has just been it."

As the conversation turned to Python and favorite sketches, Carol admitted to enjoying many of the most popular, including the Dead Parrot and Hell's Grannies. "But there are so many, and I've forgotten so many of them. I come across fans of Python—and of course they're still seeing Python in the States, they haven't stopped and have been repeated all the time—and they keep talking about sketches which I have long since forgotten, because, as I say, it's been nearly ten years now. I think, 'Oh my goodness, yes, that was a funny one, yes, I'd nearly forgotten about that one.'

"For me, the very favorite one that I personally was in was way back in the first series, and we did an episode that later won the Montreux television award. This was one of the few long sketches that worked, because on the whole, I think the long sketches in Python have been the least funny. It was all about Scott of the Sahara, which was from Scott of the Antarctic. It was very funny. Everybody was in it and had these very definite characters, and everybody was extremely funny. I played a film starlet, à la Marilyn Monroe, all blond. I loved doing that. I had to stand in a trench, and the director of the film comes up and says, 'Miss Whore, we think we'd like for you to play this scene out of the trench today.'"

Carol went into her best squeaky Monroe voice: "'You want me to play the scene out of the trench? But I've never acted out of a trench before! It's dangerous, I might fall over!' Lovely lines like 'I'm terribly sorry, I just can't remember my lines, my doggie's not well.' I loved doing that."

Despite her long history with the group, she was afraid there might not be anything for her to do in *Life of Brian,* so she was very happy to be asked.

"I was a little bit worried that I might have been left out of this one, because I haven't been left out of anything in Python. I've been in the series and all of the films, and all the records and stage shows. The only time I wasn't able to join them was when they did the show at Drury Lane—I was otherwise engaged when it came up. Otherwise, I've always been there.

"When this came up, I talked to the lads when they finally got the script together. They were very apologetic because they said they just weren't sure if there would be anything in the film for me. As usual, there are very few female parts. They've apologized over the years continuously for not having enough for me to do. The only females they do have in their films are, as a rule, elderly ladies—the Pepperpots—which they do beautifully themselves, leaving very little for the rest of us. In this particular film, there's only one main female role, and she really has to be sort of petite, and serious, and dark, and young, and I really don't fit into any of those descriptions anymore. And I said, 'That's quite all right, I'll buy that one, it's fair enough.' And they said, 'Well, the only other things there are, are the little sort of bit parts, different ladies, not big parts, just lines here and there.' And I said, 'Listen, I don't care! That's fine by me.' I would just hate to think that I'd be left out of the film, because I'm part of Python as far as I'm concerned, and I couldn't conceive *not* being there somehow. So they said fine, if I was happy to do that, so here I am, playing just a few little bits, things like 'Mrs. Jew on the Cross,' who has one line that goes something like this: 'Aaarrgghh!' So that's what I'm doing here, but it's jolly good fun. I'm loving every minute of it."

The rain had stopped by the time we finished talking and the sun was breaking through, but it was too late for another try at the beach. Before leaving, Carol invited me to have dinner with Peter and her, so I went back to my room to clean up.

The members of the unit were becoming familiar faces around the restaurant, and the waiters were gradually learning how to serve us fairly quickly and somewhat efficiently. This evening, the dining room was filled with people from the film. Most of the makeup girls, several members of the camera crew, and the usual grips and sparks filled the restaurant. John Cleese ate with Iain Johnstone (the first time I had seen him eating at the Ruspina), and there was only one couple in the dining room that wasn't associated with the film.

Carol, Peter, and I discussed the improved service in the restaurant and bemoaned the inefficient telephone system. "We've asked for a wake-up call every morning since we've been here, and I don't think we've gotten one yet," noted Peter.

"That's understandable," I said. "Whenever I get up early in the morning, I usually wake up the desk clerk."

"I'm surprised they haven't asked me to return my Miss Ruspina banner. I suppose they probably will, though!" said Carol, and she and Peter laughed. I remembered a commotion outside when I got back from filming Friday night, though I didn't bother to investigate.

"They had a contest of some sort out by the pool Friday night to select a Miss Ruspina, and I won!" Carol explained. "It was the strangest contest I've ever been in. They selected some of us to take part in it and devised all sorts of competitions. In one, we all had to go out into the audience and collect as many pairs of pants as we could from the men."

I remembered seeing an old photo of Carol in one of the Python books in which she was wearing some sort of banner, and she admitted she was a veteran. "Back when I was in high school, I was working for a modeling agency that would get us in all of these contests, mostly for the publicity. They were nothing big, but I wonder where they dug up one of those photos?"

Rival Revolutionaries, in which rain forces a change of plans— and dueling commando groups compete to kidnap Pilate's wife

I ARRANGED A RIDE TO SOUSSE with Carol and Peter, so I was able to sleep in later than usual today. It wasn't until I met them in the lobby this morning and we started riding north that I heard about the storm. ■ "I've never seen such a storm!" exclaimed Peter. "The thunder woke me immediately, and I just sat up and watched it for a time." ■ "It was incredible!" Carol added. "The crashing and the downpour!

And it continued for hours! The whole sky was filled with lightning, not short flashes, but it covered the sky for several seconds at a time."

They continued to describe the storm with great enthusiasm while I wondered how I could have slept through it all. "What a downpour! It just rained buckets," Carol went on. I looked into the fields as we drove on. The standing water covered many of them, in some cases suggesting small lakes.

When we arrived at the location in Sousse, there was no standing water; the sand was certainly damp but had apparently soaked it all in. This morning's filming was at the city wall, an impressive stone wall that surrounded a large castle and plenty of land inside. All of our filming would be done on the grounds outside the wall, however.

"It was here that Robert Powell was crucified for Lew Grade," quipped Eric. [Powell was Jesus Christ in Zeffirelli's *Jesus of Nazareth*, which Grade produced.]

The sea was not far away. Sousse was apparently a port city, as there were several large freighters docked nearby.

"Look, there's a Russian ship!" Gwen pointed out. "Two of them!" I looked more closely and spotted the hammer and sickle insignias.

"Did you see the lightning last night?" asked Michael. "The thunder woke me, and I just sat up for a while on my balcony watching it. It was fascinating. It just covered the sky!"

"My driver, who's a native, said he hasn't seen anything like it in years," marveled Graham.

"The locals claim that these torrential rains usually move in for two or three days and then suddenly move out, leaving sunny skies and hot temperatures for ten or twelve days, until the next rains. At least that's what my driver told me," Michael added.

How could I have slept through a storm like this?

Bernard and Andrew were out on the beach yesterday afternoon when the earlier storm hit, and they decided to run into the ocean, in the rain, with all their clothes on. They then went back to the Sidi, dripping wet, and started knocking on doors, looking for someone with the film who was unlucky enough to be in their room. For a while it looked as though they wouldn't find anyone, but eventually Gwen opened her door. She had been just about to get into her bathtub when Bernard and Andrew invited themselves into her room. Finding a hot bath waiting, they both stripped off their wet clothes, grabbed some of her liquor, and settled back in her bath to relax and have a drink.

The sky remained overcast throughout the morning, and there were worries that the storm might start up again. The clouds by themselves weren't enough to stop the filming, though, as they covered the entire sky thoroughly and evenly. The first scene to be shot was of Brian and Mandy walking down along the city wall on their way to the stoning, as Mandy lectures to her son on sex. On their way down along the wall, they passed several mules and a goat herder. There were quite a few animals showing up on location today for some reason, including several cattle and a number of camels.

While Graham and Terry J went through their paces, the rest of the cast sat in the canvas chairs, one eye on the scene and the other on the sky. The BBC crew arrived early, and while the filming continued, they shot an interview with Eric. After the second shot was lit, it began to sprinkle. Terry J, Peter Biziou, and the camera crew conferred, trying to decide their next course of action. A lightning bolt and thunder, followed by a sudden downpour, quickly made up their minds, and everyone scattered for the nearest available cover. As we had been filming in the middle of the huge open area outside the wall, there was really no shelter, so everyone flocked to cars, trailers, buses, or anything else that would provide a bit of cover. I took refuge in Mike and Terry's trailer, along with ten others. Terry, Peter, and Brenda discussed options for filming, while the rest of us watched the rain outside, grateful for the mostly comfortable shelter.

After the situation was discussed, it was decided to have the costumes and props sent over here from the Sidi in order to film more commando scenes. We had an early lunch, dining in one of the buses, and returned to the trailers to wait for costumes to arrive. For this afternoon's scene, the commandos would run into an almost identical group of commandos with an identical plan, led by Deadly Dirk (played by John) below Pilate's palace. Several of us were recruited to play Deadly Dirk's followers, wearing similar commando gear. The scene would be shot in a castle, similar to the Ribat in Monastir, in the center of Sousse.

The commandos all dressed and started out for downtown Sousse. The rain continued steadily, and would for the rest of the afternoon, validating Terry's decision to seek a cover set.

Inside the castle in Sousse, I was given a club, a net, and some ropes, and positioned behind John as the Deadly Dirks slunk along the hallway. (As I was too tall and a bit too noticeable, I was soon relegated to the back of the line.) We were able to accomplish quite a bit during the afternoon, so what could have been a completely wasted day turned out rather well, and we actually lost very little.

After we wrapped for the day, Peter Grant noticed several small bats sleeping on the ceiling of the castle. One of the sparks started throwing rocks at them but stopped when he was reminded that they could be infected with rabies.

I rode back to the Sidi with John and Peter Brett. Carol had gone back to the Ruspina early that afternoon. So far, Peter has done more acting in the film than Carol.

Tonight's rushes consisted of the haggling scene and various shots of the marketplace. Perhaps because of the weather, the next two days of filming have been changed to interior shooting at the Ribat. According to the revised shooting schedule attached to today's call sheet, the rest of the week will be back in Sousse.

What Have the Romans Ever Done for Us? In which the revolutionaries hold a meeting, and Garth reloads

THERE WAS ANOTHER TORRENTIAL DOWNPOUR OVERNIGHT. I slept through this one as well. ▪ By the time the crew arrived at the Ribat, the skies had cleared, though the winds, water, and mud had left a minor mess. The canvas and burlap from the market stalls had been scattered throughout the court-yard to dry in the sun, while the scaffolding, camera, and lights were set up in a corner just outside Matthias's house.

There was plenty of time before the next scene, so the rest of us sat and watched the preparations.

The BBC crew had somehow corralled John for an interview while the rest of us were talking. "Would you like to see my hair transplant?" John asked the camera, obligingly pulling his hair aside and thrusting the top of his head toward the lens. Eric interrupted him and began using the camera lens as a mirror, contorting his face as he examined himself. Iain eventually settled them enough to begin a more sensible line of questioning, but no sooner had he started than Michael arrived to provide further disruption. "What's this, a BBC crew come to interview us?" he asked, taking a seat with the other interviewees. "One of your BBC people has taken my chair, so I found I had to come over here and sit down."

When the camera finally ran out of film and Iain had run out of energy, the BBC departed. The morning tea and sandwiches were served, as everyone relaxed. "All filmmaking should be like this," Michael noted happily.

Terry J strolled over, explaining that he was concerned about the potential running time of the film. "This is going to run over two hours as it is now," he said, shaking his head. "I don't really know what we should do. Most distributors won't touch a comedy that's any longer than ninety minutes. We'll probably have to end up cutting some things, or perhaps not film a few things scheduled."

I sympathized, noting that I would hate to see anything left out because the material was all so good, and nearly everything seemed essential to the story.

"We do have a couple of other choices, though," Terry mused. "We could split it up and actually make two movies out of it, or we could just put in an intermission . . ."

As Terry strolled back toward the camera crew, Michael contemplated one of the possibilities. "Hmm, that intermission idea," Michael pondered as he lounged in his chair. "You know, perhaps we could do an intermission where we all just sit around like this while the camera films us. That way, when the audience stops to take a break and get something to eat, we all stop and sit around and eat as well. It would be easy to do, but a tremendous waste of film if it didn't work out."

"Yes, but we could just do what we're doing here," enthused Eric. "Perhaps we could use the camera as sort of a mirror, to hold up to our faces and pluck our eyebrows and such."

Matthew and Melvin approached the circle of chairs.

"Oh, no," groaned John, just loudly enough for them to hear. "It's Binns and Lind, and I suppose they want us to go up into the little room."

John always seemed to enjoy teasing them both and delighted in making their jobs difficult, particularly the part of their jobs that involved rounding up the actors to begin filming. As Melvin approached, John began talking to John Goldstone. Melvin tried to be polite and wait for a break in their conversation before telling John that they were ready for him. But John knew that Melvin had come for him, intent on rousing him from his comfortable little reverie, and saw to it that no break in the conversation occurred for several minutes, running his sentences together and pretending to ignore the assistant director. As Melvin listened more closely, waiting for a break in John's monologue, he heard this:

"So you see I've got to keep talking because if I stop then Binns and Lind will tell me to get in front of a camera again, while I'd rather sit back here some more and relax, so if I keep talking I hope he'll be too polite to interrupt and tell me to go, and perhaps he'll just get tired and walk away and leave me alone, so it appears I shall just have to remain speaking like this until he takes the hint and goes away and leaves me alone, because I—"

As Melvin caught on, he became slightly more aggressive in his protests, jumping and waving his hand in front of John, while John continued, unperturbed, pretending not to notice. Finally, John took Melvin very carefully by the throat, clutching it with both hands and pretending to squeeze very hard, and dragged him along to the set, with Melvin trying to maintain his composure as much as possible.

Eventually, all of the revolutionaries were rounded up in the room in the upper corner of the Ribat, which was serving as Matthias's house, where the revolutionaries were meeting to discuss their secret plans. Everyone not involved in the scene seemed to be lounging around the courtyard, due to the near-claustrophobic conditions in the room. I found a place and sat uncomfortably on an apple box, where I was close enough to hear, if not see, everything that was occurring inside. Of course, there were a few moments when even those on the far side of the courtyard could hear some of John's angry lines, including gems like "You fucking stupid cunt!" As the scene was quite long and involved several characters, it took quite a while to shoot. The delays, along with the crowding in the room, caused many to become irritable, and I steered clear of everyone in the little room.

Jonathan and Terry broke for lunch just in time, which gave everyone a chance to cool down and relax. John and Eric found a few moments for cricket, and the BBC started another interview with Terry G. Michael, apparently in a playful mood, walked into this one as well.

Spike Milligan dropped by the set briefly, to the astonishment of nearly everyone. [Milligan wrote and starred in *The Goon Show*, the legendary BBC radio comedy series that inspired the Pythons while they were growing up in the 1950s; he is one of their greatest influences.] He was visiting the area on holiday, heard that the Pythons were filming in Monastir, and stopped by to have a look. Anne Henshaw, who was apparently on the same flight to Monastir, tipped him off. He had some trouble getting into the Ribat, as the guards didn't want to admit him. He was standing in the road shouting, "Does anyone here speak English?!" until someone noticed and vouched for him.

John and Eric, along with a few others, went to greet him, and the BBC crew moved in. Spike started talking about *The Goon Show* and how he almost considered the Pythons to be his grandchildren with regard to their humor. He was quite wound up and talked at some length before the BBC camera. When they finally ran out of film, he expressed an interest in doing some acting in a crowd scene before leaving. Matthew and Melvin found something for him in scene 42A, which will be shot on Thursday in Sousse; he will play one of Brian's followers. They arranged for his lunch, and he left soon after.

"I can understand Iain and his crew interviewing him and all, but I wish Spike could just sit and talk, instead of feeling he has to be performing all of the time," sighed John. "He's really marvelous to just sit down and talk to, but I hate it when he starts talking like that and I can't just sit and talk to him."

It was probably a good thing that the interiors were rescheduled for today and tomorrow, as the weather today was so changeable. After an early morning cloud cover, the sun was very hot for the remainder of the morning and early afternoon. The sky began to cloud up again about mid-afternoon, though, and it looked like it could start pouring at any moment.

Filming in the afternoon continued in Matthias's house with reverses and Judith's entrance, all well under cover just in case. Because of the reverses, more of the area outside of the house had to be evacuated, so I joined most of the other grips, sparks, and hangers-on in moving down to the courtyard. Quite a few crew members lined up in the courtyard and started pitching coins. They drew a line in the dust and took turns throwing at it, and the winner was the person who came closest. They quickly had a major gambling operation going and even brought out a tape measure to check a few close tosses.

The reverses in Matthias's house took up much of the afternoon, and the revolutionaries were practically blockaded in the room. Perhaps as a result, they started behaving very sillily. At one point, the actors were prepared for another take when our sound man, Garth, announced that he wasn't quite ready because he had to reload. John and Bernard decided they would not allow this to pass unnoticed.

Those of us talking in the courtyard below were suddenly interrupted by very spirited though unmelodic singing from a male chorus, which seemed to be emanating from Matthias's house.

> **"Garth is not ready, Garth is not ready,**
> **Garth is not ready, Garth isn't ready."**

They sang to the tune of "Oh, Come All Ye Faithful," particularly lusty and inspired as they came to the chorus, which built in volume and intensity:

> **"Oh Garth he is not ready, oh Garth he is not ready,**
> **Oh Garth he is not ready, Garth isn't ready!"**

Garth was apparently growing flustered to find himself the object of this musical diversion, which further delighted the singers. As they concluded, John called out, "Are you ready yet, Garth?" "No," Garth admitted, trying to work quickly enough to avoid further embarrassment. He was unsuccessful.

"Garth is still not ready, Garth is still not ready," they began anew, harmonizing to the second verse with renewed gusto. As the second verse ended, they gave themselves a round of applause. Meanwhile Garth, increasingly flustered, worked feverishly.

"Is something wrong?" asked Bernard.

"No, I'm just reloading the tape," assured Garth. It was enough to spark a third verse.

**"Garth is reloading, Garth is reloading,
Garth is reloading, Garth is reloading . . ."**

Garth finally announced that he was ready. It had taken him significantly longer than it had the previous weeks, but he was relieved to have finished. His relief was short-lived.

"Garth is now ready, Garth is now ready," they sang, one last verse before shooting resumed.

By this time, it was late in the afternoon, and everyone who didn't need to stay around began to drift back to the hotels. It was a bit frustrating in that we couldn't get close enough to watch or even hear the shooting. No sooner had Sue Jones-Davies decided to use the ladies' room than she was called up to the set for some brief shots of her arrival. The day finished with some shots of the revolutionaries hiding, and we wrapped. Somehow, we made it through the entire filming day without a drop of rain.

Matthias's House Is Searched,
in which the Roman soldiers
discover a spoon

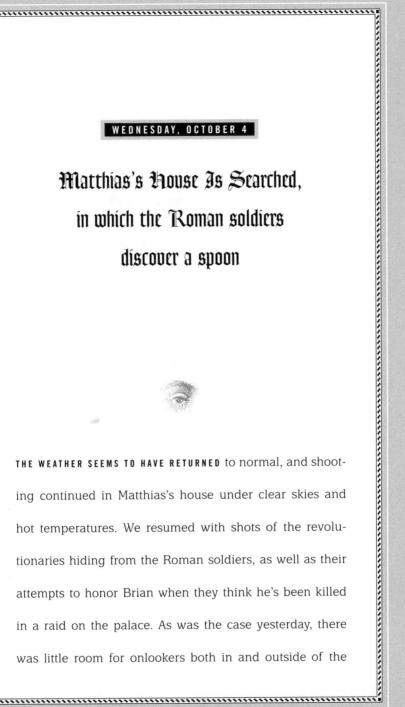

THE WEATHER SEEMS TO HAVE RETURNED to normal, and shooting continued in Matthias's house under clear skies and hot temperatures. We resumed with shots of the revolutionaries hiding from the Roman soldiers, as well as their attempts to honor Brian when they think he's been killed in a raid on the palace. As was the case yesterday, there was little room for onlookers both in and outside of the room, so the grips and sparks used it as justification for another round of pitching coins.

There was a brief notice on today's call sheet, directed to the sound department: "Python Choir to sing 'Garth Is Reloading' and other melodies as required."

Due to the tight space on the set, anyone not involved in the actual filming risked boredom. Those who were not pitching coins sat around waiting for something interesting to happen. It didn't.

The scenes in Matthias's house were officially considered to be part of the cover set, even though the weather was beautiful. Nearly every day, the call sheets listed the shooting planned for that day, along with a cover set to be used in case of rain. Oddly enough, the only day so far that the call sheets did not include a cover set was the day of the downpour in Sousse.

The morning's filming apparently went well, and we broke for a longer than usual lunch. After eating, I noticed the BBC interviewing Michael. Perhaps they felt it was the best way to prevent him from interrupting another interview. If so, they were right, as he didn't bother to interrupt at all when they grabbed the ever-busy Terry J afterward for a twenty-minute chat.

Mike, Eric, and Graham were all very pleased with the afternoon's shooting—none of them were involved in any of it, so they were allowed to leave shortly after lunch. Graham felt particularly liberated, as it was the first completely free afternoon he had been given in weeks.

The afternoon filming would involve about a dozen Roman soldiers, part of the group led by John as the centurion, searching Matthias's house for Brian. I was costumed as a Roman soldier, and when I got to the small corner of the Ribat where we would be filming, I could immediately see why the others had been so happy to flee the set. It was cramped and crowded, and the ceilings and doorways seemed particularly low. It was easily the most uncomfortable piece of filming I have been involved in so far, due to the lack of room, the heat, and the general unpleasantness of the scene.

All twelve Roman soldiers were outfitted with long spears and shields, in addition to our regular armor. Then we were lined up, single file, along a back stairway. On cue, we were to march quickly into Matthias's house, line up again, and march out while we supposedly conducted a search of the house. The camera was trained on John and Matthias as we marched past them, so it was essential that we move in and out rapidly.

It wasn't as simple as it sounded. The first problem arose when we all tried to walk through rapidly. The doorways were no more than five and a half feet high, and even the smallest soldier had to bend down. In addition, the helmets added close to a foot to each of us. Even worse than that were the spears. They were seven feet tall, so if they were carried vertically, they wouldn't fit through the doorway. But if they were held horizontally, it was a good bet that one or two soldiers at the front of the line would be hit. After a couple of attempts, it was clear that they simply wouldn't work, so we got to shed the spears.

But it was still difficult, even without the spears. We still had heavy, bulky shields, and to replace the spears, we had to draw our swords and carry them in for our search. Terry and Jonathan, who as first assistant director was often in charge of traffic control, kept emphasizing speed, "get in there and get out," and they did their best to encourage us. On the next take, there was a crush of bodies and armor, as the soldiers in the back kept pushing forward, and they became a bit unruly as they tried to push their way into the room. Someone began stepping on the backs of my heels, which was particularly painful as I was wearing sandals. Even without the spears, we still had to duck to get through the doorway, and from the sound of helmets hitting stone, it sounded like some of them had forgotten. And no sooner had we gotten the entire group into the room than we were cued to come back out, at the same high rate of speed.

"Nice, but could you do it a bit more quickly?" asked Jonathan when we had finished. The Tunisians began voicing their complains to Habib, while the English speakers asked if something could be done to prevent the massive jam-up in the doorway. We walked through it once more, slowly, this time trying to keep in step. At the front of the line was Bernard, who had apparently gotten a nasty conk on the head and wasn't too pleased with this particular scene. Nevertheless, it seemed as though there were no other shortcuts to take that would make things any easier, so we continued, take after painful take.

"What was that strange expression on your face that last time, Howard?" asked Jonathan after one take.

"I think it was pain," I explained. "Someone seemed to be stomping on my heels."

"Well, next time, don't wince," he advised.

During the scene, the soldiers search the room for Brian but return empty-handed. John's character asks Bernard what we found, and he replies, "Nothing, sir." John began thinking about it and suggested to Terry that perhaps they should have the soldiers uncover some sort of silly object.

"Let me think, now . . . How about—no—I've got it. They come out with a spoon. Yes, that's it. They uncover a spoon in the search," suggested John.

Terry appeared unconvinced, but a spoon was found for John, and he persuaded Terry to let him try it. "I think it's just the right kind of silly object," John told him. "I'll tell you what. Let's just shoot two versions, one where they find nothing, and the other where they find the spoon. We can choose the final version later."

Terry still appeared unconvinced but agreed, looking as though it was as much to keep the peace as anything else. The compromise didn't please the Roman soldiers, however, as it meant that we would have to rush through the doorway that many more times. We carried on for what seemed like hours, and in fact took the rest of the afternoon. It wasn't until close to dusk that Jonathan shouted, "That's a wrap!" They were welcome words, and we hurried back to the Sidi Mansour to return our costumes.

The evening's rushes included Brian's sermon on the wall, although not the fall onto the Boring Prophet that I had hoped to see. Brian was also chased through the marketplace; even though I knew I was a Roman soldier in the marketplace, I still could not spot myself. I'll undoubtedly be unrecognizable in many scenes I've done, but at least I'll know I was there.

John offered me a ride back to the Ruspina after rushes, and I took the opportunity to interview him, beginning by asking his reactions to the first two weeks of filming.

"I'm very, very pleased that we've managed to stay on schedule," he said. "We seem to have worked quite efficiently—in fact, I think, very efficiently. Most of the scenes I've seen rushes of or seen performed, I think we've made them work okay. A couple, I'm not quite sure how they're going to cut together, but this is always the case. Terry has probably got it clear in his mind, and just from seeing the rushes—one sequence in particular, although I haven't seen all of the rushes—I'm sure it will cut together, but I don't see it as clearly. You know, in other scenes, like the one we've just been seeing tonight, which is Graham's sermon in the marketplace, you just see how it's going to cut: 'Yes, we use that shot, then we go to that shot, then we go to that'—when you don't see that . . . I'm always just a slight worrier, I always think, 'Oh, yes, now is it going to work or not?' With the exception of those couple of scenes, which I'm sure will come together because I'm sure Terry's got them in his head, I'm very, very pleased.

"I think Terry's worked splendidly, and the crew is absolutely top class to a man. Even a guy like Roy Rodehouse, who's in charge of the electricians, he works so fast and so efficiently and so hard the whole time. The makeup people are first class, the costumes are first class, Terry Gilliam's making the film look very good. I think it's a very efficient little unit; there's a nice atmosphere around it. The camera boys are very, very pleasant and relaxed, and the wonderful thing is, nobody's too much on an ego trip; none of the technicians or camera or sound are making too much of a fuss about their own interests in the movie. Sometimes you get a cameraman who, by the time he's satisfied with a shot, all the life's gone out of the acting. They're very good; they get it all, and there are very few retakes because there've been mistakes on camera, very few retakes because there've been mistakes on sound. A very high level of efficiency."

I remembered watching John talk with Spike Milligan the previous day, and how all of the Pythons had been influenced by Milligan and *The Goon Show*. Somehow we got to discussing comedians, and specifically John's personal favorites.

"There's a lot of them," he explained. "I suppose I go through various phases. If I take it chronologically, when I was a kid at school, about fifteen or sixteen, it was the Goons. Even before that, when I was twelve or thirteen, it was the Marx Brothers. Then it became the Goons, the British radio show, then Tony Hancock, and actually about the same time as the Goons, Burns and Allen, who I think are wonderful. I think George Burns is a genius, an absolutely enchanting personality, so funny and so rich and so unusual. I was a great, great fan of Bilko, Phil Silvers, thought he was marvelous. Then, as I say, Hancock on our television over here, and then the *Beyond the Fringe* team, Peter Cook, Jonathan Miller, Dudley Moore, and Alan Bennett. Then I saw some Chaplin about that time, and I was very impressed with some of his films, terribly impressed with some of them. There was a compilation film I saw about six months ago on a plane to Australia that is just mind-boggling; it shows just how versatile he was. Very, very funny, too. Then I went through a phase of loving Buster Keaton and W. C. Fields.

"Of contemporaries, I've always thought that Billy Wilder's films were absolutely top class. I'm immensely impressed, obviously, with Woody Allen, who has always made me laugh. And I went through a phase a few years ago of liking the American comedians that one really only heard on records—Bob Newhart I thought was very funny, Shelley Berman, Nichols and May of course are wonderful. So there's really just so many of them that I reckon are good, and a very, very high proportion of them are Americans, which is interesting."

"Who do you feel you've been influenced by?" I asked him.

"I think I've stolen—and I don't mean I've stolen jokes or ideas, but one steals a little bit of the style, a little bit of the mood—and at the moment on *Fawlty Towers* I would have said I was stealing—it may surprise people to hear it, but I'm stealing a bit of W. C. Fields. I've noticed that a bit of it's in there.

"Certainly Milligan. Certainly I've noticed bits of Hancock, inflections creeping into my performance and ideas. I suppose any comedian that you've liked and watched a lot of, you've got to occasionally do a little bit of him somewhere. I don't think there's any George Burns in what I do, because that's just absolutely in another field, that's in another area. I wish I could do it, but I could never begin to. And I think probably the deepest influences were the early ones. Again, I think Peter Cook was a big influence. I would say the Goons, Hancock, and Peter Cook in this country. I'm not quite sure—Bilko's very American, but there are bits of Bilko I can catch myself doing occasionally, sometimes unconsciously. I don't think I've been so enormously influenced by the modern ones, but that's not out of lack of enjoyment of their work, but just the fact that one's style tends to be more or less formed, hopefully—perhaps not inflexibly formed—but it's more or less formed by the time you're thirty. And by the time I was thirty, I hadn't seen Mel Brooks, I hadn't seen Woody Allen."

"So your style was basically engrained by the time you saw the more modern comedians?"

"Yes, I think so. I think whatever was the basic plot out of which various different types of growths hopefully will grow was sort of rooted."

"Had you seen, or started to see, some W. C. Fields while you were developing the character of Basil Fawlty?"

"Well, it was a process that started more or less simultaneously. I bought one of those books, called *A Flask of Fields,* and I think it may have made me laugh more than any other book has made me laugh. Wonderful sequences. I had only seen *The Bank Dick* before in a rather bad print on a rather bad private projector with rather poor sound. I suddenly got interested, and in fact, the BBC has asked me to present a feature film in a few months' time, so I have in fact chosen a couple of Fields's."

We pulled up to the Meridien, where John instructed the driver to take me on to the Ruspina, and I thanked him for the ride and the conversation. We are filming in Sousse in the morning, which means rising even earlier than usual, and I expect no trouble falling asleep early.

SEPT. 16: **The Ribat (shown pre-Python) had a magnificent tower, which the Pythons would utilize by constructing an unfinished version for a chase sequence.**

SEPT. 17: **Monastir is a European resort town inside of a traditional Arabic country, where modern hotels and beaches lie next to long-established markets and houses. In the background is the Ribat, the castle that was the home base of the *Life of Brian* unit.**

SEPT. 20: **The makeup department, and even Gwen Taylor and Sue Jones-Davies cannot resist a man in uniform. It was my first day in the Jerusalem Garrison, serving under Centurion Cleese.**

SEPT. 23: Rehearsals of the ex-leper, with first assistant director Jonathan Benson (sitting in background), camera operator John Staniou (to the right of Graham), and still photographer David Appleby (far right, with camera).

SEPT. 25: Cast and crew would often relax in the sun after lunch. Current English-language magazines, particularly news magazines, were much sought after.

SEPT. 26: This shot (with John Cleese in the center, myself to the right, and Bernard McKenna to the right of me), which I requested quite off-handedly, became one of the most widely-circulated of the production.

SEPT. 27: Brian begins drawing a small crowd after he lands on the wall. Shown here: the crowd. Carol Cleveland is in the lower right-hand corner, while soldiers wait in the background for their cue to march through.

SEPT. 28: Terry G, Terry J, and Michael at the start of the day's filming. Terry G borrowed a cape from one of the Roman soldiers to stay warm. He returned it only slightly worse for the wear, coated with mud which had begun drying and flaking off his body.

SEPT. 28: Makeup artist Elaine Carew was kept busy throughout the day dirtying up Terry G as the mud crumbled from him.

OCT. 6: The Pythons always seemed to promote a collegial atmosphere on the set. From left: Kenteas Brine, Elaine Carew, Eric Idle, John Case (in makeup), John Cleese, Michael Palin, and Peter Brett.

OCT. 6: I just couldn't resist. As John Case walked around the set for the first time dressed as Pilate's wife, he was the recipient of the most amazing double-takes I've ever seen, a walking, talking tribute to the makeup and costumers.

OCT. 7: John Cleese happily mows down the Tunisian extras during a break in the filming.

OCT. 7: The Roman bust provided a convenient wicket for John and Eric during the lunchtime cricket match just outside the castle in Sousse.

OCT. 7: Michael borrowed my watch for this incontrovertible proof that the director kept him on set until 6:45 P.M.

OCT. 8: **Back in our little castle in Monastir. The Ribat came to have an oddly homey feeling to it, even though it was constantly in transition from one scene to another.**

LEFT OCT. 8: **Terry J oversaw the preparations in the recently completed Pilate's audience chamber, located in the building next to the Ribat.** RIGHT OCT. 8: **I carried with me copies of my first Monty Python fanzine, and when I asked Graham if I could snap a picture of him with one, he was happy to oblige.**

OCT. 8: **Graham Chapman's Brian is brought before Michael Palin's Pilate by John Cleese's Centurion.**

ABOVE
OCT. 8: Terry J and Michael had started writing together when they were at Oxford, and remained very close friends, so their collaborations always appeared effortless.

OCT. 10: Finalists of the 1978 "Best Legs in Tunisia" contest.

OCT. 11: Eric undergoes finishing touches as King Otto, applied by Kenteas Brine, one of the talented makeup crew.

OCT. 12: Graham, John, and Terry J discuss the upcoming scene in Mandy's garden, where John's Centurion arrests Brian. Obviously we are not ready to film, as witnessed by John's tunic.

OCT. 14-15: Michael gave his wife and young daughter a tour of the rubble in the Ribat during their visit to Monastir.

OCT. 16: John and Graham began writing together at Cambridge, and even though they drifted apart after *Flying Circus*, they reunited to collaborate on the writing of the Python films.

OCT. 16: **Fashion plates always: Michael and Terry G study up on "The Avedon Look" in the copy of *Newsweek* I found at the Hotel Meridien.**

OCT. 17: **Eric was in fine fettle as Mr. Cheeky; Terry G's attention to dungeon detail is visible here.**

OCT. 20: **One small corner of the courtyard was utilized for all of the pickup scenes filmed that day—my final day on the set.**

The Shoe, the Sandal, and the Gourd—the History of Religion Scene, in which Brian's followers follow him

TODAY'S WEATHER WAS A VAST IMPROVEMENT over our previous attempt to film in Sousse. The lights and cameras were set up outside the old city wall once again, just as they had been on Monday, but this time under spectacularly sunny skies.

■ This was the BBC's final day of filming. They began with an interview with John, which Terry G gleefully interrupted. I also overheard John asking them for funny hotel stories.

It became second nature to Terry J to give direction dressed in his Mandy costume, and none of the others seemed to mind.

The people, animals, and equipment were set just as they were on Monday, for some extremely wide shots of Brian and Mandy walking along the wall as the statue of Caesar was wheeled past them. A great deal of caution was needed in moving the statue, because one little slip would mean the end of it. It did in fact wobble slightly while it was being moved but managed to remain intact.

The camera had been placed on scaffolding some distance away to shoot the scene. Just in front of the camera, Terry G had placed two crosses, which would appear in the foreground of the shots. A very old, decaying skeleton was hung from each of them in a typically cheery Gilliam touch.

A number of utensils were hanging from Terry G's costume today, clanging as he walked. "Terry G subscribes to the ancient Chinese torture philosophy that if it doesn't hurt, it can't possibly be any good," noted John.

This morning's scenes featured Brian being pursued by a mob of would-be followers and losing his sandal as he runs from them (it immediately follows the scene in which they chase him through the marketplace after his sermon). It was filmed first in a long shot, and then the camera was aimed directly into the crowd as they ran.

During a break, I stopped Michael to inquire about a short interview; he seemed to be in a cheery mood, as he didn't have any particularly uncomfortable scenes today. When I asked for his impressions after two and a half weeks of shooting, he started emitting strange noises.

"Ooooooooooooowwwwwwwwhhhhhhhh!   Du—du—du—du—du—aaaahhhh! No! Please! I don't want to go on! Aaaaahhhh, stop it! Stop it! Oh, not the whip, anything but the whip!!! Oh, Terry, no! Sixteen hours, that's my limit, I can't hang here any longer!!" Then, just as suddenly as that performance, he calmly said, "It's been great fun, really. Mainly a lot of sitting on the beach, lying on the sand."

It occurred to me that Michael might be in too silly a mood to attempt an interview.

"There's Peter Brett now," he pointed out. Peter was sitting in a canvas chair writing in a notebook. "You ask him a thing or two. He's writing, you see, he's writing now, he's not wasting his time talking to tape recorders, he's writing his impressions. Well, I would say that, I would summarize the first two and a half weeks as pretty successful. We've gotten through the work, we're actually, I think, a day ahead. The quality of the work is looking very good. People have had to work very hard, people are working extremely hard, but I think morale is quite high. As I was saying to John yesterday, Tunisia is really one of the better places we've ever filmed in."

"As far as the cooperation you've received from the locals?"

"Yes, yes, cooperation, organization. It's just that they're a friendly lot here, there are far fewer people telling you 'You can't park here' and 'You can't film here' and 'Don't go in there, don't do this, don't do that.' Here, they seem genuinely anxious to help you. But then, I suppose that's because we've got a lot of money this time."

The reverses for the crucifixion scene would be shot outside
the old walled city in Sousse; this skeletal prop provided
the foreground for an establishing shot.

I mentioned that I had been talking to John about favorite comedians and comedic influences, and I asked Michael who makes him laugh.

"A lot of the people who make me laugh aren't comedians. They're politicians, policemen, judges, professional footballers . . . I seem to laugh fairly easily, and I think somehow, sometimes seeing someone making the effort to make me laugh puts me off. But I would say that the people I laugh at, the people who make, write, and do things that make me laugh fairly consistently, are people like Woody Allen. Peter Sellers is a very, very funny actor. Again, Spike Milligan, because of all the stuff he wrote, *Goon Shows* and the amazing wealth of ideas that he seems to be able to come up with, and his sort of staying power. He's still around doing totally anarchic shows which don't fit into any other sort of accepted pattern at all. That's great that he's still there; it gives one hope for the future. I think Peter Cook is a very funny man, a very funny writer. I've probably left out about forty people there, because one can never remember everybody that's made you laugh at some time. But those are some of them."

He also admitted a fondness for comedians from the past. "Keaton's films, especially, I've always liked. I used to like some Jerry Lewis films; I thought he was very funny. He had me in stitches in *Disorderly Orderly* and some of the movies like that, very funny indeed. Then he seemed to get sort of fond of himself and his own image. Suddenly I kept reading about how angry he was that no one appreciated him except in France, and that was a pity, really. But he used to make me laugh. Laurel and Hardy I like even more now than I used to—I've had a sort of second go at them because my children like them. There are some things in there that are great. They're a marvelous team. The one called *Brats,* in which they are actually the children and their babysitters, is wonderful.

"But there are a lot of things that you wouldn't say, 'Well, here are comedians trying to make me laugh.' There are light comedy things that one likes, or just observations. A writer like Pinter, who is normally thought of as being dark and grim, has flashes of great humor. Peter Nichols, a writer in England at the moment [he wrote *Georgy Girl* and *Privates on Parade;* the latter was later turned into a film starring John Cleese], is very, very, very funny, marvelous stuff. There are all those isolated moments that make me laugh."

"Who of all those do you feel have influenced your own comedy, if any of them?"

"All of them. Everybody has influenced my comedy, including professional footballers, judges, politicians, and anybody else who sets themselves up in strange positions of power and self-importance. As far as the actual techniques of comedy, I probably haven't been influenced by anybody any more than the rest of the Python team, as much as anybody, with the presentation of comedy and all that. For instance, Terry J and I have worked together now for about twelve years; his attitudes have influenced me a lot in actual sheer technique and writing, and what to write about.

"Otherwise, the sparks, the ideas, have to come from within. They're you, they're there. Unless you're a total plagiarist, you can't say that your perception of what's funny is really influenced by anyone else. I think it's just the technique of how you develop that perception and use it in sketches, plays, or whatever."

"Can I get into this interview, too?" asked Terry G, barging in politely.

"Are you all done with John's interview?" asked Michael.

"Oh, yes, he was very nice," Terry said with a laugh.

"There are certainly plenty of interviewers for you today," I noted.

" 'Now look, I don't want anyone sort of raising the dust on this sort of interview," Michael warned him sternly.

"Have you been talking about, uh, you know—" asked Terry.

"*Him?*" said Michael, and both of them looked toward John's now-empty chair.

"Him, yes . . ."

"Yes, him," Michael agreed. "Him who is no longer with us, but is off getting made up for television."

"Yes, he has to be so—don't tell John about this, Howard," requested Terry.

"Yes, you must keep everything we say about John now off the record," ordered Michael. "He's a total egomaniac, he's now being made up for the fourth time this morning. Do you see those four people over there now cleaning his nails, one on each hand?" He nodded toward John, who was in a chair surrounded by four makeup people. "We pay for those people, you know. It's just that he won't work otherwise. He has to have

The arrival of Spike Milligan, a comedy idol to the Pythons, caused a stir of excitement among the group, particularly when he agreed to do a cameo. Coincidentally, it occurred on October 5, the Python anniversary date; *Monty Python's Flying Circus* first aired in Britain on October 5, 1969. Here, Spike waits for his close-up outside the old city wall in Sousse. The statue in the background, made of polystyrene, will undergo a strange metamorphosis later in the filming.

this long couch . . . he's the only person who has a four-poster bed actually on location, you know? A four-poster bed. He has to have cups of coffee brought to him, he has to have champagne endlessly poured in his mouth. And he still can't act. Anyway, that's entirely off the record."

Michael and Terry were summoned for the scene; as I was one of the few people on the set who was not in front of the camera, I sat back and watched the crowd run toward the camera for about fifty yards, until they reached their marks. By lunchtime, many of them were slightly out of breath as a result of their sprinting.

We had one of our first lunches away from the Ribat today. Memmo's catered, as usual, and we all sat outdoors at tables at a bar-restaurant across the street from the location. We were even able to enjoy a beer with our meal, which seemed to put everyone in a good mood.

Spike Milligan arrived during lunch and confirmed his desire to be in a crowd scene. Matthew and Melvin took him off to costuming and makeup, while the rest of the actors finished eating and prepared for the afternoon.

Shooting led off with close-ups of the crowd discovering Brian's sandal. Spike was placed in the middle of the crowd, near the sandal. Camera operator John Stanier had to lie on the ground, next to the camera, to get his shots, but we finished before the sky began to grow cloudy.

As rehearsals began for the next shots, however, the clouds were growing increasingly heavy, and it was impossible to continue shooting. We had no choice but to sit back and wait it out. Although it didn't particularly look like rain, any shooting with those clouds would never have matched the previous takes. After an hour—one of the longest delays we had experienced so far because of clouds—Spike decided that he didn't want to be in the film as much as he had originally thought. Since he had come to Tunisia on holiday, he decided to leave and visit the catacombs instead. He was apparently rather disgruntled that the scene, which he had been told would take about ten minutes to film, had so far taken more than an hour.

The rest of us continued to wait on the clouds, trying to squeeze in whatever takes we could during patches of sun. The premature departure of Spike had caused a problem. He had been standing prominently at the

All of the Pythons (and guests) except Graham were involved in the scene, including (from left) Terry J, Carol Cleveland, Terry G, Michael, Spike, John, and Eric (partially hidden behind John). Spike left shortly after this, but the filmmakers were able to use the existing footage to include Spike's appearance, even though he had left before his close-up.

front of the crowd in the film already shot, and to scrap all of it and reshoot it without Spike would take quite a bit of time and effort. Instead, John Young was dressed in Spike's costume and put on a beard, so that he looked enough like Milligan to continue without completely reshooting the scene. Apparently, there may be enough usable footage of Spike to use for a close-up or two as a cameo appearance, even though John Young actually did most of his scene.

During one take, which was unfortunately lost due to clouds rolling in, a great commotion started in the background, and some of the locals began laughing and pointing. Two donkeys had begun to get amorous, to the delight and applause of nearly everyone. One of the animal trainers soon put a stop to it, however, and the filming carried on. Rather than wait for a complete break in the clouds to shoot the whole scene, Terry decided to film individual close-ups instead. By the time it looked as though the sky might clear up, the sun was nearly gone, so we will return tomorrow and attempt to finish everything.

Good-byes to Brian, in which his friends and followers say farewell

THE BBC CREW WERE LOADING THEIR equipment this morning getting ready to depart after a week of rather heavy filming. Iain was still unclear as to the result of their work but noted that there were a great many options. [It was later presented on the BBC as *The Pythons*.] ▪ This morning I rode with Graham and Bernard to the set in Sousse, where we discovered that the filming would continue where we had left off the day before. The first shots featured Brian, Mr. Cheeky (portrayed by Eric), and the rest of the crucifees dragging their crosses through town, to the cheers and applause of the crowd. One of Terry G's skeletons was cut loose from a cross in the foreground of the wide shot, a nice Gilliamesque touch.

The weather was still threatening to cause problems, however. While some closer shots were being set up, the clouds rolled in again, forcing us to wait for a few minutes. As soon as it looked as though we'd be able to proceed, another round of clouds came into view. This began to happen with startling regularity this morning. At one point, we nearly moved to the castle in Sousse, but at the last moment, the sun appeared, on cue, and burned off the remaining clouds.

We were finally able to shoot the centurion as he arrives to release Brian from his cross. The scene with the cast hanging from their crosses will be shot later in Gabes, but the reverses and the surrounding scenes are all being filmed here. In addition to the centurion, these include Mr. Cheeky being taken down from his cross, soldiers marching away from Brian, and then both Judith and Mandy addressing Brian as he hangs from his cross, from Brian's point of view.

Another shot featured Michael leading the group of revolutionaries to salute Brian as he hangs on the cross. Since the actors playing the revolutionaries were also playing other parts today, a number of doubles were needed as revolutionaries. I was asked to fill in as Eric's double. It seemed an odd choice, as I am a few inches taller than Eric, and sure enough, when they compared sizes, the plan changed. In a sudden burst of inspiration, Melvin had me don Terry Bayler's robes, beard, and hat, and the resemblance was reasonable.

When it was time for our shot, we walked down the hill, led by Michael, as Michael said his lines and we saluted the place where Brian would have been hanging. Then he led us back up the hill. It was simple and almost perfunctory, and over before we knew it. This was a good thing from my perspective, as my beard kept coming loose; I managed to hold it in place long enough to complete the filming. All of the faux revolutionaries were then able to slip out of costume in time for lunch.

During the midday break, there was some discussion about moving to some indoor shooting at the castle in Sousse. Eventually, though, every-one decided that the sun would stay out long enough to finish all of to-day's scenes, which would wind up everything planned for the city wall location.

There were more shots of soldiers running after lunch, but by the time the revolutionaries got into place for the next scene, patches of clouds were gathering. Although some of their bits had been filmed in the morn-ing using a group of doubles (such as walking away from the crosses as the soldiers approached), there were some considerable delays before they could finish.

During one such delay, I decided to take a short walk around town, but no sooner had I started than I was told the revolutionaries' shots were fin-ished, and the unit was moving to the castle in Sousse.

The crew had obviously been busy, as just outside the door, scaffold-ing had been erected and covered with heavy black canvas. Inside was Pi-late's wife's bedroom, filled with elaborate and ornate furnishings, with a huge bed in the center of the room. Still, it was clear that it would take some time to finish decorating the set, and some of the actors and cos-tumes were being driven in from Monastir.

I decided to use the break to head toward the docks. I could smell them before I even got close. It was a fascinating sight. Small fishing boats were huddled next to huge freighters. One of the big Russian ships was still there, though I didn't see any crew members walking about. Sue Jones-Davies said that some of the Russian sailors had been on the deck above, throwing down Russian rubles, in exchange for other foreign currency that was thrown back up to them. However, none of the sailors were allowed to leave their ship for fear of defections. As I headed back to the set, I saw fishing nets everywhere, drying along the docks, spread over the ground, and hanging from anything that might help them dry.

When I arrived at the castle, John Case was being made up for his role as Pilate's wife. I sat in one of the canvas chairs, where several other revo-lutionaries were ready and waiting. In full costume and makeup as Pilate's wife, John Case was truly spectacular, and every one of us was in awe. With his hairpiece in place, he stood seven and a half feet tall; his face was covered with white greasepaint, with red rouge delicately applied to his

cheeks in a vague attempt at femininity. Two soccer balls were stuffed into his dress to serve as breasts. Unfortunately, he had gotten into costume and makeup for nothing; none of his shots would be filmed today. There were only a few shots of the commandos running up to the entrance of the bedroom before Terry called it quits for the day. Apparently, further filming would mean changing the speed of the camera for some reason, which would somehow be more trouble and take more time than it was worth. As

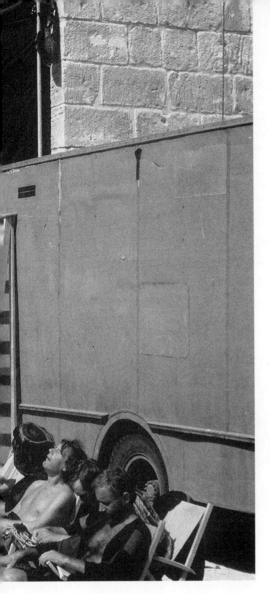

a result, we wrapped for the day without getting as much done as had been hoped.

Back at the Sidi, there were rushes from last Monday in Sousse, the day of the rainstorm. Though there were a few wide shots of the scenes outside the city wall, most seemed to be from the weather cover, with the two revolutionary groups meeting below the palace.

There had been rumors for some time that we would be seeing films

John Case, all 6' 9" of him, in full costume and makeup, is magnificent as Pilate's wife. Yes, those are indeed two regulation-sized soccer balls under his dress.

and videotapes at night after the rushes, but we had started to grow skeptical until tonight. The cast and crew, starved for entertainment, crowded into the small projection room after rushes to watch Fred Astaire, Cyd Charisse, and Jack Buchanan in *The Band Wagon*. The audience was delighted and went away with promises of more to follow.

The Kidnapping of Pilate's Wife, in which the commandos continue their assault in the bowels of Pilate's palace

THERE WERE HOPES THAT WE WOULD finish all of the filming in Sousse today. ▪ Since we were shooting in Pilate's wife's bedroom, which was an interior scene, naturally the sky remained perfectly sunny and clear. It should be a very funny scene, with the commandos struggling to kidnap Pilate's enormous wife; they leap at her, but she shakes most of them off before running down a corridor, with one of them still clinging to her in terror.

During the first takes, the commandos' thrashing about managed to knock around some of the bedroom decorations, and there were longer than usual breaks between takes to redress the set. The actors used the additional time to play word games while they waited, although Graham drew several complaints for using obscure medical terms.

John Case finished his first shots by midmorning and was allowed to slip out of his Pilate's wife costume while the commandos performed their dialogue and did more running through the corridors. His relaxation was short-lived, however, as he was snatched away to be recostumed a short time later. The commandos did a bit of fighting off and on for the rest of the morning but were allowed some free time to read or converse, with a badminton court set up nearby as well.

John and Eric started playing cricket in an open area toward the back. Eric stood in front of a Roman bust and batted in his commando robes, while John stripped off his costume and pitched to him in his underwear. As everyone finished their lunch, they headed toward the game, and soon over a dozen cast and crew members were involved. Not being terribly familiar with cricket, I lingered at the lunch table with Terry G. He had agreed earlier to talk with me, so, dodging the cricketers, we made our way back to his trailer.

"Since you are the designer of this film, are you happy with the way those elements are turning out?" I asked him.

"Well, it's getting there slowly," he said thoughtfully. "I mean, it's probably about as good as I could ever get a Python film!"

"Which things have given you the most problems?"

"Well, the schedule's quite important, and we started off on a bad foot by grabbing an extra day the first Saturday by doing the stoning. It really sort of put us behind, because it took us two days to get ready for that thing. You never quite catch up with things like that. It's really weird. I never used to feel this, but I've certainly come to appreciate what a schedule's all about. There's all these different departments, and they're all sort of geared up to that schedule, and they don't have their things ready until a day or two before they're needed. And suddenly we do a change, and it sort of throws everything into confusion, and you never quite catch up, so you're always running trying to catch yourself."

Somewhere along the way, John found a badminton racquet during a break.
Where and how is still undetermined.

"Even though you aren't directing this one, do you still feel some of the pressure?"

"Oh, yes, there's plenty of pressure in trying to get the stuff ready in time, because this is bigger than any of the films we've done before. I mean, the scale of the amount of things we've built here, and all of the bits

John Cleese gets comfortable while bowling to Eric Idle during our first
—and last—lunchtime cricket game.

and pieces . . . I mean, it's huge, it's a real epic, so there's a fair amount of work. I haven't really been able to stop the whole time down here."

"There's no animation to speak of in *Brian*. Was that due to any sort of conscious decision on anyone's part? Or was it just the way the film evolved?"

"Yes, it really was. That's what seems to be happening now. As we're doing Python, the closer we come to doing real stories, like this one is, the less room there is for animation. The title sequence will be animated, and there's a spaceship sequence that will be animated—part models, part

Eric at the ready.

animation—there's a little bit there. That's one of the problems, really. The animation was really a linking device, and now that the thing has such a solid story flow to it, there's no need to link."

Eric popped into the trailer, which he shared with Terry, at that moment and seemed startled to find an interview going on.

"We've taken over Eric's part of the world," Terry observed. Eric grabbed a book, and I asked if we should move.

"No, don't worry," he assured me as Eric ducked out. "See? He's going somewhere else."

"Okay," I said, feeling like the interloper that I was. "Well, then, speaking of your animation, who do you feel has influenced you?"

Spectators to the cricket game included Terry G, who had the intricacies of the game explained by Michael Palin, and Bernard McKenna.

"I don't know. I think probably everybody. I think I'm influenced by everything. I can't really pin it down. Walt Disney gets his share, but then, so do people like Boráček, who's a Polish animator. It's just really hard to say, because I just grab anything that interests me and try to use it. I never really think about who's influencing me or not."

With that, Terry indicated he had to leave, so I thanked him and went back to the set, where I took a walk through Pilate's wife's bedroom. It was strikingly elaborate. Two fountains stood at the entrance, and torches hung along the corridors. Huge brass ornaments hung from the canopy over the bed.

Outside, I could hear the game breaking up, and the commandos began drifting back to prepare for the afternoon's filming. Lunch was back to

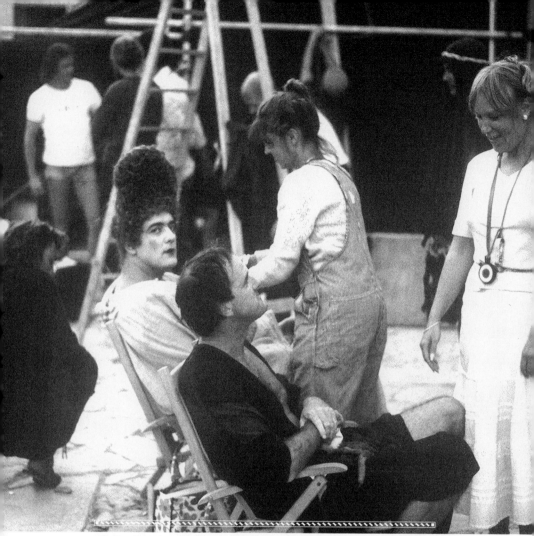

As Brenda Loader of continuity discusses the script with John Cleese, Elaine Carew of makeup sees that John Case is ready for his close-up.

an hour and a half today, and some of the makeup girls had time to walk around Sousse and do a little shopping.

John climbed back into his commando robes after playing cricket in his undershorts. "He had quite a repressive childhood, and this is his way of compensating," quipped Michael.

Filming began with shots of the commandos' legs and feet and the palace guards. There appeared to be some confusion, with some shots of the guards showing them holding spears, while in other shots they had none. Terry J was a bit worried that some of the shots might have to be done over, which resulted in a round of discussions.

Anne Henshaw will be leaving tomorrow. She indicated that when the company moved to the south in two more weeks, conditions and lodgings would be prohibitive, so my life with *Brian* would finish around that time. I would miss the last week or two of filming, but most of it would not be

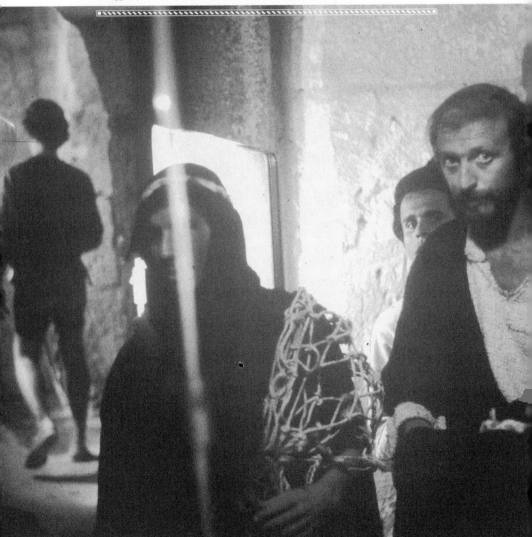

The passages under Pilate's castle, the attempted kidnapping of Pilate's wife, and the struggle between the two revolutionary groups were largely shot in the castle in Sousse.

comfortable or easy and would involve much travel. I thanked Anne for all of her help, and she invited me to stay with her family in London if I came back that way. I would be sad to leave, but I also knew it was inevitable, so I resolved to make the most of each moment until my departure.

The commandos seemed to have quite a bit of time off in the afternoon, which they spent sitting in the canvas chairs, talking, reading, and playing more word games. By late afternoon, they were all needed to shoot the reverses of the struggle in the bedroom. I was surprised at how quickly they finished, and some of the crew even started to dismantle the bedroom while a couple of miscellaneous takes were completed in the corridors.

As I stood watching the canvas come down, Melvin approached me and asked me to stand where I was; he went away and returned a few moments later with Graham, asking him to stand next to me. Melvin and Matthew studied us briefly, noting we were about the same height, then asked me to double for Graham on Monday. I will either be Brian or Biggus Dickus.

Inside the castle, the corridor shots continued. The sparks and prop men were lined up along one wall trying to create an effect that would resemble flickering torches. Instead of rolled cardboard tubes, however, they had nailed strips of cloth to sticks, waving them between the lights and the white screens. As I was taking pictures, Terry Bayler asked to see my watch. I handed it to him after he promised that he wouldn't try to sell it to any of the locals. I took another shot while Michael approached. "Here, take a picture of this," Michael asked, as he held the watch next to him. "I want proof that Terry and Jonathan kept us here until 6:45 at night."

The call sheets had several notes of interest tonight. The Ali-Spinks fight will be screened this evening. The remaining first-round players in the tennis tournament are being asked to play as soon as possible. And the table tennis draw is now on the notice board. The entertainment committee was apparently being kept busy.

I rode back to the Ruspina with John and Peter Brett. Carol didn't come out to the set today, even though this was their final day here. As it had actually turned out, Peter had done more scenes than Carol. "We had been planning to take a caravan trip down to the desert yesterday and today, but

I got too caught up in the filming," confessed Peter. "It's all right, though. I really enjoyed it."

At dinnertime, I met Carol and Peter, as well as John and June Case, who are also leaving tomorrow. We ate and retired to the hotel bar, where John became involved with trying to divide up the check, much to June's embarrassment, though no one else minded. We finally said our good-byes, expressing the hope that we would see each other again soon.

A Day Off, in which I practice table tennis

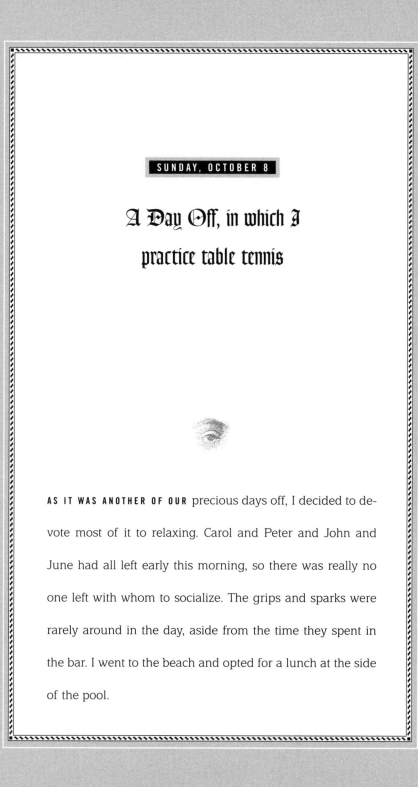

AS IT WAS ANOTHER OF OUR precious days off, I decided to devote most of it to relaxing. Carol and Peter and John and June had all left early this morning, so there was really no one left with whom to socialize. The grips and sparks were rarely around in the day, aside from the time they spent in the bar. I went to the beach and opted for a lunch at the side of the pool.

I saw Clive and coaxed him into playing some table tennis by the pool; as I was supposed to play against Melvin in the first round of the tournament, I wanted to at least make a respectable showing. But Clive decided to hang up his paddle early—not because he was losing, but because he was getting tired out chasing the ball after some of my more spirited shots.

After writing a few more letters, I headed to dinner and ran into Clive once again. He was going to go without dinner to save money, so I insisted he join me as my guest, and we split the chateaubriand for two. I passed on a showing of *The Lady Vanishes* at the Sidi and spent the rest of the night as unproductively as possible, in front of a pinball machine.

"Thwow Him to the Fwoor," in which, for the first time, Brian is brought before Pilate

I RODE INTO MONASTIR TODAY ON the minibus, which for some unexplained reason was running more or less on schedule. We were back at the Ribat, apparently for the duration of the filming in Monastir, where everyone still seemed to be groggy and lacking motivation after the rare day off. ▪ John and Michael did fit in a bit of work yesterday, according to John.

"We did another rewrite of scene 62," he explained. This is a scene in which the revolutionaries find out Brian has been captured and must decide their course of action. "It's gone through a number of rewrites, but I think this time, it's closer to the original version, but with a few of the other lines since then. It now starts out with myself, as Reg, saying, 'Item four. The attainment of world supremacy within the next five years. Francis, you've been doing some work on this.'"

John went on, doing each of the different voices. Pleased to see me laughing out loud, he wandered away to try it out on some other listeners.

Today's shooting would be in Zeffirelli's building, the one right next to the Ribat. There was no roof overhead, and much of it was being used for construction and storage of props. One small end was serving as Pilate's audience chamber, a rather small room with an extremely high ceiling, which Zeffirelli had apparently used as some sort of palace. The Ribat itself was in disarray, with the entire area outside of Mandy's house completely dismantled. It is an area in transition.

As I walked through the rubble, back toward today's set, I saw several members of the rep company getting into their armor. Terry G had apparently taken ill that day, so they were filling in for him. It seemed like a perfect opportunity to chat with some of the rep company.

Charles McKeown had just finished strapping on his armor and was in a chatty mood as I approached him to ask how he became involved with *Brian*.

"I was working in Sheffield two years ago, and I was asked to be in two short studio plays written by Terry Jones and Michael Palin. That was the first thing I did with them. They were called *Their Finest Hours*. One was called *Underhill's Finest Hour* and took place in a hospital delivery ward, in which a woman is trying to have a baby, and her doctor is more interested in listening to cricket, and all that entails.

"The second one was called *Buchanan's Finest Hour*, which was about an international packaging organization in which there were three of us inside a large crate. We never saw the audience and the audience never saw us. We sat in this crate—there was this conservative MP and his agent—I played the agent—and a French escapologist who, about ten minutes into the play, also turned out to be inside the box. Then a little later, although

Charles McKeown, always a cheery presence on the set, would go on to cowrite *Brazil* with Terry Gilliam.

she never spoke, so she didn't actually have to be there, his decapitated wife was also in the box. We thought we had been delivered to a place where we were going to make tremendous publicity and there was an audience there, but it becomes clear to us inside the box that there's nobody there at all, and something's gone terribly wrong. A little bit later, we hear the sound of a truck, and another box is brought in with the pope in it, and he's also been duped by this even larger international marketing company to be part of their publicity campaign.

"It was very funny. Those were the first two pieces I was involved in with Michael and Terry. After that, they had been writing some *Ripping Yarns,* and they asked me if I would play something in *Across the Andes by Frog,* which was fun. And then, just before I came over here, I had another

part in one of the *Ripping Yarns* from the latest series, just four or five weeks before coming over here."

I was surprised when Charles revealed that *Brian* was actually his first film.

"Since I've been in the profession, most of my work has come from the theater. I've done bits of television, but I'm principally in the theater. I've done bits of writing over the past couple of years as well, so I haven't been entirely out of work when I've been out of work."

Charles planned to focus on writing upon his return to England, he noted. "I've got a couple more rather messy plays that need a lot of tidying up, and I really ought to do that. I've been thinking about that because I suppose I have nothing positive as an actor when I get back, so I hope to do some writing."

Andrew MacLachlan attended Oxford with Terry Jones, who cast him as one of the rep company.

[Charles would go on to collaborate as a co-screenwriter with Terry Gilliam on several projects, including *Brazil,* in the years to come.]

He had to run, so I thanked him for talking with me as he headed for the makeup trailer. I noticed Andrew MacLachlan leaving the trailer just as Charles entered, so I asked Andrew if he had a few minutes to chat about his involvement with the film.

"I had known Terry Jones for a long time," he explained. "We were at Oxford together, and I thought, 'I'll have a go at acting.' So I rang him up and asked him could he help? I didn't know about the film at the time; I didn't know it was going to happen soon. And he said, 'Well, how about a bit in the film?' and I said 'Why not?' I still can't quite believe it. I've been envying myself."

"What sort of work had you done before the film?" I asked.

"Years ago, I did some cabaret just after Oxford, and I wanted to keep on doing it, but I'd come upon so many nasty people. So I then got off on a job running a language school, which I did for a year until the money ran out and the place packed up. So I took a job as a stopgap while I decided again what I wanted to be when I grew up, and that lasted ten years, doing industrial health and safety things. It was very easy and it paid quite well, but as I say, it was a stopgap for ten years. I don't know what's going to happen next. I've got one or two things in the pipeline, one a television play coming up, but after that, I just don't know."

Andrew did note that he wanted to continue acting, in part because he was enjoying the film so much. "So far it's been great fun. I can't believe something isn't going to go wrong soon. It's great!"

Andrew had to step away, so I thanked him, and found Terry Bayler available for a chat about his involvement with *Brian*.

"I'd worked for Eric Idle quite a bit in a program he did called *Rutland Weekend Television* and a program called *The Rutles,* in which I played a character called Leggy Mountbatten, the manager of the group. When it was decided that they needed a few more people, I think it was Eric who suggested me. Some of them knew my work, and Eric showed them some tapes, and they said yes. And of course I was delighted, because I always loved the Python work, since even before they were Python. Even in the pre-Python days, I knew their work individually, and they write very funny stuff."

Terry explained that he had done little film work prior to *Brian,* with one prominent exception. "The only other real film I've done was *Macbeth* for Roman Polanski—I played Macduff in that. I've done six West End plays, but in the past few years, my work's mostly been in television."

I asked if there was any way to compare working on a Python film with doing Shakespeare for Roman Polanski.

"It's always hard to compare two films, but I think there are a lot more laughs in this than there were in *Macbeth,*" he joked. "Actually, the difference is that we're working with six live writers, as opposed to one dead writer, and that creates a certain tension. No, they're wonderfully supportive, considering they have written with certain ideas in mind. They're wonderfully alert. They say, 'Well, that's a good idea,' as opposed to saying, 'Well, this is how we wrote it, this is how you'll say it.' The comedic feeling doesn't stop when they're finished with the script. They're still there saying, 'Hey, that's good when that happens,' which is marvelous."

After *Brian,* Terry said, he was hoping to do something in a slightly more serious vein. "I've been doing quite a lot of comedy," he explained. "I'd like to do something a bit more documentary now. It's been a lot of comedy this year, and I'm not only a comedy actor, I'd like to do something semidocumentary, 'man in the suburbs talking to his wife in the kitchen,' something of that sort, just to keep a balance. I think the wonderful thing is, working in, say, a documentary, you build up a sort of tension of comedy inside. You think, 'Oh my God, I'd love to do something absurd and funny.' But when one has done a lot of comedy, you think, 'Oh, I'd love to go back to basics again,' as it were, and say, 'How does this guy really talk?' And look at people in the streets and say, 'I can play him,' or listen to a guy in a pub and think, 'Yes! The way he looks, the way he talks.' I'd like to do

It was always easy to spot whether John was rehearsing or actually filming. He always avoided donning his armor until the last moment, so this tunic shot is obviously from a rehearsal.

that now. I've always hoped to do as many different things as possible, and of course, the good thing about this is that you can do lots of things, you can do heavy soldiers, older people, slightly younger people."

Terry's scene was getting close to ready, so I thanked him and he excused himself. I strolled over to Pilate's audience chamber, where preparations were well under way for the morning's scene. I studied the chamber, noting how it was elaborately decorated with erotic frescoes on each wall, with a large naughty mosaic in the center of the floor. A few of the frescoes, mostly the ones that were out of shot, were particularly graphic, including one featuring a woman with a goat. Nevertheless, one of the costumers assured me that each one of them had been taken from original Roman paintings pictured in a book on Pompeii; the set designers had even found some too explicit to be used.

The mosaic on the floor had a removable fig leaf in a strategic spot, through which the commandos would later emerge. It had been blocked off now so that no one would step on it and fall through. It was an interior set, but most of the roof was open, covered with a thin white silk to help dissipate the light. There would still be problems with the sun, and we would soon have to wait for shots between patches of clouds and sunshine.

The first scene of the morning involved Brian being brought before Pilate for the first time by John's centurion. A number of Roman soldiers crowded into the room to guard Pilate, played by Michael. I still didn't know whether my doubling for Graham would involve dressing as Brian or as Biggus Dickus. Or both. Or neither. (They are the only two real roles that Graham has in the film, so naturally they appear in the same scene.)

In the first shots today, the centurion leads Brian to see Pilate, with two guards at his side. Pilate, with his speech impediment, orders them to "Thwow him to the fwoor," and Graham is gently thrown down to the concrete floor. The first take was stopped when it appeared his knees wouldn't hold up very well if he were thrown to the floor much more, so the pillows were adjusted beneath him, which seemed to help. The throwing was a bit off, however, and the soldiers needed more rehearsal. Poor Graham endured it all stoically, though, despite all of the throwing.

It turned into a fairly involved scene, which took some time to film. All of the soldiers are to break out laughing at the mention of "Biggus Dickus," much as they try to suppress it. Nevertheless, with all of the laughter, things began to get silly, and quite a few takes were spoiled when the actors broke up at the wrong moments.

There were also problems with the clouds overhead. Chuck Finch, one of the sparks, was perched on the roof above the silk to tell us when there were clear patches or cloudy bits, so we would know when it was safe to film. By midmorning, most of the clouds were gone, and the remainder of the day was taken up by individual close-ups of the same scene. They started with the guards holding back laughter, then went on to the close-ups of Pilate, the centurion, and Brian, then back to more long shots of the same scene over again. Aside from an occasional guard snickering, the filming was mostly routine. It was a long scene, though not terribly complicated, but it still took some time to get it all on film. The scene involving Biggus was put off until tomorrow, so I didn't need to worry about doubling for Graham today.

Just two days after the BBC left, a man named Mati from Canadian radio has arrived to spend a week here to do a program on Python that will be broadcast when the film is released. Mati carried around a huge cassette recorder and microphone; we chatted a bit and, as he is also staying in the Ruspina, agreed to meet up for a drink at some point.

There were four reels of rushes tonight, the most so far, followed by a screening of Bogart in *The Big Sleep,* which retained quite a large crowd.

"I'm Surpwised to See You Wattled by a Wabble of Wowdy Webels, Centuwion,"

in which Brian is brought before Pilate for the second time, and more commandos crawl through tunnels

WE WERE BACK IN PILATE'S AUDIENCE chamber again today to finish a few miscellaneous shots from yesterday. These involved the various activities going on in the chamber, including the painters and the mosaic artist, construction workers, and Terry Bayler's interior decorator getting instructions from Pilate. These were shot from almost every angle, which gave a thorough view of the inside of the chamber.

Outside, the Python portion of the Ribat was slowly but surely being dismantled. The exterior courtyard outside of Mandy's house is almost completely torn down, along with the archway and the wall next to the larger courtyard. The rubble from the marketplace was strewn about the larger courtyard. Even the wall outside of Pilate's palace, still covered with "Romans Go Home," was coming down. All of the statues were taken from the

wall; much of the mock marble trimming was also taken from the wall and from Pilate's platform, which had overlooked the courtyard.

The first few scenes of the morning, mostly just background of Pilate walking about and observing the craftsmen, did not take long. The next scene, which was quickly prepared, involved Brian being brought before Pilate for the second time, when he is sentenced to crucifixion. It was

The interior of the Ribat occasionally came to resemble a junkyard, particularly when the marketplace was taken down. The Latin lesson, Pilate's address to the crowd, and haggling are only a few of the many remnants of sets visible in the wreckage here.

Until it started coming down, I hadn't realized how much of the stonework inside the Ribat was actually constructed by the crew out of plywood, plaster, and paint. In this corner to the rear was the courtyard where Brian and Mandy addressed the crowd, which answered them in unison, and the ex-leper scene concluded under the archway.

similar to yesterday's scene, except with the added complication of requiring both Brian and Biggus, both played by Graham. I stood by to get into whichever costume was needed.

The first shots involved only Brian and included wide shots, close-ups, and the reverses that did not involve Biggus. Although there were a few problems with clouds, they were very minor compared to yesterday's troubles. The shots were filmed from all directions, showing Pilate's chamber from every angle, which caused all of the crew to shift about constantly. Lunch was delayed in order to finish the sequences with Brian before Pilate. Graham got into his Biggus costume during lunch to shoot his scenes again, but I wouldn't need to double as Brian, as he would not be visible in those shots.

Most of the families of the Pythons were visiting this week. They seem to have waited until now in order to let the filming settle into a routine, so that things would not be quite so hectic. Eric's young son, Carey, came down over the weekend, getting away for a couple of weeks. John's ex-wife Connie Booth was bringing their daughter down later, and Michael's wife and children were coming in soon. I saw Terry J's wife and kids climbing in through the front of the Zeffirelli building and directed them to Terry; his son rushed forward and grabbed him, and Terry immediately lifted him up and carried him around the set as he finished a few last-minute details before lunch.

While the rest of us ate, Graham Bullock, our painter, was hard at work retouching the mosaic on the floor, which badly needed it. When he finished, it was colorful once again and looked great. It was blocked off while it dried, and the unit members wandered past it admiringly.

As lunch drew to a close, the commandos had to get into costume for the afternoon's filming. Graham sat in the sun in the Zeffirelli building, finishing a crossword puzzle. He was a rabid crossword fan who never considered his day complete until he had finished the *Times* puzzle, which was mailed to him regularly.

Although there was much filming yet to do, the afternoon got off to a late start due to the amount of time needed to prepare the set. In addition to the repainting of the mosaic, the trapdoor through which the commandos entered the underground, as well as their fig leaf exit, also had to be readied.

In the film, the commandos exit through a strategically placed fig leaf in the mosaic. For the actors, it was one of the most uncomfortable scenes to film, as their waiting area beneath the floor was only four feet high.

When the time came, the commandos, one by one, climbed beneath the floor through the trapdoor for a short but extremely unpleasant stay, and the finishing touches were applied to the fig leaf. The area beneath the fig leaf was lit and carpet was laid down, but it was only about four feet high and every bit as stuffy and uncomfortable as the tunnel sequences.

"Are you all right down there?" called Terry J.

"Oh, yes, fine," Michael's muffled voice answered. "It's quite pleasant, really, there are trains running regularly to Tunis every hour . . ."

"All right then, if you're all ready," warned Terry, and the camera started rolling.

Led by Michael, the commandos crawled out through the opening the size of the fig leaf. As small as it looked, none of them had any trouble crawling through. A wide shot of the whole group emerging was then followed by them all hiding from a Roman general, played by Terry J, entering the chamber still seeking the eunuch Lucillus, with Matthew reprising his role. Various close-ups of the commandos followed. The whole day turned into quite a long one, even longer than yesterday, but eventually everything was finished.

Even though the shooting days are generally as long as they have always been, things have settled into a rather comfortable routine. It's good for the filming but leaves me with less to write about—or am I just getting too jaded?

King Otto, in which a suicide squad attempts to prove its skill at committing suicide within twenty seconds

FIRST THING THIS MORNING, JOHN CLEESE gave a good report on last night's rushes. ▪ "They were very good and very funny," he enthused. ▪ "They were the scenes in Matthias's house, when all the soldiers were rushing in to search it." ▪ I was a little disappointed at having missed them, as I wanted to see if I looked as uncomfortable as I felt during the filming that day, when I was trampled, jabbed, and subjected to all sorts of other unpleasantness.

Today's filming would focus on King Otto and his suicide squad; it was one of Eric's funniest contributions to the script. Eric and the other ten extras all reported in early today for their makeup and wardrobe. The costumes consisted of the heavy leather and straw armor pieces that I had seen at the final rehearsal weeks ago. According to most of the soldiers, they were bulky and made it difficult to move. I felt a little better about wearing the Roman soldier armor for the Matthias scene.

The King Otto sequence would take place in Mandy's garden, which had been constructed in an uppermost corner of the Ribat, just above the set for Matthias's house. It was stocked with lots of plants and other greenery.

The scene begins as Brian heads into the garden to get away from all of his would-be followers on the morning after he spends the night with Judith; he finds King Otto and his squad awaiting him. The first shots involved Brian and Otto and were completed in a couple of hours, even with all of the close-ups and reverses. Conditions in the small courtyard were very crowded, and it was surrounded on all sides by very tall, steep walls. All of the spectators had to crowd into a corner behind the camera to remain out of shot. Most of the nonessential personnel only stayed for two or three takes before retreating to the large courtyard to relax. I climbed to the walkway on top of one of the walls, overlooking the courtyard, where there was plenty of room. There, I could sit back and observe all the action below without getting in the way. This smaller courtyard was also covered with a thin white cloth just above me, although there were still a few delays due to passing clouds. The sea was directly behind me, and I felt a cool, refreshing breeze from my perch. Even though it was a good-sized area that offered a nice view of the filming, the only other person with me up there was Garth, who was busy recording the sound.

When the shots of Brian and Otto concluded, Otto's men had to enter the small courtyard. They made their entrance without armor and rehearsed their marching and suicides several times before the filming resumed. They were each armed with a sword whose blade would collapse about six inches into the handle. As Eric drilled them, they practiced plunging the blades into their chests. It was fascinating to watch. On the count of "One," they drew their swords; on "Two," they opened their chest flaps; on

"Three," they raised their blades; and on "Four," they shoved the collapsing blades into their chests. Apparently satisfied after twenty minutes of rehearsing, the squad took their places and donned their armor, ready to march into the shot.

For the first few takes, they successfully marched in, overall keeping in step surprisingly well. They jabbed their swords into their chests and went through all the motions of falling and feigning death, though there was no blood used in any of the initial attempts. The actual use of blood required some experimentation.

To my surprise, Mati, the Canadian radio interviewer, was playing one of Otto's men, and it was he who was selected as the guinea pig. Peter Grant was in charge of all of the blood delivery devices and fitted one on Mati. A tube was run from his chest to his hand, where it connected with a bulb filled with the artificial blood, which the actors were to squeeze on cue. With the camera running, Mati tried it out, but the effect didn't turn out nearly as well as had been hoped. The blood didn't spurt out properly from his chest, and despite attempts to modify the device, it all had to be abandoned.

The whole bloody effect did not look very pleasant. Before today's filming, I was a little disappointed that I had not been selected to play one of Otto's men, but after seeing what they were going through, I felt a sense of relief. The artificial blood was all over Mati, everywhere except for the places it was supposed to be. There was some concern that it might stain the straw on the armor as red as Mati's skin had now become. Following the experiment with Mati, the scenes were shot without the blood, including the close-ups and reverses. The only time blood was applied to anyone was for the close-ups of the rep company members who were playing Otto's men. I don't know how the fake suicides will look on film, because there was very little blood involved, but I'm sure Terry J and Eric have something in mind.

After all of Otto's men have supposedly committed suicide, one of them is supposed to fart, which starts the others giggling. Bernard swore that he was going to eat and drink appropriately and store up enough gas for the real thing. Unfortunately, the fart will have to be dubbed in later, as Bernard "choked" at the crucial moments.

Despite the complications with the scene, Eric seemed happy to finally have a lot to do today and really immersed himself in the scene. From these preliminary indications, though, it looks like *Brian* will have much less blood spilled than *Grail*. Of course, very few films have *more* bloodletting than *Grail,* as the film as a whole reveled in excessive, over-the-top violence—which resulted in some of its funniest scenes.

After a relatively short lunch break, the scenes with the suicide squad were finished in short order. Otto's men were all released, though a few

The King Otto scene was the creation of Eric (center), and was one of the most controversial scenes in the film. Actually, it was cut, at Eric's behest, because it did not move the story forward, and the characters only appear briefly in the final cut of the film.

brief close-ups of Brian and Otto remained. John and Michael were having a delightful day, as neither one of them had to come anywhere near the set.

The Otto scene was finished by midafternoon, after which everyone moved back to Pilate's audience chamber for a few short bits that hadn't been completed yesterday. Terry J got into his general's uniform, and Matthew slipped into a tunic to reprise his role as Lucillus. It was a very simple scene, with the general seeking Lucillus, but it took time to film

Graham takes a break during the Otto scene to confer with Terry. Graham's energy was, at times, astounding during the filming, even though he worked virtually every day, and had a sizeable medical practice going after shooting each day.

from all the different angles and distances. It even included a close-up of a doorknob slowly turning. It had turned into another late day, but an extremely productive one.

Call sheets were thicker than usual today, as they included a list of the hotel accommodations and room assignments for Gabes. My name was absent, of course; if I decided to go on to Gabes, I'd have to make all of my own arrangements. Though it would be great to stick it out to the end, I thought I should look at it realistically. Even if I could afford it, I had been assured that Gabes would be more trouble than it was worth. There were very few accommodations, and I might not even get into a hotel. Although

Clive vowed to go south even if he had to "sleep in a cave," I knew the unit wanted to travel light and was only taking essential people. I decided to stay throughout the rest of the filming in Monastir and head back to civilization after that, as the vast majority of the filming would be completed here.

There was another note in the call sheet, warning us that there were three extra shots that could be filmed at any time in the near future. There was a close-up of Brian landing, looking down at the Boring Prophet, and then standing; Brian's look at the foot of the steps into the marketplace; and another shot of the writing on the wall, which would be undercranked this time to make it look a bit faster when it was projected.

Retakes, in which we redo shots in Brian's bedroom, falling from the balcony, Brian's arrest, and still more commandos crawling through tunnels

MUCH OF TODAY WAS SET ASIDE for retakes of previous scenes, and a few assorted smaller scenes. The first involved the scene in Brian's bedroom as Brian and Judith first wake up, with a number of close-ups that either weren't previously filmed or didn't turn out. The filming got under way quite early this morning, possibly because the first shots were so simple and required little in the way of setup. The sky

threatened for a time, even pissing rain for a few minutes, but it really had no effect on the interior scene, and we finished by the midmorning tea break.

There are several retakes planned over the next week or so, but there is enough confidence in already completed scenes to continue with the demolition in and around the Ribat. The area outside of Mandy's house is cleared of everything but a few smaller pieces of debris, and the wall in front of Pilate's palace is starting to come down as well. His speaking platform was completely demolished early this morning, and now the mock wall that we had built—the covering about two inches in front of the real wall—was being pried off, with "Romans Go Home" still painted on it. I almost feel wistful. There will be some definite problems if a scene needs to be reshot here, as the construction crew is literally tearing everything apart in order to haul it away.

Graham had to follow his bedroom scene with the considerably less comfortable reshoot of his fall from the balcony that collapses beneath him. It took time to set up properly; huge mattresses were scattered on the ground beneath the balcony in case it collapsed prematurely.

The first take went very well. Graham walked out onto the balcony to hide from the Roman soldiers, just above the scaffolding and mattresses positioned below him. Terry indicated that the shot was fine, and Graham stepped back inside. Peter Grant then loosened the wooden supports beneath the balcony, so that on the next take, the balcony would collapse under Graham's weight.

Graham didn't seem to exhibit any signs of nervousness as the camera began to roll once again. He stepped out onto the rickety wooden balcony, just as he had before. Right on cue, the bottom and the sides collapsed, just

The early rehearsals for the reshoots of the balcony did not require Graham to step out and apply all of his weight to the balcony; as a result, the platform with the mattresses remained on the ground below for safety. (When Graham actually performed his fall, the mattresses were on a platform just a few feet beneath him, so the drop was very minimal.)

as they were supposed to, and Graham fell into the mattresses safely. After a request by a hesitant Terry, he even agreed to do another take.

The crew then began setting up some two-shots in Mandy's garden. As they began working, I noticed the construction at the far end of the small, narrow courtyard, at the opposite end from Graham's collapsing balcony. There was a spaceship being constructed out of several large pieces of polystyrene! Huge blocks of the white material were being formed, shaved, and sculpted to create the top half of the ship (the bottom half would apparently be buried deep in the ground after a crash landing). It was part of a sequence of animation that ended with the crash, and Graham crawling from the wreckage as it changes into a live-action scene. The familiar statue of Caesar was lying on its side, and I watched as it was being carved up in order to supply material. It was strangely sad to see it go, but it had served us well, and since it had outlived its usefulness in that shape, it was simply going to continue to serve the film in a modified form.

Next to Graham's collapsing balcony was a larger balcony where another set was apparently being created. We had all eaten up there when the regular dining area was being used to film some of the corridor scenes. A couple of old, rustic wooden tables and benches were carefully placed to give it a more authentic look. Below it, closer to the ground, bars were placed in the windows for some other, unspecified, upcoming filming.

I sat with Terry G, Peter Grant, and Clive at lunch, where Peter entertained us with stories of working with the eel during the filming of *The Deep*. "Ah, yes, the eel," said Peter, in a tone that indicated it was not the first time he had been asked about it. "All it had to do was dart out of a crack for its scene, but it refused to do it. I was underwater in a large tank for protection and had a fish that we hoped it would go for when it was released. No good. It went for me every time. Finally, we all got fed up. The thing was starved for about a week. We had a fish right there for it. It was released again. It went straight for me . . ."

Over lunch, the conversation drifted back to Python, and I asked Terry about the time when Python first appeared on the *Tonight* show several years ago, before they were known in the United States. "I think it was '73. We had just finished our Canadian tour and ended up in L.A. and somehow got booked to be on the show. I think John had gone back to England by then. Joey Bishop was the guest host, and he introduced us by saying, 'Now here are five lads from England. *I'm told* they're very funny.' Can you imagine being introduced like that?" laughed Terry.

"Anyway, we all came on, and they showed a couple of tapes of us, and it was a disaster! The audience just sat there with these wonderful blank looks on their faces, and they didn't know what to make of us. They just sat there staring with their mouths hanging open. It was great! What a total disaster—complete silence! I suppose we shouldn't have expected much, though. After all, I think the first sketch they showed was something with Eric in drag, and the audience had no conception at all of what was going on. We all had a good laugh about it later."

That reminded me of an appearance Terry made on *To Tell the Truth* a couple of years ago, the game show in which a celebrity panel tries to uncover two impostors from a group of three guests. "It was really strange to be on it, because I used to watch it years and years ago," recalled Terry. "Two of the panel had to disqualify themselves because they recognized me. Then I got one vote, and one of the impostors got the other vote."

For some reason, we had gotten a rather long lunch break, but eventually we had to report to Mandy's garden. John Cleese was called in for the afternoon to film the scene in which he arrests Brian while he is talking to Judith. I climbed back up to my usual perch on top of the wall, as the filming got under way with wide shots of Brian, Judith, and John.

John, as the centurion, enters the scene at the end of the shot, slapping his hand on Brian's shoulder and saying, "You're fucking nicked, me ol' beauty!" as he arrests him. During the initial takes, only John's hand is visible in the shots, so he didn't bother to put on his armor. Instead, he gleefully finished them all wearing only his tunic.

I watched from above, taking some photos, and snapped one just as John's hand struck Graham's shoulder. Unbeknownst to me, it was a take rather than a rehearsal, and Dushko, the sound operator, gave me a scowl. I was snapping pictures more freely now, having found a reliable source for 35 mm film a couple of blocks from the Sidi.

The reverses of that scene came next, and four soldiers joined the shot to stand behind the centurion. John reluctantly slipped into his armor,

This is the final fate of the large
polystyrene statue, last seen
outside the city wall in Sousse. It
was cut up, and is being turned
into the remains of a UFO that
crashes after picking up Brian.

The demolition continued in the Ribat; in just two days, the marketplace was nothing but rubble, and Pilate's platform was now gone. (From the pile of trash, I snagged my only souvenir —a plaster cast that had been affixed to one of the torches along the wall.)

A photo that is burned into my memory, and the only one that I almost ruined. I was yelled at (and rightly so) for snapping this while the camera rolled, as John slaps Graham's shoulder and says "You're fucking nicked, me ol' beauty." I thought it was a rehearsal because John was in his tunic, but because it was such a tight shot on Graham, only John's hand was visible in the shot, so he did not need to don his armor.

looking slightly annoyed; I noticed that he always seemed to spend as little time in his armor as possible.

After the reverses were finished, we moved on to the ending of that sequence, as the centurion and his men drag Brian away, while Judith runs for help. By midafternoon, we had completed the entire sequence in Mandy's garden, but there was still more work to do before we wrapped for the day. John was released, but Michael was called in as the unit moved across the road to the smaller Ribat/animal compound. The rest of today's scenes were to take place in the hypocaust, the area of arches and tunnels under the palace, where the commandos had to do still more crawling. Not all of them seemed happy to be back in uniform, as they were loaded down with lanterns, power packs, and weapons.

"I have this recurring nightmare," Michael confessed as he was being outfitted. "The filming is all finished and I'm at the airport getting on the plane back to England. As I'm about to climb into the plane, somebody comes up to me with all of my commando gear, saying, 'Just one more take please, Mike, one last time.'"

At the far end of the courtyard, currently under construction, was Ben's cell. It was a large wooden freestanding structure, circular, about ten feet in diameter and nearly twenty feet high. The inside was caked with all manner of dirt, moss, slime, and other filth, with a few old bones scattered about the floor of the cell.

"This whole area is like a huge personal torture chamber for me," Michael confessed as he looked across the courtyard at the large wooden framework. "I have to play Ben in that, and crawl through these tunnels here as a commando."

Most of the other commandos had been on the set since midafternoon; they had been called to the set to be measured for their crosses and decided to wait for their scene. Despite a slow beginning, as the commandos were loaded into the wrong tunnel, the filming finished rather quickly— and with a minimum of complaining, though the usual bumps and groans occasionally emitted from the tunnels beneath the black canvas. As we wrapped for the day, the call sheets were handed out, informing us that we'd be spending the entire day tomorrow filming the scene in Ben's cell. It was the only sequence planned.

That evening, I decided to ride back to the Sidi to watch the rushes and the movie for the night. They were showing *Them!*, the fifties science fiction story about giant ants, which may have been intended to make us feel a little better about the insects we had to deal with each day on the set. I rode in with Mati, and we watched the rushes of the city gates of Sousse and some of the palace corridors. Waiting in the hotel bar for *Them!* I ran

into Melvin, who beat me handily at table tennis, knocking me out of the tournament. I accompanied Mati and Clive to the Coq, where we had an excellent dinner, including the spectacular fish soup, and several bottles of wine. We missed the movie but no longer cared. We then asked the front desk to get us a taxi and ordered more drinks.

Eventually, the lobby began clearing out, and there was still no taxi. Mati had repeated his request, and the desk clerk called again. It was almost midnight. Mati grew furious, as the clerk explained in broken English that late at night, it sometimes took a long while to get a taxi, and he was

The cord from the power pack was run down the sleeve of Michael's shirt and connected to the lantern. Once he was connected, he and the other commandos had to keep hold of their lanterns on the set. A quick test, and the lantern worked. He claimed that all that electricity forced him "to be very careful when he has a pee."

doing his best. Clive and I let Mati do the talking, and he came back to inform us that the whole town was closed up, we couldn't get a taxi, and there were no empty rooms at the Sidi.

I suggested that we sit there and wait, and if worse came to worst, we could sleep on the couches in the lobby. They seemed rather comfortable, and Clive was already falling asleep on one of them. Mati would have none of it and suggested we start walking the twelve miles back to the Ruspina, in hopes that we would encounter a taxi along the way. I was unconvinced and Clive was half-asleep, but at Mati's urgings, we began walking.

We had walked at least fifteen minutes without hearing the sound of a car. Finally, we heard a vehicle approaching and flagged it down, running into the street and virtually blocking its path as soon as we saw it was a taxi. The three of us climbed into the backseat. There was another man sitting next to the driver, and both were clearly drunk. The driver indicated he would take us to the Ruspina as soon as he dropped off his friend. We rode along quietly, figuring even this was better than walking all the way back to the Ruspina.

"He works at Sahara Beach," the driver said, indicating his unconscious friend, as he attempted conversation. "Waiter." That explained why they were out so late. The Sahara Beach Hotel was the largest tourist hotel in the area, with a bar that stayed open until 2:00 A.M.

Our taxi careered through the streets at breakneck speeds. Clive had a look of blank terror frozen on his face, while Mati worried that the driver would try to charge us for this side trip. Fortunately, there were no other cars on the road, and we sped away in the opposite direction from the Ruspina, into a section of Monastir I had never seen. I had visions of them pulling guns on us and dropping our bodies into the Mediterranean, unless we crashed first.

"I think they're lost," whispered Clive.

After ten minutes, he dropped his passenger at a little house along the beach and circled back to the Sidi Mansour to recover our bearings. Somehow, we managed to direct our driver back to the Ruspina, where we gladly paid him the normal fare as we exited.

Our Friday the Thirteenth had gotten off to an appropriate start.

"This Calls for Immediate Discussion," in which Judith rouses the revolutionaries, the marketplace is reconstructed, and the commandos prowl the palace once again

THE WEATHER PROVED CONSISTENT WITH TODAY'S date. At half past seven this morning, the rain began coming down in buckets. After arriving at the Sidi, I rode out to the small Ribat, where Ben's cell was waiting. But there were only a handful of people walking around in the mud at the location, so I hopped back on the minibus and returned to the Sidi. The rain had made filming the scene in Ben's cell impossible, so Terry and the others would have to choose a cover set.

It seems that the surest way to get rain here is to not plan for a cover set. The only two days of filming that we had heavy rain were the two days there was no cover set listed on the call sheet.

At last, scene 62 in Matthias's house was selected, and crews were dispatched to prepare it. I stopped in the production office, where I was given Python postcards that had just been printed for the cast and crew, then settled into a chair in the hotel bar to address a few of the cards.

In addition to the weather, today was a rare day for another reason: It was Graham's first entire day off since the filming began! He was in the bar examining his camera, while a few of us sat around giving advice. He had just gotten a new flash attachment, and we offered well-intentioned but not very useful comments.

"No, we won't read the directions unless there's no other way," Graham responded to one suggestion, and he set off the flash several more times. He made an adjustment and tried it again, but it wouldn't go off. "What's wrong now? Oh, I see—there's too much light to use the flash now, so it shuts off automatically. It's smarter than I am!"

By midmorning, the rain had nearly stopped; at the same time, we were called to the set at the Ribat for Matthias's house. Despite the promised day off, it seemed Graham would have to come in later.

"That's all right, I don't mind," Graham insisted. "I wouldn't know what to do with all the time off anyway."

Michael had been more than an hour in the makeup chair when he found out the scenes with Ben wouldn't be shot today, but he took it all good-naturedly. He was called to the set dressed as a revolutionary instead.

Michael's family arrived on the set for the first time. His sons instantly fell in love with the Ribat. Within the first five minutes of their arrival, despite his best efforts to control them, they were waving down at us from some of the uppermost walkways of the castle.

John Cleese came striding onto the set in a playful mood. Mati approached him, intending to interview him, but John started in before Mati could ask a question.

"Would you like to hear about my day?" he asked. "I was looking forward to what was practically a day off, having only to come in around four o'clock to say one line. Instead, I was called about eight this morning and told we were shooting on a cover set. They sent a car for me, which drove me to the set, where I sat around for a bit. After a short while, I was sent back to my hotel with the explanation that the cover set couldn't be prepared due to the weather, which I feel seems to defeat the purpose of having a cover set. As soon as I got back to my hotel and got started on a good book, I was called back to the set to actually film the scene. And here I am."

Filming finally began just before noon, with the scene in which Judith informs the revolutionaries of Brian's arrest and attempts to stir them into action. This was the scene that had undergone several minor rewrites, the latest by John and Michael not long ago. Filming conditions were again crowded, but what I could hear of the dialogue sounded very funny indeed. Once the filming started, no one wasted any time, and shooting in the hot, humid little room was finished quickly.

The afternoon filming seemed to take a little longer than usual to prepare. After finishing the morning's scene with reverses and close-ups, all of the filming in Matthias's house was completed soon after, which left time for a couple more scenes.

A makeshift archway was constructed, and there were a few more shots of Graham running through the marketplace and spotting Judith. These were filmed without the marketplace or Judith actually being there, which made things a bit more difficult. Graham had to run into the crowd, stop at the archway, and then look around until he spotted her. All the while, a number of locals were paraded in and around the crowd to simulate a busy marketplace. One of the locals received a nice round of applause for walking through the background with a pumpkin balanced on his head.

The unit worked efficiently and finished rather quickly. Filming soon shifted to one of the topmost corners of the Ribat for still more shots of the commandos walking through corridors. This also took time to set up, and as it was Friday afternoon before a two-day weekend, people began acting silly. I was hit by what felt like bits of gravel as I approached the set. I saw a half-opened bag of corn that was serving as the ammunition; even

The fickle weather forced us to delay filming in Ben's cell, and substitute a brief scene in Matthias's house, being prepared in the background on the second story.

Graham waits in the arch. He is to run through the marketplace looking for Judith, a shot made more difficult without Judith or the marketplace.

Jonathan started throwing corn while the corridors inside were being readied. We were all on the walkways above the small courtyard where the spaceship was being constructed, so those of us on high did the mature thing: We agreed to a cease-fire and started dropping handfuls of corn onto the workers below, who scattered and ran for shelter.

The crew soon grew bored once again and started pitching coins, throwing them against the wall to see who could come closest. Even Terry J took a crack at it, and exhibited a natural talent, giving the coins a slight

There were so many delays and changing set-ups that even Terry J had time to join the high-stakes, floating game—pitching pennies with crew members and locals.

spin just as he threw them to improve his accuracy—something I doubt Zeffirelli would have thought of.

The upcoming scene utilized the commandos in one of the higher levels of the palace climbing some stairs, narrowly escaping a drunken Roman who was coming down them. Despite problems with a fountain that refused to run properly, there were no major difficulties, and the shot was finished quickly. Terry felt we needed to shoot this scene in order to make it look like there was at least someone living in the palace—in all of the previous shots of the commandos, they've scarcely run into anyone.

As we wrapped for the day, the commandos received yet another promise that today would be the last of the commando filming. Call sheets were handed out that included a revised shooting schedule to cover the remainder of our time in Monastir. There was also an invitation to a middle-of-production party tomorrow night at the Sidi, with entertainment "to be provided." I heard a group of sparks joking among themselves: "Does that mean you're going to be flinging cakes tomorrow night?"

A Day Off, in which there is a chat with John Young, a visit to the beach, and a floor show

AT LONG LAST, ANOTHER DAY OFF, and naturally, it rained off and on all morning. I decided to take a taxi into town and, after a stop to buy some film, headed to the Sidi. Since I wouldn't be going to Gabes, I stopped into the production office to check on my flight arrangements. Time has flown, and it hardly seems possible that I will be leaving in one more week.

I walked into the bar and saw John Young, who agreed to an interview.

"I'd always wanted to be an actor," said John. "Of course, I'm sixty-two now, and when I started in the business, I was sixteen. So I've been at it a long time. A lot of my previous experience would be uninteresting now. Apart from starting off in repertory and going off with the forces during the war, I came back and I've been mainly in the theater since then. It led to other things, such as broadcasting, television, and a few films, and there we are! It's going on like that. Of course, I'm married and my wife is a theatrical agent in Scotland, which is where I've been working mainly, and my son is also an actor. He does the same sort of thing that I do, working in Scotland mainly as a base."

"How does this film compare with some of the previous films you've done, as far as the way Python works and their approach to filmmaking?"

"I think their approach to filmmaking is now quite experienced and good, since this film is absolutely on schedule, and one doesn't expect that when you're halfway through. They're great people to work with. All the scenes are discussed, and one approaches a scene without having nerves, either. I think they must sort of take all the nerves themselves—they put other people at ease, and I find it extremely pleasant with them. And I enjoy playing comedy!"

Unlike most of the other rep company members, John had experience with a previous Python film, playing two roles in *Holy Grail*.

"I was asked to play someone who could have been John Cleese's father, and he threw me onto the death cart for ninepence," explained John. "Well, that was only one day's work. They came back about a fortnight later and said another part had turned up, a part in modern dress, that of an eminent historian who had his head lanced off by a knight. That worked as well. In fact, I died twice in *Holy Grail*. Then, to my great surprise and joy, I was asked to come to Tunisia and be in this film, which delighted and excited me.

"Of course, I was only involved in *Grail* to this small extent, but this film has a complete story line running through it. In *Grail*, of course, there was a smaller cast. The Pythons played several parts each, as they're doing in this film."

"Do you enjoy playing multiple roles?"

Scotsman John Young had several memorable moments in *Monty Python and the Holy Grail* (he was the modern-day historian who was attacked by a knight on horseback), so the Pythons came calling when they were casting *Brian*.

"Yes. I'm quite sure that apart from the Python films, there's no other film company or film people who would employ actors to play several different parts. I think the makeup department does a wonderful job, because even from my own eyes, there are two things I do in it, and I look entirely different in each one."

As I thanked John, one of the crew members, Brian, offered me a ride back to the Ruspina, and I gladly accepted. As we drove along, he explained that they were setting up for the party tonight in the dining room at the Sidi. "They're supposed to have quite a show planned for us, but no one is telling what it is," he explained, noting that John Goldstone was saving it for a surprise.

By the time we arrived back at the Ruspina, the sun was emerging. I decided to return some books to John Cleese, and the typewriter to Michael, and when I walked into the lobby at the Meridien, I ran into Michael and all of the Palin clan, loaded with beach toys. I left the books and typewriter at the desk, then headed outside, intending to walk back to the Ruspina along the beach.

Terry J and his family had joined the Palins for the afternoon, and everyone seemed to be enjoying the sun. Michael's sons stopped me as I walked along, pointing out to sea. About fifty yards out, Terry's wife was in one of the little two-man paddle boats with one of the children. They were paddling slowly and looking over the side.

"They saw a jellyfish out there," explained Thomas Palin, "and now they're trying to find it again."

I was a little surprised that a jellyfish would be that close to shore, as the water was still very shallow, but Michael confirmed the sighting. "Apparently they spotted one a little while ago," he noted. "Just a small one, though."

I decided that even though it was late in the afternoon, I would change clothes and come back out to the beach. As I was about to leave, I noticed Eric's son, Carey, playing with the other children. "When I got back to the room today, I saw William on the phone," explained Michael. "I couldn't imagine who he was talking to at first, because I didn't think he knew anybody down here. I was afraid he'd called London or something, until he told me he was just talking to Carey upstairs!"

By the time I changed and made it out to the beach it was nearly four o'clock, and most of the people were beginning to leave. The hotel man who handed out the beach mats refused to give me one and kept repeating, "Four thirty we close!" I tried to explain that I only wanted it for half an hour, but to no avail. Instead, I found a white plastic beach chair that looked suspiciously like those at the Meridien and sat down to begin reading the latest *Newsweek*.

A short distance away, I could hear the Palins and the Joneses; by this time, they were practically the only ones left on the beach. As the children played and the wives chatted, Michael and Terry were making each other laugh.

"We're now talking to a man who is attempting to break the decibel record for human speech," said Michael, who had suddenly become an interviewer.

"That's right, yes, I am," Terry responded at the top of his lungs. Michael provided the commentary as Terry continued to shout.

"One hundred five . . . up to one hundred nine now . . . and . . . yes, he's about to reach—one hundred twelve decibels!" Michael observed.

It was like watching a Python sketch being created before my eyes. I sat back and watched the performance, delighting in their inventiveness and exuberance and the spontaneity of it all. Once again, it struck me how lucky I was, to be privileged enough to witness Palin and Jones creating comedy. If the Beatles had stopped by and started jamming on the beach, I couldn't have felt luckier.

Soon, the sun began sinking and the air grew cooler, and the tourists retreated to their hotels. I showered and changed clothes; then Mati and I shared a taxi to the Sidi for the party. No one seemed to know what the entertainment would be. Terry emphasized that he and Michael had *not* been rehearsing a new sketch on the beach for the party; he speculated that Sue Jones-Davies, who sings in a rock band, might be performing.

A number of tables had been lined up for us in front of a makeshift stage, and I joined some of the sound crew at one table. The Pythons all sat at a table in the center; Eric had his son with him, but the other children had apparently been left with babysitters. In the next room, a lamb was roasting on a large spit, and the drinks were flowing freely, pausing only when dinner was served. Afterward, the lights came down, and our impresario, John Goldstone, announced, "Please welcome, direct from the Sahara Beach, Four Guys in Disguise!"

The recorded music started and the performers took the stage. I was amazed to see it was a drag show! I wasn't sure what I had been expecting, but it wasn't this. This was apparently the same act that performed for the English tourists at the Sahara Beach. I had never seen a drag show before but had to admit they were very good. They lip-synched and wore elaborate costumes for each number, entertaining us with ad libs between sets, even climbing on some laps and stroking the hair of a few men in the audience. They were well received by everyone except Carey Idle, who fell asleep midshow.

They exited to a rousing ovation, and then Garth brought out an elaborate sound system. Tables were pushed to the side to form a dance floor, and the place was soon crowded as everyone was on their feet, dancing late into the night.

Another Day Off, in which there is a final visit to the beach

A LATE MORNING FOLLOWED A LATE night. I managed to place a call home to let my parents know when I would be arriving; then I napped a bit more. Eventually, I decided to head to the beach so as not to sleep away the entire day. ▪ I walked along the beach, noticing an impressive sand castle near the Meridien, the proud work of the Palin boys. "You ought to put them to work designing and building

Ribats," I suggested to Michael, and we both marvelled at the size of their structure. He laughed, and I walked on, eventually returning to the Ruspina. I decided to lie on the beach for a little while longer. As I would be leaving in less than a week, it was my last chance to lounge along the Mediterranean under the Tunisian sun.

Sharing a Cell with Ben, in which Brian is confronted by a longtime prisoner

FILMING TODAY BEGAN WITH THE SCENE originally scheduled for Friday but postponed due to the rain. ▪ Ben's cell was erected in the small Ribat/animal compound and dressed with all manner of filth and decay. Michael had only undergone half of the makeup for Ben on Friday, but this morning, he got the full two-hour treatment. Ben is a prisoner who has been hanging from chains in a dungeon for what

There was always a makeup person nearby to dirty Michael up a bit between takes.

looked like decades. Michael made quite a stir when he finally arrived on set, as it was the first time that most of the unit had seen him as Ben.

He was dressed in rags, literally, so torn up and full of holes that the few bits of rotting cloth that held the holes together resembled nothing so much as a spider's web. He wore a thin white wig and a long grayish white beard. Streaks of gray and white greasepaint covered his body, giving the impression that he had not been exposed to sunlight in a very, very long time. Scars, scabs, and running sores were everywhere. His cell, and the bit of archway outside of it, needed some finishing touches before the filming could begin, so chains were hung and bones scattered about the cell. Part of the archway needed paint as well, so unit painter Graham Bullock touched up a few spots and tossed bits of sand onto the wet paint to give it a rougher appearance.

Michael walked into the courtyard to show off his outfit to those who were interested, pointing out the more picturesque sores.

"I refused to wear anything that was still living, though," he noted. "I felt a line had to be drawn somewhere."

The cell itself was small and cramped. In addition to Michael and Graham, half a dozen people were crammed into the cell for the filming, along with the lights and camera equipment that had to be placed inside. When it was almost time to begin, Michael got into place, and chains were attached to his wrists. (Although he would not actually have to dangle from them, his arms soon began to grow sore as they were held stiffly in place throughout the shooting.) Unseen by filmgoers was the small device, resembling a bicycle seat, that supported all of his weight; it was hidden by his rags during filming.

Before we could begin filming, Michael and Graham were released from the cell for a few minutes while the set was dressed—or dirtied, in this case. I used the time to run to Tunisair a couple of blocks away to arrange a flight to London. As the Sunday flights were full, I had to book a Saturday plane to England. When I returned, everything—and everyone—appeared to be in place.

The first shots of the day involved Ben in his cell, with Brian lying there looking up at his fellow prisoner. No sooner had we gotten under way at ten thirty than the camera broke down. Fortunately, the repairs

Graham and Michael discuss the scene to be shot that day. Michael had to undergo the makeup and costume the previous Friday, but the rain completely altered our schedule.

were made quickly, and filming resumed. It was followed by a two-shot of Ben and Brian, and both were finished by lunchtime. It had been a short but successful morning of filming.

After lunch, I walked to the production office to arrange airport transportation, which turned out to be easy since quite a few others were leaving on the same flight. As I walked out the door, I ran into another figure leaving the makeup house. He was dressed in a worn leather outfit and looked nearly as filthy as Ben. He was wearing a bald cap that covered

The plan was to complete the scene in Ben's cell today, to save Michael the ordeal of more filming as Ben tomorrow, but it would be a challenge.

most of the top of his skull, with long, scraggly hair growing on the fringes of the bald spot. A huge, open scar ran from the back of his head, over his skull, and all the way down to his nose, giving a bizarre, split-skull effect. I strained to look beneath the makeup.

"Hi, Howard, what do you think?" it asked. "This is the jailer."

"Terry?" I stammered, finally recognizing another Gilliam creation. "Wow, it's, uh . . . incredible . . ."

He continued walking through the lobby to his car outside, attracting stares much like those given to a car wreck. It seemed like quite a bit of preparation for a rather small role, with his primary function being to spit in Brian's face, but Terry would not go unnoticed.

I headed to the lobby in his wake but then noticed Barry Took exiting the elevator, likely heading back to the set. Barry Took had been with the BBC when Python began and was in part responsible for putting Python on the air. The Pythons seemed to look up to him as a sort of father figure. I hadn't actually met him, though he was pointed out in the hotel bar a couple of days ago, so I introduced myself, and he agreed to a short chat.

"I had met John and Graham when they were with Tim Brooke-Taylor and Marty Feldman doing a thing called *At Last the 1948 Show,* and I had met Michael Palin and Terry Jones because they had all worked on *The Frost Report,* for which Marty Feldman, who I was currently writing with, was the script editor. I knew them as individuals. Terry Gilliam had done some stuff with the Marty Feldman series that Marty and I had written, a thing called *Marty,* and they all, in fact, had contributed occasionally to the scripts for that. So I knew them from that end of it.

"So it just struck me that of all the twelve or fifteen very talented men around, the people who had the most influence on each other—and that was my thinking—would be John and Graham on one hand, and Michael and Terry on the other. Fundamentally, it would be the impact of those two different sorts of brainwaves coming together that would make the comedy. And they added another couple of ingredients, and that became Monty Python. Once they were formed and running, I got out of the way," explained Barry.

"What was the initial reaction from the BBC to Monty Python when they saw what they had unleashed?"

"Well, Tom Sloan, who was then the head of Light Entertainment, his first comment to me after seeing the first two programs was 'Does John Cleese have to say "bastard" twice?' And I said, 'Well, yes, if he chooses to, that's the whole nature of this program. He's such an intelligent man, he would not have said it had he not thought it artistically correct.' And he said, 'Oh, that's fine.' And that was the only true criticism I'd had at the beginning. They were much, much enjoyed by the very top people at the BBC; they thought it was a terrific show. And even though it wasn't immediately popular, particularly amongst the lowest ranks of the hierarchy, they persisted with it; people like David Attenborough and Huw Weldon persisted and persisted and made them keep it on and booked a new series, because they thought it was enchanting comedy, just the sort of thing the BBC should be doing at that time. And from there it just grew and grew and grew and became a huge success in every possible way. End of story, as far as I'm concerned. I just stand back and admire them now. I just think they're wonderful."

"Did some of them come to you initially with the idea for the program?"

"No, no. I went to them and said, 'Would you like to do a program with these other people?' so that each of them individually would get to work with these other people. And they all said yes. They all had qualms about it, they didn't want to feel trapped by a group show that they then could not get out of, so I said, 'If you don't like it, there's nothing to hold you. You can leave.' I wanted to have a very free feeling.

"They couldn't think of a title. I think they wanted to call it *Whither Canada?* at one stage, and all sorts of things like that. Then it was settled on, and they said, 'No matter what you call it, as long as the words "flying circus" are in it, because that's on all the notes and memos that are going around internally at the BBC, it's called the Circus. It will confuse the BBC if you call it anything else now, so it doesn't matter what you call it as long as the words "flying circus" appear in it.' So they went away and invented Monty Python, and there it stayed."

He explained that despite the name, "Circus" actually had nothing to do with "Cambridge Circus," the university show that featured John Cleese and Graham Chapman. "It actually came from Baron von Richthoven's Flying Circus in World War I. Some of the people at the BBC had been calling it 'Baron von Took's Flying Circus' for a time as well."

Difficult as it may be to believe, Took said he had no particular program in mind when he lined up the group for the show.

"It was whatever they wanted to do—entirely that. It was what *they* wanted to do. That was the whole new conception, really, that I brought to the BBC. If you get people with talent, I say go with that. Don't ask what they're going to do; let them do what they feel is absolutely apt. The antithesis of censorship or control—that's what I wanted to impose. It sounds a contradiction, but I wanted to say to them, 'Look, if you let people run free, they'll produce better work than if you constrain them in old-fashioned formulas.' They say, 'You can't do that because it's never been done before, but then contrary to that is 'We must do that because it's never been done before.' And I said, 'Once you give these men their head, they're so bright, they will produce this very ingredient. They're bound to—how could it not happen?' I said optimistically, before it had ever happened. I happened to be there at the time, really. That was all.

"I think they're wonderful. I still do. Enchanting. Every piece of evidence suggests that the initial guess was the right one, and that's lucky. I've started many shows off and had the most dismal failures in the end."

Barry excused himself and headed off to the set. He was apparently here for a week's holiday and made it a point to visit the set. He was obviously one of the Pythons' biggest boosters, and must feel like a proud father. Or uncle. Or at least a midwife.

Although Mati, the Canadian radio man, left over the weekend, we weren't lacking journalists this week. There was a man here from *Melody Maker,* and upon my return to the set this morning, I met Charles Alverson. Charles was here for a week to do a story for the Sunday *Times* on Python and seemed to know the group rather well. I had never met him before, although I was familiar with at least one of his works: With Terry G, he had cowritten *Jabberwocky,* Terry's first post-Python film, a couple of years ago, and the two seemed good friends. Charles and Terry were working on another new project together and had been writing the screenplay whenever Terry had a break from his work on *Brian.* As I chatted with Charles, Terry, still wearing his jailer's makeup and costume, approached us.

"Have you heard the latest?" asked Charles. "*Jabberwocky* has been sold to Poland. How about that?"

"Poland! Wow, that's great." Terry smiled. "We finally made it behind the Iron Curtain. Any word on Italy yet?"

"No, nothing more. The deal is still in the works, but nothing has happened yet."

I left them to talk business while I walked over to observe the preparations at Ben's cell. The next shots would be close-ups of Graham in the cell, so Michael was able to shed some of his rags and relax in the sun. Michael's wife and daughter stopped by the set for a few minutes, but when he approached his little girl in his costume and makeup, she started to cry. Michael tried to talk to her and calm her down, but he was still unable to convince her that he was her father.

Everyone continues to be amazed at how much more smoothly the *Brian* filming is going than *Grail*'s had. Graham's partner, David Sherlock, explained that "morale was really terrible as it dragged a week, two weeks into the film. The cast and crew were really being worked hard, very hard, and they had lost a lot of feeling about what they were doing about a week and a half into the film. They still hadn't seen any rushes, so they didn't really get an idea of what they were doing. Terry J and Terry G were really pushing them awfully hard, although I don't think they realized at the time just how the crew felt. Finally, it got to the point where they were all just about ready to mutiny, to walk out.

"Somehow, Graham seemed to sense it. So that night, Graham had the whole cast and crew meet in the bar and started buying drinks for everyone. They were there drinking for hours, far into the night. Graham started up a sing-along, and I don't think he let anyone else buy a drink all night. Graham is really quite shy, so the whole evening was really kind of hard at first. But that night, the whole unit seemed to develop a sort of unity that had been lacking before. They developed a strong bond that made them keep going. Of course, the next night the rushes finally came in, and everyone got a chance to see what they were working on, and they saw they had a winner, so they went all out for the film from that point on."

Most of the afternoon's shooting involved short bits with the jailer, the centurion, and Ben and Brian, along with the necessary close-ups, reverses, and wide shots from all angles. John Cleese arrived about midmorning to do his walk-on as the centurion, and the Roman guards were brought in as well. Filming slowed somewhat during the afternoon due to an assortment of minor problems. In addition to delays in setting up the shots, there were camera breakdowns, a noisy camera, and chickens, pigeons, and ducks making noise in the background.

I walked around the set during the breaks, taking a few pictures. I noticed Michael and Terry G, both covered in rags and filth, sitting side by side

This peculiar-looking structure housed the set and the crew for the filming involving Ben's cell. I was surprised that it was not shot in an existing building, but it needed to be enclosed, dark, and taller than most existing structures, so this was constructed in a courtyard of the Ribat.

in the canvas chairs, so I gave them my copy of *Newsweek* to use as a prop. Both David Appleby and I took some nice shots of Ben and the jailer reading the magazine intently, studying the cover-featured "The Avedon Look."

Our previous problems and delays were now joined by a black, threatening cloud cover. It hung over us for a little while but then finally blew past without dropping any rain. "God has been good to George Harrison's money," observed Michael. The forecast was calling for rain tomorrow, though, which wasn't good, as there was still plenty left to film in Monastir.

George Harrison was, of course, the reason we were all here. If he hadn't been a Python fan, he wouldn't have offered to raise the money to produce the film. Python has often been called the Beatles of comedy (and to a few, the Beatles are the Pythons of rock), and it's ironic how the members of each group are such fans of the other. There are few, if any—and I include myself here—that are as big a fan of Python as George. My only regret is that I've never had the opportunity to meet George. Of course, considering what a fan I am, it's probably just as well . . .

While Graham was in the cell for his close-ups, Michael, John, and Terry G sat outside with the crew, waiting for their turns.

"This is what happens when you can no longer do juvenile leads," noted Terry, indicating his filth and rags. "I'm doing my own Dorian Gray portrait. I'm living it—you go back to a little room . . ."

"I think you're a matinee ghoul," quipped Michael, who then turned to John and said, "I remember him being very beautiful when he was dressed up as the one who appeared in the ministers sketch, remember, with the long cigarette holder and all?"

"That's your idea of beauty?" Terry asked accusingly. "It's a little bit of a giveaway—"

"No, that's your idea of beauty, not mine," insisted Michael. "I just thought you were quite an elegant man, with that long cigarette holder—"

"No, I think it's just that the extremes of the spectrum are mine. There's no middle ground."

"I agree with you," said John, "but it's just that I've never seen you down at the other end."

"Oh, no. Remember—which is the one with the Scottish Louis the XIV? I thought I did a wonderful butler in that, a real class butler."

"I don't think we saw your legs, though," Michael pointed out.

"I know, but—well, actually, we did. They were inside the stockings. I think I know what my limitations are. The more Richard Burton–ish type parts are mine, the Calibans of the world."

"The terrible thing about having a jailer who looks like that," observed John, "is that you know he's not apt to be too worried about how you look. Do you see what I mean? I mean, if he's got a complete crack down his skull, I mean, he isn't going to bother much about you. 'I've got a sty right here,' you know."

"Perhaps the brains could sort of ooze out," suggested Michael.

"A sort of suppurating brain," giggled Terry.

"No, just a brain. It wouldn't have to suppurate," said John.

"Sorry, I've done it again," laughed Terry. "Oh, no! There I am, at the beautiful end of the spectrum again."

"Have you ever been anywhere nice?" asked John pointedly.

"Oh, yes, I spend most of my holidays going to lovely places."

"Where do you go? What sort of places?"

"Did you see the film *The Duelist*? It took place in this lovely medieval city. Tivoli, the gardens of Tivoli."

"Oh, yes, very beautiful," noted Michael. "He went there covered with soot, a great scar down his head."

"I've been in most of the world's great beautiful places," noted Terry.

"Oh, well, then, I take it all back," said John.

"Terry G, they're calling for you," said Michael, indicating Jonathan. It was time for him to throw Graham in the cell some more.

Michael pretended to notice John in part of his centurion costume. "Look, John's in to work, of course. I thought he stopped by to sort of see how we all were. Jolly nice. I was rather touched. I thought, 'Well, I didn't expect to see him socially like this.'"

"Well, your kids have been reminding me all day that I'm working," responded John. "First thing this morning I came down to the swimming pool. 'I thought you were working,' one of them calls out. Little Carey Idle comes up to me and says, 'Do you know what a German policeman says to his chest?' I said no, and he said, 'You're under a vest.'"

"Very good," laughed Michael.

"Now for a five-year-old, you know, that's very good. I don't know where he got it from. Eric swears he didn't get it from him."

The conversation turned to the upcoming table tennis tournament, and Michael turned and began talking to some of the rest of us.

"Yes, I guess Mimoun was once the Tunisian national champion at table tennis," Michael noted, making sure that John was within earshot.

"What's that you say?" John asked concernedly. "What about Mimoun?"

"Oh, we were just talking about how he was the national champion at table tennis," said Michael innocently, all the while knowing how much John had been looking forward to the tournament, and also knowing he was set to play Mimoun in the first round.

"Mimoun? Really?" asked John, taken in by it all. "You mean the driver Mimoun? I'm supposed to play him!"

A few of the others turned away, and John suddenly looked relieved.

"Oh, all right, I see. You're having me on, aren't you?" John smiled. "Very good . . ."

The time seemed to be passing fairly quickly, and it looked doubtful as to whether all of the scenes with Ben would be finished today. That meant Michael would have to spend another two hours in the makeup chair tomorrow to become Ben. He seemed to take it all in stride, though, as he sat back relaxing with John.

"I think it would be fun to form the Holland Park Schadenfreude Society," John mused. "It could meet Friday evenings and have a good giggle about all those things happening to others. 'Schadenfreude' actually means 'shameful joy'—you take joy in other peoples' misfortunes. Say somebody you really like has an accident, or his wife dies of cancer or something, you have a good laugh about it and you feel better. I think it's probably an underdeveloped art."

Everyone else considered this as John was called off to do some acting. Michael remained behind, and I began wondering how it was that he had roles nearly as unpleasant as those of Terry Gilliam. "When you guys wrote the film, how was it decided who would play what?" I asked. "You seem to have gotten stuck with so many of these filthy parts."

"Oh, I don't know—I mean, this is a far cleaner film for me than

Jabberwocky. Jabberwocky was nine weeks of shit and toothblacking," Michael joked. "I've had Pilate to do in this, who is clean. I have a Roman to do tomorrow who's clean. The Roman parts are great, much sought-after, because they are clean, though they have to wear fairly heavy tunics. Pilate didn't even have to wear a heavy tunic!

"I absolutely balked at the idea of playing Brian. Whenever the casting of Brian came up, I went very quiet, because I just didn't want to do a sort of quintessential, naive, whatever it is Dennis [from *Jabberwocky*] is called. Once it was established that Graham would play Brian, then it was just everybody doing the usual Python thing of playing their own creations, generally speaking. And then you pick up a few roles, and you lose a few as well. I'm very happy. I think I've got some nice things to do in this. Ben's a bit horrible, but it's a funny scene, and I'm glad to be doing it. It's just that the conditions leave a lot to be desired!"

I knew that with *Monty Python's Flying Circus,* there may have been a tendency for the group members to play the roles that they had written themselves, but Michael seemed unclear about such casting in *Brian.*

"I don't know, actually, I can't really put a figure to that. Terry and I wrote the Ben scene, and I play Ben in that ... and we wrote the Pilate scene, and I play Pilate. Most of the Mandy scene, on the other hand, was written by John and Graham, but Terry's playing Mandy, so it's not quite a rule."

Michael was soon called off for more Ben filming, and the day dragged on. He had expressed some hope that we would be able to finish the scene today in which he hangs upside down as the crucifees pass by. But the time had dragged on this afternoon and we were unable to get to it, which meant that Mike would have to undergo the makeup and costume for Ben yet another day.

Instead, the last shot of the day was another run-through of the Ben scene, this time shot from just below Michael's armpit. It was an unpopular shot for some, including Graham, who had already had a long day, especially as they felt it probably wouldn't even be used. Nevertheless, a hole was cut in the wall below Michael's armpit for the camera, and the scene was reshot from that angle several times before we wrapped.

It was dark by the time everyone started packing and call sheets were

handed out. Apparently there is no film tonight, and our rushes are stuck in customs for some reason, though we'll probably have them by tomorrow night. I met two neighbors of Graham's called Roger and Pan who had come down for the week to watch the Pythons at work. The three of us rode together back to the Ruspina, which many seem to be calling the Rasputin.

Michael (speaking with producer John Goldstone) was shadowed by makeup and costume people between shots; he insisted that he would not agree to wear anything that was still alive.

"Out of the Door, Line on the Left, One Cross Each," in which Brian and Mr. Cheeky meet their jailer and Brian is dragged to his cell

THE INTERIOR OF THE DUNGEON WAS erected just next to the main courtyard, about halfway below ground level at the Ribat. Wooden gratings were set up on the windows outside, with lights shining through them, casting effective prisonlike shadows inside. Romans and crucifees were all costumed and made up, as were the necessary Pythons. ▪ Eric and Graham were dressed as Mr. Cheeky and Brian, and Terry G

The jailer sequence was an interior scene, but had to be lit from the outside;
Michael enjoyed the opportunity to finally play a cleaner role,
particularly on the heels of Ben.

was in his bald cap and scar as the jailer. Terry pointed out some round bits of gold metal on his chest, proudly confiding that they were actually just bottle caps that had been flattened and painted. Michael arrived shortly after the others. He was grateful to be assaying one of his cleaner roles in a nice lightweight Roman toga as Nisus Wettus, who guides the crucifees through the line on their way to be killed.

Filming started with scenes of the prisoners as they lined up to be questioned by Nisus and the jailer, just before they are led away to their crosses. Most of Eric's Mr. Cheeky scenes were done first, as Eric would also have to portray the jailer's assistant in the same scene. Brian's shots were next, and those lasted well into lunchtime.

Despite today's predictions of rain, the day turned out beautifully—a

Eric's shots as Mr. Cheeky were filmed first, as his fellow crucifees waited in line with him; after days in which he was little used, today he would make up for it by playing two roles in one sequence.

good thing, because even though it was an interior scene, it had to be lit from the outside. Despite another slow start, it went very smoothly. The grips and sparks seem to be doing their coin pitching on a more regular basis lately, though I'm not sure whether they are becoming more efficient or simply enjoying the gaming.

John Cleese arrived on the set around midmorning with Connie Booth and their daughter, and he showed them around the set. Their flight down was apparently not the best, and to make matters worse, the airline lost Connie's luggage.

After the early lunch break, Andrew and Terry Bayler were called in to play guards, and filming proceeded with more of the morning's scenes. Eric changed costumes, from Mr. Cheeky to the jailer's assistant, having finished all of the Cheeky scenes in the morning.

The Ribat is filled with a surprising amount of activity, considering we are leaving at the end of the week. More of the stalls from the marketplace were constructed along the sloping walkway where Pilate's platform had once overlooked his Forum. Work on the "unfinished tower" has begun, and the spaceship has been painted a bright yellow, with wreckage strewn about and charring added to it. From glancing at the shooting schedule, there seems to be a lot of filming to be finished by next Monday, when the unit moves to Gabes. Time is really flying by, and it hardly seems like I'll be leaving on Saturday.

After a few more shots that included Roman soldiers, the crew moved over to a large underground room beneath the area where Mandy's house was located. Most of the cast was released for the day, but Graham, Terry G, Bernard, and Andrew had to stay around. I saw that Charles Alverson was hanging around the set, and we started chatting while we waited for the crew to set up inside. Enjoying the irony of an interviewer interviewing another interviewer, I asked Charles about his friendship with Terry Gilliam.

"I was working in New York City in 1962 for Harvey Kurtzman on a magazine called *Help!* I was his assistant editor. *Help!* was going from monthly to quarterly, and I was leaving to take a job. Somehow Terry came in from California just out of college; he'd just graduated from Occidental. I'm not sure whether it was his first job or not. But Harvey, who was doing *Little Annie Fanny* in those days as well as now, was at the Algonquin Hotel with a bunch of people—Arnold Roth, Jack Davis, and there was Terry. He had somehow gotten to Harvey and hit Harv up for my job, so Terry took it over.

"He stayed in my flat. I had an apartment on East Seventy-sixth Street, and he slept on my couch for a while until he got a place, I think in the Village. So we got to know each other fairly well, and did some work together on *Help!*—not writing together or anything, but helping Harvey. We never wrote anything together until *Jabberwocky*.

"He did work for me once, though. There used to be a magazine in New York called *Monocle*, a political satire monthly, and they used to do a newsletter called *The Outsiders*. I edited an issue of it, and Terry did the art direction and cartooning. That was pretty good stuff."

It wasn't until after Charles had moved to Britain that he began to work with Terry, he explained.

"Terry always had an idea of making a film, something out of the *Jabberwocky* poem. In the summer of 1975, when I was still living in Wales, I went to a party at Terry Jones's house, and Terry was saying that he'd decided to do it as a live action film. Then I moved to Cambridge in September of '75, and he came up to see me and asked me if I'd like to write it with him. And so we started there. We wrote over the next four or five months, and it was pretty well finished by February or March 1976. It seemed to go fairly well. We write fast together, we write fluently. It was a good experience."

I noted that the film really has little to do with the poem and wondered how they came up with the basic story line.

"Terry basically had the beginning scene, in which Terry Jones gets killed, and he had the end scene, and he had a few points he wanted to make en route, and that's all—nothing positive. So we just started from the beginning of the story, in which Terry Jones gets killed, and sort of worked it out. It was just a process of saying, 'Who's our hero? What's he doing? What does he want to do? Why does he do this?' It was just worked out scene by scene, arguing and fighting out the socioeconomic premises, and we, of course, made a lot of mistakes. We wrote much too long a script, much of which never got filmed. That's really the working process.

"Terry used to come up to Cambridge. I was working in my garage then, and we had scenes with me behind the typewriter and Terry sitting in front of me, reading a magazine, until I got pissed off at him and made him do some writing. He had never written before; Terry had never been a writer. He'd written captions for his animation, but he'd never written any continuity, and so we'd say, 'What about this? How about that?' Then Terry would go back to London and I'd work by myself in Cambridge; I'd do three or four more scenes. I'd take them around to London and we'd work on them at his place, up in his studio, and he'd rewrite me. Eventually from just sitting there throwing ideas, he'd sit face-to-face with the typewriter and hand things back and forth for rewriting. Terry's a much better rewriter than a writer. When he gets an idea, once you put that idea down and give it some decent clothes, he can shift it around and make it work. That's his real strong point.

"I think the more he writes, the better he'll write. I'd never written a screenplay before, either, and we both sort of learned as we went along. I taught him what I knew about writing, which isn't very much, but mostly it was me laying down a basic scene and him improving on it, or suggesting, or saying, 'How the hell can we get over this point?' Of course, neither of us knew what we were doing—that was the main thing, we didn't have a clue. And we learned a bit!"

"Were you happy with the way the film turned out?"

"No, not really. I've seen it five times now. I've seen it four times during the editing, four different versions. I saw it a year ago spring when I came back from America after the preview, about the beginning of May of 1977. That was the fourth time. I liked it then, and I stopped some people in the cinema at Leicester Square and asked them what they thought without telling them who I was, and they liked it. That was encouraging.

"But then, about a month ago, I saw it again in Cambridge, and I didn't like it. I thought it very imperfect. Some of it is badly written, some of it doesn't play, other bits that were written well enough weren't played right. So I think it could have been a lot better, and Terry thinks so, too. But it's hard to be objective about your own work, and how it's illustrated and made real. I think Terry did a good job in a lot of things. I think he does brilliant images. I don't like the way he handles a camera very much, but he'd never done it before, he's learning. I couldn't do it. I couldn't do half as well as he did. I know that. I like to kibitz anyway. And I think the next one, if there is a next one, will be much better."

"What would you change if you had *Jabberwocky* to do over again?"

"I think I'd recast quite a bit. I didn't like Harry H. Corbett as the squire, and much as I like the girl who played Griselda, I thought she went way over the top. I thought one of Terry's problems was controlling the cast and making sure he got exactly the performance he wanted, because an awful lot of it's crude. And as much as I liked the girl who played the princess, I felt she was too American, her accent changed. Maybe we didn't give her the right words to say, but it was a bit dopey, dopier than it should have been. But some things were very good. The best things were the images. The pictures were beautiful.

"I wasn't really convinced by the fight with the Jabberwocky. Mind you, I knew, but I just felt Terry goes in too much for static shots—you see the whole of the character, you know what he's doing. That kid in the knight suit—there were three knights, three different sizes—the kid in the final one was just running at clear air, empty air. I would have done it with a bunch of random detail shots—the blade cutting through the leg of the monster, the leg flaring out—and put it together as a composite, rather than show the whole thing. Because I thought it was a boring fight. I didn't believe it, I didn't believe he was in danger. I don't know how it looks to somebody who doesn't know the film, but I'd like to have seen a better film. I don't know how to describe it. It should have been a lot better written, because we didn't know what played and what didn't. I think we'd do it better this time if we did it again."

"Terry mentioned a script that the two of you were working on for a new film. How far along is it?"

"Well, we've done a fifty-page treatment, which is like a glorified detailed outline. Right now it's nowhere, there's been no money raised for it. The treatment is not as good as it could be, either. It needs to be rewritten. I'll probably rewrite it when I get back. It's a bit too jokey. I made it very jokey and Terry didn't cut enough of the jokes, but I'll redo it. He's going to do a sample scene of some of the fantasy and try to sell it to some backers. But it's a very strange film. It's not going to be an easy film to get someone to finance, although I think there's interest in Terry as a director because of *Jabberwocky,* and the fact that it's just been sold to Argentina and Poland, which is good. A little bit more money.

"The new one is a long way from being a film, and I'm not sure it ever will be, although he certainly wants to do a film. Whether this is the one, I don't know. He doesn't seem keen to do other people's films. That's one thing about the Pythons, they don't want to do anybody's things but their own. So that's about it. It's a very long shot, and I'm going ahead with my own stuff. If it happens, great, but it's going to take money."

Charles excused himself and headed back to his hotel, and I decided to walk over and watch the filming. It was obviously the scene in which the

Roman soldiers, led by the jailer, drag Brian to the cell that he will share with Ben. I watched as Bernard and Andrew, as the soldiers, pulled Graham along. In order to make the dragging on the stone floor as comfortable as possible, Graham was on a wicker mat, with pads beneath his costume for his elbows and his butt. In addition, there were ropes run down his back and along one leg, so there would be as little actual pulling on Graham as possible. It was first shot along one wall, then along the other before we finally wrapped for the day. Some of the grips and sparks were busy waving their cloths in front of the lights for the torchlight effect, making for crowded quarters. I looked around the set as we wrapped, noting that Terry G had decorated it with several interesting-looking torture devices.

I decided to stay in town and view the rushes at the Sidi, which were of the interior of Pilate's audience chamber, with the commandos climbing in through the fig leaf. These weren't the rushes that were to be shown last night—those are still stuck in customs, and it may be a week before we can get them out.

"Crucifixion Party! . . . Wait for It . . ."
in which there are crucifees marching in the rain, the unfinished tower, and lots of reshoots

IN RECENT WEEKS, I HAVE CONSISTENTLY been the first breakfast customer in the dining room. All of the morning waiters know me and bring me my food and drink without my having to order it. The highlight of the breakfast is always the freshly baked rolls, still hot from the oven, topped off with butter and marmalade. Even if the rest of the food is terrible, I can always rely on the bread.

As I sat eating, I noticed that the next wave of rain, which had been predicted for a while, had finally arrived. As it was only a slow drizzle, it didn't seem as though it would have much effect on the shooting schedule.

The light rain continued off and on all morning, never long or hard enough to disrupt the filming. I was one of eight soldiers today, marched up the stairs leading to the dining area shortly after we arrived. We were taken onto the balcony, where two wooden tables and several benches had been arranged for us. There were empty wine flasks, pieces of fruit, and loaves of bread to serve as props. Our job was to sit there, pretend to eat and drink, and laugh at the crucifees as they marched along the grounds beneath us.

It was absolutely ideal filming conditions for us soldiers, without a doubt the most comfortable scene for me personally. I chose a seat at the end of the table, and Roger and Pan sat near me. We were even allowed to remove our helmets. As the rest of the unit went through their rehearsals in the rain, we sat and watched, warm and dry, some of us even munching on some of the bread and fruit. (Even though Melvin had instructed us not to eat the food, a few of the locals had already started in on it.) From above, I had a perfect vantage point to view the activities in the courtyard below, where the slow drizzle continued. The crucifees milled about restlessly, leaning against their crosses, and the end of the small courtyard was cluttered with people and equipment. Michael was walking around the set with a clear plastic rain bonnet covering his head, so that his curly wig wouldn't be ruined in the rain.

The first shots of the day focused on Michael as Nisus Wettus, as the crucifees started out from the dungeon, carrying their crosses. This involved a tracking shot, so the tracks for the camera had to be laid out so it could be pulled back as the crucifees shuffled along. Despite the weather-related delays, Michael remained in good spirits as he strutted about, waiting for the first take of the day. Jonathan called to Graham to get in his place; Michael issued a long introduction for Graham in which he referred to him as, among other things, a "former Petula Clark writer." Roger and Pan confirmed that this was one of Graham's earlier jobs, one he would just as soon forget about, although there seemed little chance of that with Michael announcing it to all of Tunisia.

The moment the drizzle let up, everyone got into position to shoot. Christine had been sitting with us, her tape player serenading us with

The light, misting rain that continued off and on for much of the morning required us to shoot between the raindrops, but forced Michael to protect his wig.

Linda Ronstadt, but Jonathan ordered her out of sight and earshot. The first take was a wide shot of the crucifees, which took several attempts to complete; it apparently proved rather difficult to get a good shot of Michael through all of the crucifees.

After the wide shots and close-ups of Eric and Graham with their crosses, as well as of Bernard as a Roman officer, the camera panned up from the crucifees to reveal all of us in the soldier's canteen, generally making fun of the poor unfortunates below. Terry J had originally instructed all of us to jeer at them, but derisive laughter seemed to work better on film. Roger got the okay from Terry to throw a piece of pomegranate down into the mob, and we got our shot completed in two takes.

FACING PAGE: The cast and crew were crowded into the smaller courtyard in the Ribat.
The crucifees (lower right) wait for a break in the rain; the tracks are down for the camera to
follow alongside them when they begin their march. In the background, the construction of the
UFO continues. ABOVE: Clive and I were among the Roman soldiers who were to jeer at the crucifees
from a nearby balcony. Considering the inclement weather, it was a perfect observation post, even
though the shots didn't make it into the film.

When all of those scenes were finished, the rain started coming down
harder, and the crew moved upstairs to the highest tower in the Ribat, un-
loading gear in the walkway right next to it. About twenty yards down from
the real tower was our unfinished tower, which was still not ready for filming.
In the script, Graham is chased by two Roman guards and runs up the stairs

The prop crosses were much lighter than those the actors would hang on in the final sequence, but they were still awkward to lift and drag along their route through town.

in the tower. When he finds the tower is still under construction, it is too late to avoid falling. Therefore, the unfinished tower that is being built is only about fifteen feet high, and Graham will do most of his running up the steps inside the real tower. Today's running was shot inside the real tower, as Graham runs up the steps and passes a workman, played by Chris Langham, as he flees the soldiers. As it was shot without sound and only showed Graham running up steps, it was finished quickly, and we broke for lunch.

Our false tower was situated right next to the real one. Ours was to appear under construction, all the better for Graham to appear to fall from the top (and be picked up by a UFO).

After the lunch break, Michael returned to the set as Ben, prepared to be hung upside down. He was hoping it would be the last time he would have to portray Ben and assured us all that getting into the costume and makeup was less fun than it looked. His family had accompanied him to the set once again, and, as before, little Rachel wouldn't go near her father. As soon as he indicated he was ready, the crucifees were all lined up, and he was hung in place just before the camera rolled. He was then let down between takes to reduce his discomfort as much as possible, so the shots with Ben were as quick and painless as possible.

This seemed to be the day for short and varied scenes that had to be completed this week. Ben's shots were followed by still more shots of Brian painting "Romanes Eunt Domus" on the wall, with corrections by John. It was rather difficult to set up the shot correctly, as Brenda couldn't seem to find any shots of Graham or John doing the writing on the wall, and no one could recall for sure which hand held the brush. Matthew finally had to radio back to the production office to contact the cutting room to see how it actually worked on film. Once everything was sorted out, the painting and corrections were finished in two takes. The shot only involved the actual painting of the slogan, so John was even able to wear his blue jeans while filming it, which seemed to delight him.

The last scene of the day was prepared just inside the corner of the area that had once been the courtyard outside of Mandy's house. A group of soldiers were lined up for shots of their search for Brian, as Brian hides from them. Just as the last take was completed, the rain began to pour. We had finished nearly everything we had planned for today, except for retakes of the crowd's reaction to Brian's preaching. The weather for those has to match the same bright sunshine under which the original scenes were shot, so, with luck, those will be finished tomorrow.

I shed my armor and stayed to watch the rushes at the Sidi, which were a number of odds and ends of various scenes. Most seemed to be from last Friday, including Brian and Judith in bed, Brian's fall from the balcony, and the commandos hiding from a Roman as they creep through the corridors. A videotaped soccer match was scheduled to be shown tonight in the TV room upstairs, and I decided to head back to the Ruspina.

The Ex-Leper Returns, in which there are still more reshoots, including Brian addressing his followers one more time

MY UPCOMING DEPARTURE ON SATURDAY IS really starting to hit me. I don't want to go. I feel sad, not only to be leaving the Pythons and the excitement of the film set, but leaving everyone else I've come to know around here. I'm really going to miss them. ▪ I had to report to the crowd makeup house early today to be a peasant. They couldn't find a suitable hat for me, so instead they grabbed a braided sash and fashioned it into a makeshift turban.

The finishing touches are applied to the UFO, which bears little resemblance
to the statue of a few weeks ago.

When I arrived on the set, the sky was clear and blue. Although we
had an extremely early call today, due to the number of scenes that had to
be finished, we still didn't start filming until two hours after our call. A
great deal of time was needed preparing the marketplace for the ex-leper
scene, which would be the first shot of the day.

The marketplace was arranged much differently than it had been for
the other scenes down in the courtyard. There were rows of stalls along the
walkway, where the front of Pilate's palace had originally stood. The stalls
ran from the top of the wall to the bottom, then turned a corner and ran
along one of the adjacent walls in the courtyard and extended through a
passageway to the smaller courtyard. Over a hundred extras were needed
to occupy the stalls and wander about while Michael, Terry J, and Graham

walked along the stalls as the ex-leper, Mandy, and Brian. It was the same path that had been charted out when I walked with them before, on the last day of rehearsals nearly five weeks ago.

As one of the extras, I stood up at the top of the walkway while I awaited my instructions. The locals were assigned to various stalls, and the rest of us were instructed to find a stall or two to frequent while the scene was being filmed. I chose one halfway down the walkway, and Clive stopped not far from me. I loaded a couple of bundles of yarn around my shoulders and sat while I waited for the filming to begin.

Terry's original thought had been to shoot it all in one long take, without a break. There were several problems in such a long, continuous shot, in addition to all of the extras seemingly everywhere. Recording the sound was difficult because there was really no way to use a boom mike with a cord long enough to allow the proper freedom of movement, and so a wireless mike was set up for the boom. It was more difficult to use than the regular mike insofar as getting the sound right. The crowded conditions and lack of maneuverability contributed to the problems. We needed eight different takes before there was finally enough good footage. A few selected close-ups and reaction shots followed, and we broke for lunch. The ex-leper scene needed to be completed as soon as possible to give us enough time for the rest of the day's planned filming.

At one point, I thought we had finished, as we had all been told to take a break, so I pulled off my robe and unwound my headgear. I was sitting listening to Eric, John, and Bernard carrying on when I heard my name being called. I jumped up, grabbed my costume, pulling on the robe as I hurried, and realized that I would never be able to get the turban right. I got into place and started struggling. Clive tried to assist me, but it was hopeless. Just then Nick, one of the wardrobe men, happened along just ahead of the camera and actors.

"Oh, dear, Howard," he said, horrified. "What's happened here? Come undone, did it?" I nodded weakly, and he wrapped it up and pinned it just before the camera was due to come by. I looked away from the camera as it passed through, so I don't think anyone noticed a thing.

When we finished, I made absolutely sure before taking off the costume and heading to lunch. Since the weather was holding up so well, the retakes of the crowd reactions to Brian's preaching were planned for immediately

At last, we would be filming the beginning of the ex-leper scene, the long tracking shot first rehearsed nearly five weeks ago, the day before filming began.

after lunch. There was one minor problem, in that Carol Cleveland and Peter Brett, both prominent in the earlier shooting, had left almost two weeks ago. Since they had stood out and even had lines, Gwen and David Appleby were recruited to stand in for them. After makeup and the proper costumes, they looked as though they would fit in very well.

All of the shots looking into the crowd were then redone, with all of the extras from the morning, myself included, gathered together to walk back and forth in the background. Some of the locals had to be roused from their afternoon naps for the sequence, and we were all lined up and kept flowing back and forth by Matthew, Melvin, and a few others. I had the silk rope wrapped around my head again, and for the third time, it was arranged in a different configuration. During a break in the action, I had a seat next to Garth, David, and Clive.

"Is this the first time you've been recruited to do some acting?" I asked David.

"Well, yes, actually. I've been asked before, here and there for other pictures, but I've always balked at it. It was the beard here, you see. They needed someone with a beard to replace Peter Brett, so I didn't really have much of a choice."

The conversation turned to the weather, as it was becoming very hot, and Garth and David both agreed that they preferred hot-weather filming to very cold.

"The cold weather is really the worst, I'd say," David noted. Garth agreed, noting, "The hot weather is a little uncomfortable, but it doesn't really bother all of your equipment as much. Besides, it's really easier on everyone when it's warmer."

The next shot was set up, and the soldiers were queued up and marched through the crowd, while the actual filming ended with a reverse shot toward Graham. Garth did a wild track, recording the sound, of the extras walking back and forth, and we wrapped for the day after that was completed. For all of the filming we did, we finished rather early, and it actually made for a pretty short day.

There were no rushes tonight, but I stopped by the Sidi to buy a few final souvenirs. When I got back to the Ruspina, I threw my things together but decided to leave most of my packing until tomorrow night. Tomorrow will be spent scrambling to finish the scattered shots that remain. I would have liked a big finish to my stay here, but maybe it's better to go out quietly.

I found myself reflecting back on the past few weeks. There was now a strange dichotomy in my relationship with the Pythons. I looked up to them as the comedy geniuses I loved in their TV shows, films, books, and records. They had become comedy gods. On the other hand, here I was, working, drinking, and laughing with them. They were becoming good friends. I was having trouble correlating the Pythons I watched on TV with the friends I was lucky enough to be working with on a daily basis. It almost seems like the actors on *Flying Circus* are different from the people I've been living with for the past several weeks; the TV images have become larger than life, while the Pythons, as persons, have become . . . well, part of my life. And I still can't believe I'm a part of it all.

Tidying Up, in which there is Graham falling from the tower, people rushing through the marketplace, more of the crucifixion party, and a special visitor

TODAY WAS MY LAST DAY WITH the Pythons on the film. They will have to struggle along by themselves during the next two and a half weeks in Gabes and Carthage. ▪ But if I have to leave, this was a perfect way to go out. ▪ It started typically enough. There was an early call on the set this morning, with plenty of short bits that needed to be finished. I pulled on my peasant costume and arrived as early as I could, in order to make the most of my final day here.

Terry J had to scramble to make sure everything was finished at the Ribat, despite weather that was not always helpful to the shooting schedule.

Shooting began today with Graham rushing off the top of the unfinished tower. Only the front half of the tower had been finished, as the back side wouldn't be in shot. Chris Langham, who had also been doing quite a bit of acting lately, played a workman sitting near the top steps of the tower in the first few takes. As the camera rolled, he dropped his hammer and then started down to retrieve it.

Following his shots, Graham took his place near the bare wooden framework behind the tower and waited for his cue to rush up and fall off. As with the earlier fall from the balcony, scaffolding was erected a few feet below the end of the stairway, with huge, fluffy mattresses piled on it. On cue, Graham rushed up the steps, walked off the top stair, and fell safely down on the mattresses. While he didn't particularly care for all of the falls

The construction crew did an amazing job constructing a shorter version of the real thing, which made the sight of the unfinished back side of the structure even more startling.

The view through the lens made it appear riskier than the reality; there was actually a large mattress sitting on a platform just out of sight of the camera.

he had been required to perform, Graham took it all in stride, obligingly standing on the top step looking petrified while David Appleby took photos. After Graham's close-ups came shots of the Roman soldiers following behind him. All of the tower shooting was finished surprisingly quickly, and everyone moved back down to the marketplace set again.

The marketplace was still standing from yesterday, and the length of it that was not on the sloping walkway was soon teeming with extras for the rest of the morning's shooting. As a peasant, my job was to mill about while various members of the cast rushed through the crowded marketplace for various reasons.

The first shots involved Sue Jones-Davies handing out pamphlets, followed by a shot in which she attempts to run through quickly after she has stormed away from the revolutionaries. We had quite a bustling market, and Sue really had a hard time getting through. She had to try to push people aside to get through the crowd; she likewise had to work to force her pamphlets on us, as we had all been instructed not to want them.

It went slower than expected. There were some difficulties using the boom mike in the scene, due to the low-hanging obstacles. Another interesting problem arose after a few takes. When we were filming Sue running through the crowd, pushing people aside, the first couple of takes were quite good. But the more we filmed it, the more people knew where she was coming through and moved out of her way so that she would not have to push them aside. Terry J had to stop everyone and direct us to stand in her way, forcing her to push us aside, instead of being so obliging.

The rest of the morning was completely taken up with people rushing through the crowd, including the revolutionaries (all of whom had to be roused from their hotels in order to make it to the set). Those of us wandering in the marketplace were told to switch our positions so that we wouldn't be in the same place during different scenes. I was quite happy to move around and even bow out of a few scenes. In recent weeks, I had come to appreciate the hard work involved in being an extra. In addition to much standing around and doing the same scenes over and over, it was difficult to know when one was doing a good job. The extras seldom received much direction, as opposed to the actors—understandable, and yet the extras were often a bit in the dark about what they needed to do in the next scene. An extra usually only knows when he is *not* doing a good job.

Just before lunch, there was a short rehearsal for the actors who had to carry crosses through the marketplace. They walked through the scene and learned all the blocking without all of the extras standing in the way. There were still a number of shots left on the schedule to finish today, including the crucifees' journey through the marketplace, the centurion and his soldiers rushing through the marketplace to retrieve Brian from his cross, and Brian's escape from the spaceship for the animation sequence.

Leaning against the makeup trailer, I noticed a large dummy dressed in Brian's costume, which was presumably going to be used for the fall from the tower. The manikin was so authentic that anyone rounding the corner without paying attention might easily assume it was Graham standing there. It was slightly unnerving; although it was visibly shorter than the real Graham, there was a strong resemblance.

During lunch, many of us took our trays over to sit on the steps of the mosque next to the Ribat. The sun was out, and it was a beautiful day. As we began eating, the midday prayers were broadcast from the speakers just above us. Today was Friday, the Muslim holy day, so people headed to the mosque to worship. All of us eating there suddenly had to scoop up our lunches and move, looking rather lost as we balanced our trays and looked for a less heavily trafficked area to finish dining.

The first scene after lunch would be the crucifees dragging their crosses through the marketplace while Michael, as the souvenir salesman, plied his wares, and Terry J, as a saintly passer-by, got tricked into holding a cross and forced to join the procession. Unfortunately, just as we were set to begin, a large bank of dark, threatening clouds rolled in. Everyone sat around waiting to see if the sky would clear, which was looking increasingly unlikely.

I decided to take advantage of the delay to interview Sue Jones-Davies, and we walked to a quiet corner of the Ribat, where I asked how she became involved with the film.

"I honestly don't know why they approached me," she confessed. "They were going to do it in May, and I think they had another actress in mind then. When it was all rescheduled, they started to look for people again, and I really don't know why they asked me to come on and audition. I think they must have just looked through *Spotlight* and seen pictures. I had worked with them before, but on such vague things, I don't think they would have remembered me from any of them. I'd done an Amnesty International concert with John Cleese as part of a band, but I would have thought they'd have just assumed I was a singer from that, and not rung me up as an actress. So I was pretty surprised, but very pleased, too, when I eventually was picked, because I had to do auditions. I did the first audition before I went to Australia and didn't hear anything. My agent said, 'Well, you have to go within a week because they've got to know.' And I heard nothing and assumed I hadn't got it. Then when I came back from Australia about two months later, they said they wanted to see me again. So I did two more auditions. It was very long and drawn out, and I assumed I didn't stand a

Graham applies the finishing touch, by way of his pipe, to the dummy Brian,
who will be hurled from the tower in his stead.

chance. By then you think, 'Oh God no, it can't be,' so I was really delighted.
It's the first film I've ever done, and I think it must be a really nice introduction to filmmaking, because it's much more relaxed than I imagine most
films are."

Although it was her first film, it was far from her first performing.

"I've done mostly theater work, quite a bit of telly now, and a lot of
work with the band I sing with—quite a variety of things. But I prefer theater and singing to the telly work, which I find a bit claustrophobic.

"I've always enjoyed singing on stage, but I never thought after university that that's what I would do. I thought I'd go into journalism—well, I
wasn't sure what, but that seemed the most likely thing. Then I went up to
the Edinburgh Festival my last year at university, and the revue I was in
was transferred to London. That happened, and I was also offered a rock
record contract from the same revue, so suddenly I found myself going to

London and almost being channeled into that profession without really doing much about it—and finding I liked it and thinking, 'Well, I may as well
make my money this way, as I enjoy it, rather than try to do it in a more
conventional way.'"

Sue noted that she had previously appeared in a British series called
Rock Follies, which had been broadcast in the United States on PBS.

"I'm in the second episode. I join the trio and eventually become a duo,
just Julie and myself, the others getting squeezed out," she said with a
laugh. "Very nasty politics! It was great fun doing it, lots of singing, lots of
acting, just nice people to work with."

She noted that she was likewise enjoying her time with *Brian.*

"I don't exactly get flogged to death from it, working one day, swimming two days, working the fourth day! It's a wonderful introduction to
filming, because it isn't tense. Maybe it's tense for other people, but because I don't have that much to do, it's very pleasant out here in the sun
and the sea. And the flies," she joked as she brushed one away.

"You said earlier that you didn't really know any of the Pythons before
you auditioned."

"Well, John Cleese has the same agent as myself, and I'd met him sort
of briefly through that, as I say, when we'd done the Amnesty concert, but
I don't know him, really. I'd worked once with Eric for about a week two or
three years ago, with the band again, but I didn't really think he'd remember me from that long ago, especially as it was in a singing context rather
than an acting context. So I just assumed they'd looked through *Spotlight,*
because my agent said it definitely wasn't John who suggested me to
them, so he's as mystified as me, really. I think they just flipped through
and picked out people who they thought looked dark."

"Do you hope to work with the group again?"

"I don't know, really, because they don't write much for women. Most of
their women characters are usually played by them, so I wouldn't really think
it's very likely. This is a specific woman they wanted for this type of part, but
I shouldn't imagine she'd reappear much in other Monty Python things. It
would be lovely if it were to happen, but I wouldn't really expect it to."

"Chris has gotten sucked up into the filming, it seems," I commented
on all of the acting bits her husband had been doing.

Sue Jones-Davies's background is primarily in music,
but she made a powerful figure of Judith in *Brian*.

"Oh, he's enjoying it," she laughed. "He was hoping, before he came out, he would be able to do—well, he wanted to be able to say, 'I've been in it,' but he didn't think he'd wind up doing quite this much! He's working more than I am now!"

"Yes, and when Carol and Peter came down, he ended up doing more than her."

"Right! That's ridiculous, isn't it?" she laughed. "I mean, I can't play anyone else. I'm stuck—well, I'm not stuck with Judith, but you know, they just want me to be seen as that one character, so they can't rope me into playing other women characters. So in a way, that's very nice, it means I get to be just the one. I don't work that much, really."

"You're the only member of the cast who doesn't play more than one part. It's strange. Even Graham does . . . Do you have any favorite scenes so far?"

"Well, I loved doing the crowd scene from the window over there," she said, pointing to Mandy's courtyard, "because just looking down at all those people, so funny, having not even rehearsed it much, suddenly to open that window and see that mass. It hits you, it takes on a whole new perspective. I enjoyed that. I enjoyed most of the scenes in different ways. I found some difficult because I'm not used to having to do close-ups with people not there. I mean, I've never done that before, and I find that a bit disconcerting. You know, all of a sudden you're doing something, and you find you're not doing it *to* anyone, or looking in an area that you didn't before. I find all that very instructive, but very confusing . . . I can't think of any of the other ones I've done. I enjoy all the market scenes; I have to push my way in and run up steps and all that, and that's a gas. Well, I enjoy all the 'getting cross' bits with the revs . . . I seem to be getting cross all the time in this film—that's all I ever do is yell at people—a very unpleasant lady!"

We decided to see what was happening with the filming plans. Sue headed to the set; I felt like walking around a little more, to soak up the atmosphere on my last day here. The spaceship looked nearly ready to go, I thought, and would surely be shot tomorrow. I strolled to another corner of the Ribat where more construction was going on. There was a room being constructed in the area near Mandy's garden, where only a large open area had previously been. A heavy black canvas had been pulled over it to help serve as the roof for what is becoming Mandy's house, where the revolutionaries and others try to exploit Brian after the crowd starts to follow him. As I walked around up there, I heard music coming from a loudspeaker in the courtyard, and it definitely wasn't Muslim prayer music.

As I walked down, I realized it had to be a recording of Eric singing the closing song of the film, "Look on the Bright Side of Life." It was a smash around the Ribat, and most of the unit hadn't heard it before; even the locals began whistling and clapping along in time to the music. Terry J and a few others were on the sloping walkway, still trying to determine what would be shot next, and so, bowing to popular demand, Eric played it again.

"Did you write it yourself?" I asked him after it finished playing.

"Yes, as a matter of fact. It turned out fairly well, I suppose, kind of a whistler," Eric explained.

"Did you write the other song? The one for Otto's men?" I asked. When he nodded yes, I asked if it was going to be used.

"No." He shook his head. "I'm afraid it doesn't look like it. I wrote the original song, you see, and no one was completely happy with it. So Mike wrote a song, then John wrote a song, and then I think Mike wrote another one. Don't think any of them will be used, though. Kind of a shame. I liked mine, really, kind of a German band thing." He sang a couple of lines before turning to Garth. "There's no way I could get a copy of that now, is there? I'd really like for George to hear it."

Throughout the previous five weeks, there were constant rumors circulating that George Harrison would be coming down to Tunisia for some of the filming. There were rumors about other celebrities as well—Graham had mentioned Ringo—but apart from Spike Milligan, no one had materialized. Rumors had been the heaviest about George, though, as he was helping to finance the picture. It figured, I thought. If George came to visit, it would undoubtedly be while they were in Gabes, and I'd miss my chance to meet him. It was too late to change my schedule, though, and it was only one disappointment in the middle of weeks of wonder.

When it became apparent that there would be little or no chance for sun the remainder of the day, Terry decided to release everyone except those needed for the scene in which the centurion and his soldiers rush through the marketplace on their way to rescue Brian from his cross. John Cleese was quickly snatched away from the comfort of the Sidi Mansour and costumed, while Roy Rodehouse and a younger spark called Chuck were recruited to play the peasants that the soldiers bump into. It seemed that nearly all of the crew had now found a place in front of the camera.

Following that bit of filming, we wrapped for the day a bit earlier than usual in anticipation of a rainstorm. John had agreed to a farewell interview, so I lingered near his trailer, but he was somewhere in the Ribat preparing for tomorrow. I spoke to Connie Booth, who was waiting at his trailer as well, and arranged to meet John at the Sidi later. There would actually be quite a bit of filming to squeeze into the last two days in Monastir. According to the call sheet, the spaceship scene, the scene in Mandy's house with the revolutionaries, and today's unfinished scenes were all scheduled tomorrow. A notice on the call sheet indicated that unit members might be required to work overtime to complete the day's shooting. I suddenly felt slightly less sad about leaving tomorrow, knowing how much hard work would have to be finished.

I returned my costume to the makeup house, debating whether to go back to the Ruspina and pack or stay at the Sidi for a drink or two. It wasn't a difficult choice, as it was my final day, and it seemed like a good chance to say my good-byes to everyone. I headed into the bar, where some of the crew had already gathered, and mingled a bit. Rushes had been set for six o'clock, and it was already getting close to that, so I grabbed a beer and walked to the projection room with Clive.

A few others were starting to gather to view the rushes, but it was soon after six o'clock, and there was still no indication that they would be starting soon. I walked out to the lobby to see if anyone knew the reason for the delay. Terry J and Michael were standing outside the production office, and I was about to speak when I overheard them talking.

"Eric said he'd be here by six. I suppose we can wait a little longer," Michael said.

"Oh, yes. I hope he gets here soon," Terry agreed. "I'd hate to start without him."

Connie Booth joined John Cleese in Monastir, where they spent much of their
spare time working on the second season of *Fawlty Towers*.

"Is everyone waiting for Eric?" I asked apprehensively.

"Well . . . sort of," explained Terry. "You see, George just got in late this
afternoon, and Eric was going to bring him over to see the rushes. He just
called a little bit ago and said they were on their way."

"Oh, okay," I nodded. As I turned to go back to the screening room, I
did a double take. George? George Harrison? The former Beatle turned
Python movie producer? No. It couldn't be. I had given up all hopes of
George visiting the set, but I knew that it had to be the case. The Beatles,
like Python, were such huge figures to me that I never dreamed I'd be in
the same room with one of them.

I tried to calm down as I took my seat in the screening room. I had a
feeling that the word had spread around the room, and there was a sense
of nervous excitement, even though everyone was very well behaved.

The waiting was torture. Every time someone entered the room, I couldn't help shooting a glance to see if it was Eric and George. But after another half hour, there was still no sign of them, and so the rushes were finally started without them. These were the interior of Ben's cell, but I was finding it awfully difficult to concentrate on them. Every time the door in back opened, I fought the urge—usually unsuccessfully—to turn around.

At long last, the door opened and I heard a slight rumbling in the back. George had entered the room. Wait—no, it wasn't George, it was Eric—the hair length had fooled me. Tania entered after him, then Carey. Finally, I noticed a smaller figure, with shorter hair, follow behind as the group filed into a row of empty seats in the back. George.

In retrospect, it was probably just as well that I wasn't introduced to him first in the lobby. I'm sure I'd have made an idiot of myself, stammering, drooling, too agog to say anything intelligent. Instead, I sat watching the rushes while he sat across the room. I had a chance to calm myself, breathe deeply, occasionally glancing over to reassure my subconscious that he was still human. It was like Beatle Decompression.

Nevertheless, I was pretty hyper and found it difficult to keep still for the rushes. At one point, the projector broke down again, so I decided to race to the bar. John and Connie were just coming in, so I took their order for drinks as well. I carefully returned carrying drinks for myself, John, Connie, their driver, Clive, and Terry G, who was sitting next to me. The rushes had resumed, so I tried to avoid blocking the screen while I handed out the drinks, nearly spilling one on George's back. Yes, it was him, all right. I had seen him in concert from the last row of the Chicago Stadium in 1974, but this was infinitely preferable.

I gave Terry and Clive their beers and sat to watch the remaining rushes. As they drew to a close, I slowly drifted out of the room, assuming George had already been whisked away. To my surprise, I found myself just a few feet away from him. I quickly pulled out a copy of my Python fanzine and shoved it in his direction. He accepted it, and I introduced myself. He seemed to be in a very happy mood, genuinely glad to be here. He thanked me, flipped through the zine briefly, and stuck it in his briefcase as Terry G approached him and began chatting. Everyone remaining in the room slowly filed out, coming to a stop just outside the production office, where several conversations were going at once. Terry J was talking about the rushes with Michael and seemed a little disappointed.

"Well, Ben seemed to blend into the wall behind him," he explained. "Worst of all, though, Ben's feet were out of frame in every shot. It makes it appear as though Ben were standing, when he actually was off the floor. I'm afraid we won't be able to reshoot any of it, though, with our schedule here running so tight."

I hadn't noticed it during rushes, but his expert director's eye noticed that there wasn't a shot of Ben's feet dangling above the floor.

People started drifting away, and it looked like things were breaking up when Eric said, "Why don't we all go down to the Coq for dinner? It's a great local restaurant, wallpaper peeling off and everything, but the food is great."

Everyone was agreeable, until Graham remembered that "today is Friday. This is like Sunday to them. They're closed tonight."

There were a few disappointed moans, and no one seemed to know what to do until Terry J announced that John Goldstone was talking the hotel people into putting several tables together for us. I felt rather underdressed, wearing the same tank top and cut-offs I had worn on the set all day. Unlike most of the others here, who were staying at the Sidi, I couldn't just run upstairs and change clothes. But no one seemed to mind, and I resolved not to worry about it, either.

Most of our group started toward the bar to wait for our tables, and I realized George was next to me as I walked along. "How was your flight down?" I asked, doing my best to find some common ground for small talk.

"Pretty good," he said, "though our plane had a long layover in Nice." He explained that he had chartered a plane down here that flew directly into Monastir, rather than going by way of Tunis. He had been accompanied by his manager and fellow producer Denis O'Brien. "Denis and I just came down for the twenty-four hours. I took a break from mixing an album, but I'll be going back tomorrow afternoon."

Somehow I found myself at a table with Eric, Denis, and George in the bar. George had been passing around a picture of his son Dhani, who had just been born a couple of months ago. He was a typically proud father, flashing the pictures toward anyone who expressed even the most casual interest. Eric opened his briefcase and presented George with the contents—a tiny, baby-sized Gumby suit, complete with a tiny pair of wire-rimmed glasses, a Gumby hat-handkerchief, tiny boots, and clothes with miniature suspenders. Hazel Pethig, the Python wardrobe genius, had made it specially. George was delighted. They sat back and talked while I chatted with Denis, as I didn't want to intrude upon George and Eric's privacy.

As they talked, I noticed that George had pulled out the Python zine that I had given him and started paging through it, stopping to rest on the section dealing with the various Python records. "Where are yours?" he asked Eric as he searched for the listing of Eric's recordings. "There's the soundtrack for *Grail* . . . I can't wait to hear the sound track for this film! 'Fuck this, fuck that, fuck, fuck, fuck!'" he joked.

Our tables were ready, so we headed to the dining room. The tables had been set up in a large U-shape. George, Eric, and Denis sat at the middle table, while I sat off at one of the side tables. There were about eighteen of us altogether. I sat next to the reporter from *Melody Maker* and across from Graham. Terry G was nearby, and his wife, Maggie, had gotten out of her sickbed to enjoy the night. Over at the other side table sat John and Terry J, while Michael and Helen had gone back to the Meridien.

It was a festive occasion, and spirits were high. George asked Graham about their mutual friend Harry Nilsson; George hadn't talked to him in quite some time, so Graham started bringing him up to date. Suddenly, all of our conversations were halted by a trio of Tunisian musicians—the same three who seemed to be omnipresent at the Sidi. They may have been acclaimed local artists, but unfortunately, our untrained Western ears found their instruments and voices shrill, discordant, and unnecessarily loud, so much so that we were unable to converse, even with the people sitting next to us. George finally decided on the best course of action. He took one of the dinner rolls and wadded up little bits of dough, which he then stuck in each ear as a makeshift pair of earplugs. They seemed to do the trick, and several others followed suit.

The trio finally left us to resume our conversations, which by this time had been hopelessly forgotten. Eric showed everyone the Gumby suit that had been specially made for Dhani, which got an appreciative round of applause from everyone. Just as we were all finishing our dessert, the musicians

I handed out copies of *The Complate Monty Python*, my Python fanzine, to George
Harrison and Eric in the bar at the Sidi Mansour, and was even bold enough to
ask George to sign some for me—which he was happy to do.

came back. In went the earplugs, and this time the complaints were more vo-
cal and serious.

The musicians were followed by the man with the balancing beer bottles. Once again, he had them all balanced on his head, this time on a single board, as he danced around, until he finally started tipping them off,
one by one. He selected a girl from a nearby table to stand next to him and
catch the last few bottles as he rolled them off the board. Everyone watched
with mild curiosity. The girl was nervous, and so, sure enough, she dropped
one of the bottles, which smashed on the floor and stopped the barefoot
dancer. The first one to his feet to lead the standing ovation was George.

Our entertainers finally got the hint and left the room with considerably
less fanfare than had accompanied their entrance, and we could safely remove our earplugs. Terry G seemed particularly wound up at his end of the
table, and he had shoved two flowers into his ears for his earplugs.

George and Denis had bottles of Dom Perignon brought in, and Denis proposed the particularly well-received toast: "Let us all eat, drink, and make merry tonight—for tomorrow, the money runs out!"

Graham had ordered a bottle of tonic water from a waiter who hadn't been seen in at least half an hour, so I ran to the bar and got one for him. On my way back, I noticed Carey Idle looking at me. I had bought a pound of sweets earlier and passed them out that afternoon, and I remembered that I had promised Carey more of them. I retrieved them from my bag and gave him a handful, then passed them out to everyone who wanted one.

"Didn't you want to ask me some questions earlier?" John Cleese reminded me as I walked past him. I had almost forgotten. I quickly grabbed my cassette recorder. Things were getting a bit too raucous for any sort of serious interview, so I decided to limit myself to a couple of questions.

Noting that it's been nearly six weeks, I asked, "John, how has this experience been compared to *Grail*?"

He screwed up his face a bit and replied, "Well, it's much easier on the nerves. We get much more time off. We still work every day, but we do get time off. We don't start at seven o'clock every morning, and on the mornings when we do start at seven o'clock, the sun is usually out. There's a few chairs to sit around in when we actually do have a break, and there's often sun to sit in. So it's a bit of a doddle, really."

"What's next for Python?"

"I think the bill!" Eric shouted over.

"I have no idea. We have to get this out about April, I suppose, and after that, make another film in four years. Unless this one's a disaster and no one will give us the money for it."

Carey had approached us, lured by the sight of the cassette recorder, so I asked if he wished to say a few words. John and I coaxed him a bit, but he declined. "What does a German police officer say to his chest?" I asked him. He immediately responded with "You are under a vest," and John broke up laughing.

Things seemed to be slowly breaking up, and our exit was accelerated by another visit from the Tunisian musicians. In the lobby, I said good-bye to Terry J and Graham, who left for their rooms, and to several of the others. Terry G had a word with George before he left, as George had agreed to come out to the Ribat tomorrow to do a short bit in the film.

"When are you going back to London, then?" asked Terry.

"Well, we should be finished about four thirty, and then just go out to the airport and bug off."

"Terrific. Are you going back to London?" asked Terry. George nodded yes, and Terry noted, "It's a pity you couldn't have stuck it out a bit more."

"Well, I'm mixing now, you know. And I wanted Denis to come, too, and he's been in L.A. since last Sunday or Monday, so he's only over for five days or so . . . Anyway, at least we got down here."

I realized I'd better get a ride to the Ruspina lined up so I wouldn't get stuck here again. John was happy to offer me a lift in his car, but then he ended up riding in another one. I rode back to the Meridien with Connie and a couple of other people I really didn't know. My only regret of the night was that I hadn't gotten a chance to talk to Gwen, as George's arrival had rearranged everyone's plans. Gwen was an incredible actress and had played such diverse roles in the Rutles film as Chastity and Leggy Mountbatten's mother—if I hadn't seen the credits, I'd never have believed they were played by the same person.

After making proper introductions, I started talking with Connie as we rode along, and she reminded me that she was really an American. "You first got involved with Python through John, of course, didn't you?" I asked.

"Definitely!" laughed Connie. "It was shortly after we were married that John started doing Python."

"Did you start acting in the first series?"

"Yes, I think I did. I don't remember now, exactly, but I think I did a Canadian sketch, the Mounties—me being American—singing. I had to learn an English accent for one thing. Little tiny bits, mostly."

"You seem to have appeared sporadically, doing a bit or two, then you were off for a time."

"Well, there was no reason, really," she explained. "I didn't think I was that suited for much of the stuff that they did. If something came up that they thought I was right for, I did it."

"It was mostly between you and Carol Cleveland for the female parts."

"No, Carol was hired to be their steady lady. And I never was. I was only in for little bits that I might be right for. Carol was also very good at different types of voices, and I only did American parts, and a couple of times English."

"You really just jumped in whenever there were a few extra bits."

"Yes, or something that I could do. But I've never really felt that Python wrote for women. They wrote for men to do women. They thought that they played women much better than women did."

"Did you enjoy doing the sketches with them?"

"Yes and no. I was very flattered to be amongst Python, because I admired what they were doing. But I always felt—well, I was never particularly funny. They were the funny ones, you were always the fall guy, the straight guy, the dumb blonde, and they were the ones being eccentric or interesting."

We soon arrived at the Meridien and got out of the car to wait for the other two to join us before heading into the bar. As we entered, I saw Michael and John Stanier talking at the bar. We all ordered drinks and stood around the bar, ignoring the large dancing area and the tables inside. For one final time, I heard John Cleese asking everyone if they had any funny hotel stories, as he and Connie had another *Fawlty Towers* to write. The two of them then went upstairs after just one drink, since it was growing late. I said good-bye and thanked them for everything.

Carey started playing with my cassette recorder once again, so I turned him loose with it. A small band in the back was playing "Guantanamera" for a handful of couples on the dance floor. Eric and George heard a bit of it and jumped in, singing their own version of the chorus as loudly as possible, changing the lyrics so that they were as obscene as they could make them. They were having a great time, and no one else seemed to notice them. Carey was walking around with my recorder, prompting Eric to ask George to give Carey a lift back to England tomorrow afternoon. Most of the other wives and families were leaving this weekend as well. I diverted Carey from the machine with a couple of paper airplanes, which proved to be a mistake, as he began sailing them across the bar.

Despite the number of people we had encountered throughout the night, amazingly, no one outside of our unit seemed to recognize George.

The hotel band, which had not taken any notice of him either, started playing the Lennon-McCartney composition "And I Love Her."

"Listen, there's one of yours," teased Eric. "It bloody well isn't!" denied George, with as much mock indignation as he could muster.

Eric and George began heading for the exit. As George had earlier expressed some interest in getting a copy of my Monty Python fanzine that had been autographed by all of the Pythons, I handed one to him, and he seemed very appreciative. "Well, I think I'm going to go upstairs. I'm getting a bit tired now. I don't know how he does it," he said, indicating Carey, who was running energetically through the bar.

"I don't think he's ever going to get tired," I noted.

"It's his last night," explained Eric. "He's going home with you tomorrow, so I won't see him for a little while. I'd rather he went without sleep and saw me, than have him sleep a lot and not see me."

"I'm going to bed," George announced to Eric. "I'm knackered. I feel a bit, sort of, coagulated. So we'll just catch up with you about nine, or ten, or—"

"Ten thirty, or eleven thirty, or lunchtime . . ." Eric added.

"Maybe we'll wake up in time for the plane," George decided.

"Are you going to take my friend, then?" he asked, indicating Carey, who overheard and started to protest. "No, tomorrow," Eric reassured him. George said he'd be glad to, and he and Denis headed upstairs for their rooms after a final good night.

Things slowly started to calm down as the party broke up. I had one more beer and remembered I still had most of my packing to do. The minibus was picking me up at nine in the morning, so I decided to head to the Rasputin and turn in. I said my good-byes to Michael and the remaining crew and walked the short distance.

Somehow, I miraculously managed to fit everything into my pack and suitcase. As I lay in bed, I reflected on the past six weeks. I couldn't help but feel awfully sad to leave everyone, but I was consoled by the fact that I had gone out with a vengeance. I felt very lucky as well. How many people get to meet their heroes at such a young age, let alone live and work with them on one of their major projects? I still found it hard to believe that I was actually in North Africa with Monty Python. It was little more than three years ago that I had been just another fan, watching them faithfully on television and writing to them, in hopes that I might be lucky enough to get a letter in reply. The past couple of months had all been a dream. As I rolled over and started to drift off to sleep, I knew that, schmaltzy as it sounded, none of those dreams could compare with the dream I had been living.

SATURDAY TURNED OUT TO BE ANTICLIMACTIC, which was hardly surprising. I rose early, though not as early as Michael and John, who had already left for the set by the time I arrived at the Meridien to catch the minibus. A group of farmers from North Dakota were just arriving at the hotel, serving as an ironic counterpoint to the Beatle sleeping upstairs in the same hotel.

Sunrise in Tunisia. While I waited for my ride to the airport, I walked around the Ruspina one last time, and snapped this shot of the swimming pool area.

Roger and Pan had all of their luggage piled in the lobby waiting the arrival of the minibus, so I threw mine into the pile and picked up a few more last-minute souvenirs. It soon pulled up and we quickly loaded our gear, then headed north to the Tunis airport. After we arrived, we found we had little time to dawdle, and I barely had enough time to change my money before we boarded.

The flight back to London was uneventful. I sat across the aisle from Roger and Pan, and we arranged to meet at the Angel Pub near Graham's home in Highgate on Monday. I left them at Victoria Station and took the tube to Anne Henshaw's place, having gladly accepted her offer of a place to stay during my three-day layover.

The next three days in London were quiet as well. I didn't feel much like playing the tourist. I had already seen most of the attractions that I cared to see, could afford, or had time for. To me, the main attraction of London was visiting friends, but since most of them were currently in Tunisia, I didn't see much point in staying around too long. I walked through Trafalgar Square and Piccadilly Circus on Sunday and ate my first McDonald's burger in more than two months, which gave me a greater appreciation of the Tunisian food. Then I stopped off at a cinema that was showing a double feature of *Monty Python and the Holy Grail* and *Jabberwocky*, which seemed irresistible to me. I paid my money and watched both films, hard to believe that only two days ago, I was walking around with the real-life counterparts of these screen images. I paid more attention than ever to the credits, spotting the names of people who had become friends.

I spent much of Monday sightseeing, then headed north to meet Roger and Pan at the Angel Pub. I was passing Graham's house along the way, so I stopped to talk with someone staying there who had just returned from the set on Sunday. "The filming went quite well Saturday," he assured me. "It was a little bit cloudy at first, but I think they were able to get everything done. George was out on the set in the afternoon. He played one of the people in Mandy's house, in there with all of the incurables and women taken in sin."

I headed on to the Angel, where I sent greetings from Graham after spotting a few familiar faces. I had a couple of pints and then headed back to Anne's place.

In the morning, I took the tube to Heathrow and caught the flight back to the States. I was careful to keep all of my notes, tapes, and film close at hand for the time I'd be able to write *Monty Python's Tunisian Holiday*.

AFTERWORD

I KEPT UP AS WELL AS I was able, considering I was near Chicago and the Pythons and crew were all an ocean away. I sent off a few letters after I returned, which I knew they would receive after they all returned to England. ▪ The first to reply was John Cleese, in a letter dated November 24:

*Very nice to get your letter. So pleased you enjoyed your stay. Things
got a good deal less enjoyable towards the end, as the weather and
hotels deteriorated rapidly when we went south, but I think we have
done alright despite this. We saw a rough assembly on Monday and
were pretty pleased. A lot of work to be done of course, particularly on
the end, but a good proportion of it works very well indeed.*

I kept in touch with the progress of the film largely through letters as it
entered the postproduction stages. I began the major task of sorting
through everything that I had gathered in Tunisia, and I compiled another
volume of my Python fanzine. I received another letter from John dated
December 18, which meant quite a bit to me as I knew he was awfully
busy trying to finish the next six *Fawlty Towers.*

*I heard from Mike Palin—I was not there—that the first public showing
got a good response, although there is some very heavy cutting to do
around the raid on Pilate's palace. You had better not publish this yet
as Terry Jones may not know that this is how everyone feels!*

Eric came over to host *Saturday Night Live* in December; it was nice to
see a mention of Tunisia in his opening monologue for the show. It was
also a bit strange to see him on television—it was the first time I had seen
any of them since I left Tunisia. He looked exactly the same.

I rang up Michael in New York on the twenty-fourth of January and
caught him in a less busy moment. Rather than chopping the film into two
segments, or inserting an intermission, both of which had been discussed,
the film was being edited down to about ninety minutes, he explained.
Much of the raid on the palace would go, as well as part of the haggling
scene and some of the chase through the marketplace, as well as, probably,
the ex-leper scene. I told him I was sorry to see them go, but he explained
that much of it was repetitious and overly long, and the other scenes were
good but not really essential to the story. He noted that the ex-leper scene
might be more trouble than it was worth to keep in the film.

Just after I spoke with Michael, a letter arrived from Clive, back in England and determined to break into the film business. He had made it to

Gabes and Carthage and noted that, among other bits of shooting, he did a wild track for Garth of armor clanking. It was, he noted proudly, the very last location recording for *Life of Brian*.

It took time to edit the film down to an hour and a half. Although the ex-leper and most of the haggling remained, the kidnapping of Pilate's wife and the King Otto scene were cut (they can still be seen on the *Life of Brian Immaculate Edition* DVD, along with another deleted scene of shepherds watching their flocks near Bethlehem). While some of the cuts were painful, the Pythons all agreed that the changes ultimately improved the film.

Late the following summer, I went to New York when the Pythons came over for the U.S. opening of *Life of Brian*. The movie had actually begun screening the previous month at a couple of theaters, but the group didn't promote it until its wider American release. Although there were no formal events, I got to see and visit with most of the Pythons, John Goldstone, and even George Harrison.

The opening week was accompanied by protests from religious groups who, for the most part, either hadn't seen the film, had completely misunderstood it, or chose to exploit it for their own purposes. I had gotten wind of a protest demonstration and decided to attend incognito, in order to give the Pythons a report of the proceedings. I even got a copy of the address given to the crowd, which underscored how badly they had misunderstood the film and its message.

Although there were scattered bans and boycotts in America and Europe, *Life of Brian* was well received by critics and fans alike and did fine at the box office, which ensured the Pythons backing for another movie. Still, their follow-up, *Monty Python's Meaning of Life,* was not released until 1983. In the meantime, they revived and revised their stage show in the fall of 1980 for *Monty Python Live at the Hollywood Bowl.* I drove out to L.A. in a rusted-out ten-year-old Chevy Impala for the event, met up with the Pythons once again, and even ended up joining the show, making a brief appearance as a Pantomime Goose each of the four nights.

Through the years, the Pythons had gone from idols to good friends. I was living in Chicago throughout the 1980s and 1990s, and Graham Chapman was a frequent visitor as he traveled the United States with his lecture tours (which actually began one memorable night in Chicago). I saw the

In New York in September 1979 for the opening of *Life of Brian*, I observed
the protest rally targeting the film.

The protestors marched from the Warner Communications building to the theater
showing *Life of Brian*. The protesters are forgotten, *Brian* endures as a classic.

I was recruited to help fill the stage during a strange sequence in the Hollywood
Bowl show that they referred to as "Idiotting."

Michael Palin, John Cleese, and Neil Innes watch from the wings at the Hollywood Bowl, about to present the Church Police sketch.

others on their occasional trips through Chicago, and I made frequent journeys to London to visit as well. The most poignant was undoubtedly in December of 1989, when I went to Graham Chapman's memorial service; his death of cancer on October 4, 1989, devastated all who knew him. There were a few tears, but there was much more laughter, as Graham would have wanted it.

I went on to write several best-selling books, including *The First 200 Years of Monty Python, And Now For Something Completely Trivial, Life (Before and) After Python,* and *The First 280 Years of Monty Python.* I've attended the Python anniversary celebrations, and they are kind enough to make sure I am always included when there is an event of Python significance. There may not be any more Python films or TV shows, but seeing

the five surviving members onstage at the Aspen Comedy Festival and at the Broadway opening of *Spamalot* brought a lump to my throat. In turn, I have done my best to chronicle the projects of them all, both individually and as Monty Python.

Of course, my life with Python was capped off by my years serving as personal assistant to John Cleese. It's hard to imagine a more satisfying experience, both on a professional and personal level, and I will always be grateful to John for the years that we spent together on a daily basis.

In the end, of course, *Life of Brian* has stood the test of time and is acclaimed as a classic. With each year that goes by, I am increasingly proud of my infinitesimally small role in the production. With the publication of this journal I hope to offer a firsthand view into the creative process of the Pythons, a part of comedy history that will never be repeated.

INDEX